Impossible Bodies, Impossible Selves: Exclusions and Student Subjectivities

D1434886

Inclusive Education: Cross Cultural Perspectives

VOLUME 3

SCOPE OF THE SERIES

This series is concerned with exploring the meaning and function of inclusive education in a world characterised by rapid social, economic and political change. The question of inclusion and exclusion will be viewed as a human rights issue, in which concerns over issues of equity, social justice and participation will be of central significance. The series will provide an inter-disciplinary approach and draw on research and ideas that will contribute to an awareness and understanding of cross-cultural insights and questions. Dominant assumptions and practices will be critically analysed thereby encouraging debate and dialogue over such fundamentally important values and concerns.

Impossible Bodies, Impossible Selves: Exclusions and Student Subjectivities

By

Deborah Youdell
Institute of Education,
University of London, U.K.

 Springer

A C.I.P. Catalogue record for this book is available from the Library of Congress.

ISBN-10 1-4020-5484-X (PB)
ISBN-13 978-1-4020-5484-6 (PB)
ISBN-10 1-4020-4548-4 (HB)
ISBN-13 978-1-4020-4548-6 (HB)
ISBN-10 1-4020-4549-2 (e-book)
ISBN-13 978-1-4020-4549-3 (e-book)

Published by Springer,
P.O. Box 17, 3300 AA Dordrecht, The Netherlands.

www.springer.com

Printed on acid-free paper

Printed in the Netherlands.

To my mum, Pat
And to optimism

CONTENTS

Contents

SERIES EDITORS' FOREWORD

For at least the past 25 years, issues about inclusive education have generated a great deal of discussion and debate. The importance of inclusive education has been a centre of controversy and advocacy in the disability movement and has generated a significant amount of research and analysis in Faculties of Education in both Northern and Southern countries. One of the key concerns of such work has been the question of all children to be educated together.

The questions raised by this book are essential to discussions concerning the nature and experience of inclusion and exclusion. Drawing on a wealth of insights and understandings from the Sociology of Education, Youdell engages in a serious process of deconstruction of key discourses and categories. Underpinning the analysis is a passionate desire for a just educational system. These questions raise the bar in how the issues are framed and clearly outline the complex competing constituents of the education system. Who gets excluded in the classroom and the way in which they are excluded are fundamental questions of an education enterprise that has fallen prey to a market system of education. Addressing this hegemonic economic analysis favouring ideas that the economic well-being of nations is dependent on schools training a productive labour force is contested as is the reliance on a need for technology and specialized pedagogical theory as the evidence base to judge the capacity of children to learn and the ability of people to participate in the current education systems. This volume achieves clear and concise insights into the construction of difference and inequality that marginalizes and defines children in the school industry. It exposes the powerful interests involved. These are insights, the author argues that are intended to assist in bringing about change to the education system.

Through the use of perceptive Episodes taken from ethnographic fieldwork carefully crafted nuanced insights, ideas and interpretations are offered. Evidence of the reproduction of the status quo is provided through the rich ethnographic material from schools in London, England and Sydney, Australia. Youdell explores gender, sexuality, race, social class, disability, ability, ethnicity and religion as the basis of the construction of the 'bad' student and 'unacceptable [impossible] learner'. This gives us material from the classrooms to show how, for example, the teacher constructs Paul, the 'impossible learner' in the framework of special or normal/abnormal; how a teacher constructs, Steve, the 'bad learner' in the context of white-working-class excessive masculinity; and of Marcella, Naomi and Marcia, 'bad students – non-ideal learner' in the environment of racism. The professional discourse evidenced in these and other cases shows how students are excluded from the education process. Exclusion and inclusion are not understood as fixed universal realities, but rather, as open to varying degrees of challenge and reconstitution by the participants involved.

This thoughtful text provides us with a range of serious and thought-provoking questions and a good many answers. It digs much deeper than much of the literature in the field of inclusive education to make an essential analysis of the systemic construction of the outcast in the education system. It doesn't stop at how we can make educational inclusion happen but constructs a picture through rich ethnographic data of how exclusion is woven and who is affected by these patterns. It is an indictment of the marketization of education and liberal notions of accountability and standardized testing in the school system. Finally, this book is about the education system itself and how it systemically (generously the author suggests that this may be unintended) demarcates the included and the excluded. To do this the author steps outside the context of the system to make us reflect more fundamentally on the education industry.

The book is an important addition to our series. It provides us with a critical methodology to understand inclusion and the ethnographic material to support its findings. We believe the book offers a broader analysis than much of the existing literature on this topic and it will stimulate further debate and investigations into these fundamentally important issues.

Len Barton
Marcia Rioux
September 2005

ACKNOWLEDGEMENTS

I would like to start by thanking all of the students and teachers at Taylor Comprehensive in London, UK, and Plains High in Sydney, Australia. Without their willingness to let me into the daily lives of their schools, this book could not have been written.

My enormous thanks to Len Barton and Marcia Rioux, the editors of this series, for believing this book needed to be written and read and for helping it to be the best book it could be. And to Springer, for embracing a book that did not quite fit the education mould.

I also offer enormous thanks to David Gillborn who has been an unending source of sound advice, belief and friendship. Along with Sally Power, David also supervised my doctoral research (some of which appears here in a new form in my analyses of practices in Taylor Comprehensive). My gratitude to both Sally and David for supporting the exploration of the ideas, methods and analyses that this book is built on. My thanks also to Stephen Ball and Mairtin Mac an Ghaill who examined my PhD and insisted that the ideas I was developing merited sharing with the education community.

Particular thanks also go to Sue Saltmarsh who was Research Assistant to the Plains High study in Sydney and who, along with generating a share of the data (some of which appears in this book), has always excited me with her scholarship and encouraged me in love and shoes. I also acknowledge Macquarie University, Sydney, Australia which provided the financial support for the Plains High research, and the encouragement and insights of all of the members of the School of Education there.

There are a great many colleagues, some of whom are also dear friends, who deserve my thanks for stimulating and challenging me intellectually; reminding me that the work we do is necessary; and making me smile. I thank all those colleagues at the Faculty of Education, University of Cambridge who engaged me in debate and pushed me on my ideas during my time there, and I thank all my current colleagues at the Institute of Education, University of London who do the same. As well as those people I have already mentioned, my special thanks go to: Mike Apple; Gregg Beratan; Jane Cullen; Kalervo Gulson; Valerie Harwood; Deana Leary; Mary Lou Rasmussen; Geoff Whitty; Paul Wood; and David Woodhead. And to Lyndsay Upex for my Endnote Library and Sarah Wishart for proof reading.

Students also constantly offer me opportunities to think again about ideas and explore new directions. My appreciation to all of the students I have worked with, especially the students who have been part of various Master's programmes that I have taught. Also to Natalie Heath, Chris Tooley, and Teresa Winstead whose doctoral research has run alongside the writing of this book – our conversations have undoubtedly made this a better book.

I also want to thank my friends and family for their absolutely endless love, support, and belief. Some of the people I have already mentioned are amongst my dearest friends. My love and gratitude also to Linny, Glenn, Pat, Chris, Steve, Ben, Bob, Milli, Molly, Natalie, Rhiannon, Kate, Sue, Misa, Helen, Julia, Brian and Stevie G.

Finally, I want to acknowledge the wider community of thinkers – some friends, some colleagues, and some strangers in other disciplines, places and times – to whose work and ideas this book is indebted. In the face of the demands of the contemporary education scene, I thank this community for insisting on keeping space for creativity and playfulness; for thinking, trying out ideas, and making connections; and exploring possibilities for enduring constraints to be shifted.

KEY TO TRANSCRIPTS AND TEXTUAL CONVENTION

TRANSCRIPTS

Data generated through my ethnographic work are presented here as 'episodes' – extended representations of data that combine the conventions of sociological transcriptions and theatrical scripts. This approach is discussed in detail in chapter 3.

Outside quoted speech, background or contextual information appears in italicised text. Biographical information about individuals appears as italicised text within (round) parentheses. Within quoted speech, background or contextual information appears in [square] parentheses. Detail of the ways in which quoted speech is delivered, non-linguistic utterances and bodily postures, movements and gestures are indicated through italicised text within (round) parentheses. Emphases and raised voices are indicated by CAPITALISED text. That material has been edited out is indicated by [...]. Where episodes offer detailed representations of extended discussions these draw on audio recordings supplemented by fieldnotes (written during and/or shortly after the event). Where episodes offer detailed descriptions of students' attire and/or appearance these frequently draw on photographs as well as fieldnotes.

TEXTUAL CONVENTIONS

I have sought to minimise my use of 'single inverted commas' in order to indicate the problematisation of a term or concept. However, it seems neither desirable nor possible to completely jettison this convention. When such problematisation seems necessary, single inverted commas are used only on the first occasion that a given term or concept appears within a section. Single inverted commas are also used to indicate the citation of published works.

Due to this dual use of single inverted commas, "double inverted commas" are used where students' or teachers' talk appears within the body of the text. Where I adopt terms and concepts drawn from pupils' and teachers' talk within the text, these are enclosed in "double inverted commas" on the first occasion that they appear within a section.

LIST OF EPISODES AND FIGURES

INTRODUCTION

The 'educational exclusion', and potential 'social exclusion', of some students is a central concern of contemporary education policy in the UK, with similar concerns evident in a range of Western nations. These educational exclusions are also a key concern of this book. Rather than understanding exclusion as the result of life-circumstances and an array of concomitant deprivations, however, this book looks inside the school to examine how school processes act unwittingly to exclude particular students from the educational endeavour.

These educational exclusions are framed by the contexts of contemporary education, namely the marketisation of education and the accountability mechanisms, apparent consumer choice, and individualisation of the learner that are features of this. In examining the school-level processes through which educational exclusions are effected, then, this book intersects with current debates in education that are concerned with these trends.

The marketisation of education has impacted contemporary schooling profoundly and has been proliferated through global processes of policy borrowing (Taylor *et al* 1997) and policy imposition (Stiglitz 2004). As a result, pseudo-markets in schooling are evident not just in the UK but across English speaking nations including Australia, New Zealand and the US (Apple 2001, Taylor *et al* 1997, Whitty *et al* 1998). These markets bring with them a range of demands and ways of thinking about education that have major implications for educational exclusions. Not least of these is the enormous importance placed on high-stakes standardised tests[i] in education markets where these are used as both mechanisms for ensuring accountability to the centre and the basis for consumer choice (Apple 2001, Ball *et al* 2000, Ball 2003, Whitty *et al* 1998). The demands of high stakes testing in the market context have created an environment in which both abstracted and common-sense models of intelligence and ability have been elaborated anew and individualised models of learners and learning have been rearticulated (Gillborn and Youdell 2000). As this book will show, these models frequently elide 'who' the student is, nevertheless, they are deeply implicated in the production of both particular students and educational exclusions (Youdell 2004a).

Marketisation, high-stakes tests, the revival of 'intelligence' and the individualisation of the learner have been subject to extensive scrutiny by critical educationalists who have demonstrated the continued significance of social and biographical identity categories such as social class, gender, race, ethnicity, disability and, more recently, sexuality for educational inequality (see Arnot 1998, Barnes *et al* 2001, Gillborn and Mirza 2000, Gillborn and Youdell 2000, Rasmussen *et al* 2004). Having been removed from the policy agenda during periods of intensive educational reform under explicitly rightist neo-liberal governments (Gillborn 2002), these population groups and their differential educational outcomes have begun to resurface in official educational discourse. This is not to suggest that social justice has returned to the centre of educational concerns. Rather, categories move in and out of the policy frame as exigencies demand (often in the form of significant fractions of the electorate) and as concerns for population groups are subsumed within or replaced by new official discourses – most significantly in the UK the discourse of social inclusion. These moves then, and the debates that surround them, provide further terrain for this book.

As well as intervening in education policy silences over the inequalities that have remained and been exacerbated by market reforms, education scholarship concerned with student identities has sough to better understand the processes though which the subject, or person, who is schooled comes to be meaningful. This has involved the increasing take up of post-structural understandings of the self and an engagement with discussions of the global-local intersections of cultural forms and the relationships these have with global economies. These are ideas that are drawn on and developed in this book as it demonstrates that *'who' a student is – in term of gender, sexuality, social class, ability, disability, race, ethnicity and religion as well as popular and sub cultural belongings – is inextricably linked with the 'sort' of student and learner that s/he gets to be, and the educational inclusions s/he enjoys and/or the exclusions s/he faces.*

The book suggests that these educational inclusions and exclusions are effected through prevailing discourses coming together in ways that create 'truths' about students as learners. One result of these processes is that some constellations of identity markers – for instance feminine, middle class, White – come to be synonymous with the 'ideal learner' who is thereby set up for educational 'success' in the terms of prevailing educational and policy discourses. Another result of these processes, and the one that forms the central concern of this book, is that other constellations of identity markers – for instance working class, masculine – come to foreclose the possibility of educational 'success', that is, the student is produced as an 'impossible learner'.

This argument, and the theoretical tools that underpin it, are at the heart of the title of this book. The main title, *Impossible bodies, Impossible selves*, alludes to the idea that persons are not 'who' they are because of some natural or essential nature, some inner state. It insists instead that persons come to 'be' 'who' they are by being intelligible within discourses, the bodies of meaning that frame social contexts.   Impossible bodies and impossible selves, then, are outside those frameworks of meaning. They are unintelligible, they are not persons. This set of assertions owe much to the work of Judith Butler, which I discuss in detail in chapter 2, as well as to my own earlier work (See Youdell 2003, 2004a, 2004b, 2004c, 2005). The subtitle, *exclusions and student subjectivities,* is more straightforward. It draws these ideas about how persons, or 'subjects', come to be recognisable together with a concern for processes of educational exclusion. It suggests that students' subjectivities are entangled with schools' notions of different 'sorts' of students and learners. This lays the ground to suggest that student identity in terms of social, biographical and sub-cultural markers *and* the sorts of students and learners they are are tied together in identity constellations that constrain, but do not determine, who the student is or whether they are intelligible as a student at all. Here, then, lies the theoretical possibility, indeed requirement, for the school to constitute the *impossible   learner*. This assertion forms the central discussion of the book.

This book is also part of a series of books entitled *Inclusive Education: cross cultural perspectives*. In engaging the issues at stake in this series, the book steps outside inclusive education as it is usually understood (as concerned with the education of students deemed to have special educational needs) and refocuses on a broader concern with inclusion, a notion that is at once taken up and contested. In doing this, the book takes the UK as its primary focus with Australia a major second thread. The discussions offered, however, attempt to reach beyond these two contexts and draw in parallel concerns and issues from the US and elsewhere. The book does not aim to offer a comparative account of educational inclusion and exclusion in the UK and Australia and beyond. Rather, it reaches across settings in order to identify the global processes that are at play and to tease out global/local intersections. It also explores the usefulness of the analytical tools employed and analyses offered across contexts and in the light of local/global forces. Ultimately, the book remains one about educational exclusions in wealthy industrial nations. This is not to say that the tools offered will not have some utility elsewhere, but it is not the goal of this book to lay claims to that.

Part One of the book, *Subjectivity and Exclusion*, offers a framing for the book by exploring current policy debates concerning educational inclusion and exclusion; outlining key research into educational inequality; and providing a detailed theoretical framework for the analyses and arguments that follow. Part Two, *Researching Subjects, Making Subjects* provides a discussion of the processes of researching these issues, including a consideration of methodology and the ethnographic method as well as explication of the implications for fieldwork and analyses of the theoretical location of these researches. It goes on to provide a demonstration of how school-based ethnographic research into subjectivities and inequality is made to 'work' from constructing data to developing arguments. Part Three, *Educational Exclusions: bad students, impossible learners and intelligible subjects* provides close readings of a series of moments in UK and Australian schools identified as moments of educational exclusion effected through the constitution of subjectivities whose identity constellations include, or even insist upon, the constitution of 'bad student' and 'impossible learner'. Part Four, *Navigating Educational Inclusions and Exclusions,* reverses these concerns, and offers a series of close readings of ethnographic moments that can be understood as constituting students as potentially good students and acceptable learners, but constituting these through simultaneous constitutions outside the bounds of intelligibility in terms of social and sub-cultural selves. In doing this, it demonstrates the negotiation of these positions through students' practices and shows the slipperiness of these constitutions. As such, it also emphasises the possibilities of being constituted a good student and a learner at the same time as being constituted as desirable in social and sub-cultural terms. Finally, Part Five, *Interrupting Exclusions,* explores how these analyses might inform political practices and considers the strategies that educators might deploy to facilitate the loosening of the constitutive ties between student subjectivities and educational exclusion.

PART ONE: SUBJECTIVITY AND EXCLUSION

Making sense of educational exclusion requires an account of the broad policy contexts that frame the school-level processes and practices that are under scrutiny in this book. This contemporary context also needs to be located against the backdrop of ongoing concerns in critical education research with educational inequalities, inequalities that have been and continue to be marked by students' social and biographical identities including race, ethnicity, social class, gender, sexuality, special educational needs, and disability. The combined concern with policy contexts, school-level processes, and the identity categories around which educational exclusions and inequalities orbit also demands an understanding of the person – the subject – that can account adequately for the interplay of individuals, groups and institutions; engage both intent and its limits; and understand constraint without suggesting determination.

Part one of the book, then, offers these framings. Chapter One outlines the contemporary policy context and its significance and explores a number of accounts of educational inequalities that help to situate the arguments that are offered by the book. Chapter Two goes on to detail the understandings of the subject that are at the heart of the analysis offered in later parts of the book. This is a necessarily theoretical discussion that sheds significant light on how and why apparently mundane and everyday practices inside schools are so central both to educational exclusions as they currently are, and to the possibility of interrupting these exclusions.

It is my hope that these chapters serve not only to frame my own analysis, but also to offer a useful introduction to contemporary debates concerning education policy and educational exclusion and inequalities as well as theoretical explorations of how the student comes to 'be' 'who' s/he is.

CHAPTER 1

WHO'S IN AND WHO'S OUT?

Inclusion and Exclusion, Globalised Education Policy, and Inequality

SETTING THE SCENE

This book makes a series of arguments about the processes through which subjectivities are constituted; how these intersect with school constitutions of students and learners; how these school-level constitutions are implicated in educational inclusions and exclusions; and how market sing policies across national contexts frame these naturalised processes. These arguments are made in the intersections of key strands of contemporary educational debate.

First, the book takes up debates about education reform; the global reach of neo-liberalism as it is played out in education policy; and the impacts of these reforms on schools and communities. Second, the book engages debates concerning current patterns of educational inequalities and the likely causes of these. In doing this it engages what often forms a parallel (but intimately connected) debate about social exclusion and the capacity of education to promote social inclusion. And third, it engages debates about the nature of the subject; the status of categorical identities such as, but not limited to, race, class and gender; the promise and limits of identity politics; and post-structural political alternatives. While at times this third set of debates can appear abstracted, they are frequently deployed in empirical analysis and political activism, increasingly so in education. Furthermore, they intersect concerns about the material educational inequalities and exclusions faced by particular groups of students who remain identifiable and identified by identity categories even as discourses of social inclusion push these categories to the fringes and post-structural theory and politics calls these categories into question.

Before moving on to outline in detail the argument made in the book, it is useful to set out these framing debates in more depth.

NEO-LIBERALISM, GLOBAL POLICY PROLIFERATIONS, AND THE SHIFT FROM INEQUALITY TO EXCLUSION

There is now a significant literature that explores the nature and implications of neo-liberal reforms of education across English speaking contexts. See, for example, Apple (2001) on the US; Ball, Bowe and Gold (1990) and Whitty, Power and Halpin 1998, on the UK; and Marginson (1997) and Welch (1996) on the Australian context.

This body of work traces the extrapolation of neo-liberalism since its rise during the late 1970s and 80s and its complex relations with traditional liberalism, neo-conservatism, entrepaneurialism and the new middle class, nationalism, and the religious right. A core activity of this neo-liberalism has been the opening up of public services to at least pseudo-competitive relations (Whitty *et al* 1998), alongside the borrowing of neo- and post-fordist private sector models of management and efficiency (Halsey *et al* 1997).

A key component of this overhaul of education across national contexts has been a process of simultaneous centralisation and decentralisation. Control of curriculum and assessment has been centralised while responsibility for financial management, recruitment of staff and students, and performance has been migrated out to the school. These simultaneous centralising and decentralising trends have been key components of state-led drives for efficiency and accountability. Indeed, the standardised high-stakes tests introduced alongside centralised curricular have become the measures of a schools efficiency and effectiveness. That is, performance in these tests has become the measure of a school's success.

Not only have these standardised high-stakes tests been promoted by governments as an important mechanism of quality assurance, they have also been offered as a key indicator of the quality of schooling for parents and students, themselves reconceptualised as consumers of educational products. With school choice a staple of neo-liberal education markets, diversification of school types has been promoted at the same time as school funding has been tied to school enrolments. This marketisation of education is at the heart of neo-liberal education reform.

In thinking about school choice it is important to recognise that choice markets do not exist in all locales, despite government efforts to promote these (Youdell 2004a); that choice is often contained within particular local competition spaces (Taylor 2002); and that differing degrees of choice are likely to be available within differing locales (Heath 2005). It is also important to be mindful that parents do not all share common grounds for choice and that some motivators for school choice do not line up well with government models of the sorts of choices that parents will make (Gewirtz *et al* 1995). Despite these nuances, however, the underpinning rationale for the development of an education market place in which parent-consumers select educational products remains that the supply-demand relations of a rational free market will promote both diversity and quality.

The underside of this argument, again well rehearsed in the literature (Gewirtz *et al* 1995; Whitty *et al* 1998), is that those schools that do not perform well in high-stakes tests, and those schools that are not chosen by consumers (and these may or may not be the same schools) are also subject to the mechanism of the market. That is, schools that do not perform will lose customers and funding and, in theory at least, they will close down: in the parlance of the market without customers the school will be bankrupt.

However, this is an extended and ordinarily incomplete process, and one that is peopled: non-performing schools still have students, even if they do not have as many as they would like or need. Schools with an under-supply of students find themselves under-resourced and in the position of accepting students who cannot access more desirable schools for which there is surplus demand. These students, it is suggested, are likely to be those considered by schools to be least likely to perform well in high-stakes tests and so contribute to the school's reputation. As such, the school with surplus-supply caters increasingly for those consumers believed to impact negatively on its reputation. This is a cycle of decline that has been referred to as residualisation (Marginson 1997); the sink school made anew in the education market place. While such residualisation is clear in some competition spaces (Ball 2003), it is important to recognise that choice is not always demonstrated to intensify stratification within education systems (Taylor 2002).

So far this account has not engaged the implications of producer practices. One of the criticisms levelled against schools by policy makers in the early moments of neo-liberal reform in the UK as well in Australia was that of producer capture – that schools had become self-interested organisations detached from the needs of economy, employers, and students. Neo-liberal reform, it was argued, would correct that imbalance. While centralising the curriculum and setting performance targets and introducing parental choice of school, neo-liberal reform also encouraged the diversification of school types and re-engaged with the possibility of selection into state schools. This has been struggled over and the right to select students into state schools on the basis of supposed special aptitudes continues to be restricted. Nevertheless, through limited formal selection mechanisms and other admissions policies – such as attendance of siblings, residential proximity, and special needs – it is argued that popular schools that receive applications in excess of available places are able to secure for themselves a student population that is deemed likely to perform well in high stakes test (Whitty *et al* 1998). In this sense then, it is the school that is the consumer selecting between different sorts of students, with a view to maximizing its overall performance in high-stakes tests.

As this outline of neo-liberal reforms of education suggests, these reforms and their impacts are not restricted to the UK. Elsewhere in the wealthy industrialised world, reforms of this kind are being developed. And while these differ in relation to their specific contexts, the turn to market models and new mangerialism to promote educational quality is evident across contexts. See, for instance, in New South Wales, Australia *Securing their Future* (Aquilina 1997), in England *Excellence in Schools* (DfEE 1997), and in the US *No Child Left Behind* (US Department of Education 2001). Reforms of this sort, replete with the language of account-ability, standards and high quality education for the total population, evade engagement with another reality of the market model: in a competitive environment where education is a positional good there are necessarily winners and losers – some children will inevitably be left behind.

In the UK and Australia standardised tests and locale- and national- level comparisons of performance have been in place for some time. As such, data exists to allow the investigation of which students are winning in the education market place and which students are losing. Research by Gillborn and Mirza (2000) in the UK usefully demonstrates how, while overall performance as measured by high stakes tests have improved, particular populations are persistently benefiting disproportionately from these improvements (see figure 1). This research shows performance to be marked by social class, race, and gender, while girls outperform boys from the same background; the most marked gaps are between social class and race/ethnic groups. Students from professional middle class backgrounds and White,

Indian and Chinese ethnic backgrounds continue to be substantially more likely to reach the target grades in high stakes tests than students from manual working class backgrounds and Black, Pakistani and Bangladeshi backgrounds. Similar patterns are evident in Australia, with a small discrepancy between the attainment of all boys and girls, while low socio-economic status, minority ethnic background, and regional and remote locations are all strongly associated with lower attainment irrespective of gender (Collins *et al* 2000).

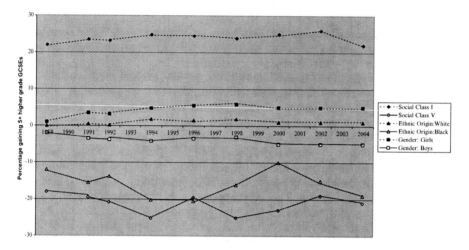

Figure 1. Educational Inequalities by race, class and gender
After: Gillborn and Mirza 2000: 22

It is important to note that not all educationalists that have considered these patterns of differential attainment agree that their most salient feature is the expansion of inter-group gaps. For some, intra-group improvement over time is the focus, and is the basis for claims that the education market place has not see the intensification of educational inequalities (Gorard 2002). Nevertheless, when education functions as a positional good and attainment in high-stakes test is a key device for sorting and selecting into post-compulsory schooling pathways, it seems reasonable to argue that the most salient indicator of advantage and disadvantage is the gap between those doing most well and the rest of the school population.

Research focusing on overall attainment is not designed to demonstrate the processes through which these uneven patterns are produced. In the UK, my own work with David Gillborn (Gillborn and Youdell 2000) examines the ways that these reforms articulate with and impact on school-level practices is. Based on ethno-graphic study in two schools, we show how the demand for performance in high stakes tests at the benchmark set by government is provoking schools to turn to practices of selection and targeted resources allocation. We suggest that, in order to maximise attainment at the benchmark, schools use once discredited ideas of intelligence, recast as common-sense notions of ability, to identify, and justify the identification of, those students who are performing just below the benchmark. These students are then targeted for additional resources and special interventions aimed at facilitating performance at the benchmark. This, we argue, is educational triage: students expected to perform comfortably at or above the benchmark are diagnosed as 'safe' and left to succeed; students expected to perform below the target are diagnosed as 'hopeless' and left to fail; and students expected to perform just below the target but believe to have the 'ability' to make the improvements necessary to push them over the benchmark are diagnosed as 'suitable for treatment' and targeted for intervention. Practices of educational triage can be identified operating at bureaucratic, institutional, and classroom levels in the Australian context (Youdell 2004a). And these practices have also begun to be identified in the US in the context of the *No Child Left Behind* legislation and its State-level fore-runners (Booher-Jennings 2005, Lipman, 2004). In the Gillborn and Youdell (2000) study schools, the safe were disproportionately White, middle class and girls; the hopeless cases were disproportionately Black, working class and boys; and the suitable cases for treatment were disproportionately White, middle class and boys. Research of this sort suggests that market reforms, and the competition and high stakes tests that are core features of this, are impacting on the organizational practices of schools and provoking institutional practices that contribute to the reproduction of educational inequalities.

Neo-liberal education reform, then, is a trans-national, if not global, phenomena, with the proliferation of market based models of state education as well as the exportation of western education products to low-income nations acknowledged features of these globalizing processes (see Apple, 2001; Taylor *et al* 1997). This is, of course, not to suggest a global monolith of neo-liberal education policy. Rather, national and regional specificities and local refractions mean that neo-liberal reforms take on particular shape in different locales. That these market models are implicated in deepening inequities across setting is now beginning to be clear (Dale and Robertson 2004; Gillborn and Youdell 2004; Sleeter 2004).

In order to contribute further to understanding the local/global intersections of neo-liberal educational reform and its inequitous effects, this book works across two locations in which I have undertaken ethnographic research – the UK and Australia. This selection is not arbitrary (both nations have been at the forefront of neo-liberal reform of public services) but other setting would have surfaced. This is because the goal of this book is not to enumerate exhaustively the situation regarding education reform and inequality in these two national contexts. Rather, it is to demonstrate the continuities and breaks in the processes through which inequalities are produced across these setting and to provide tools for understanding similar processes elsewhere.

So far in this discussion I have used the notions of equity and inequality and linked these to particular population groups understood in terms of identity categories such as social class, race and gender. While these population groups are in use in the lexicon of education policy after a period of significant silence in relation to these (Gillborn 2002), a new conceptual category for thinking about – or perhaps more accurately not thinking about – inequality has entered contemporary policy discourse in the UK. This is the notion of social exclusion and its pair social inclusion. These notions are concerned at core with those on the periphery of society within wealthy industrial, or perhaps more accurately post-industrial, nations. While in the current moment these notions are found specifically in UK policy, they are pertinent beyond the UK context. The particular shape of these concerns over those on the fringes of Western society is an expression of the individualisation of failure that underpins neo-liberal models of competition and so might be extrapolated to other wealthy (post-)industrial nations (See Youdell 2004a). Furthermore, past experience of policy borrowing suggests that such notions, or the discursive manouvres that they are expressions of, are likely to be taken up elsewhere if they promise to meet exigencies faced, in this case the need to navigate the space between welfarism and personal responsibility.

This trans-national relevance is further reinforced by the slipperiness of the terms. Social exclusion can be synonymous with multiple disadvantage; it can be recruited to think about non-participation in the economy, production, politics and the social realm; and it can be deployed to define the exterior of the social mainstream, to delimit a *normative centre* of society. Ultimately it appears as a conservative notion: critics have argued that it is one in which the socially excluded person is require to fit – albeit with some assistance – into economic, productive, educational, and social fields that are left unquestioned (Levitas 1998). Not only do the economic, political and social structures that might act to exclude go unchallenged, these are givens located beyond the terms of debate. As such it has been suggested that the discourse of social exclusion provides the UK's New Labour government the opportunity to ameliorate the worst impacts of the market without engaging with poverty or inequality *per se* (Levitas 1998).

Within policy discourse framed by a notion of social exclusion, education is positioned as a key tool for promoting social inclusion through the development of skills, attitudes, qualifications and goals for participation. At the same time as making the pragmatic claim that education might prevent social exclusion, however, social inclusion discourse acknowledges that educational exclusion might precipitate social exclusion. The socially excluded, then, may well have been, or be, the educational excluded – not just in terms of formal removal from schooling but also in terms of non-attendance at school and disengagement from the educational process. Again, it is evident that the model understands exclusionary mechanism to be located in the educationally excluded student, and so specialist interventions or more extensive reforms, such as diversification of the curriculum (see, for instance, Tomlinson 2004), are aimed at promoting inclusion in an education system that is not itself called radically into question. In this frame, concerns with educational inclusion and education as a tool for social inclusion do not allow for a more fundamental questioning of how the institution of formal education, and school institutions, are themselves implicated in excluding students from the educational endeavour, from schooling, through their own processes and practices.

In this book, then, there is an acknowledgement of the significance of the contemporary discourse of social exclusion that frames the UK policy context, and the individualised notions of non-participative, non-citizens that seem to parallel this in other nations. There is a rejection, however, of the notion of exclusion and inclusion as conveyed in this official discourse.

The book takes up the notion of educational exclusions but understands these in a rather different way, insisting that they must be engaged as ongoing exclusionary processes. In this frame, it is not a case of identifying students in a state of, or at risk of becoming, educationally excluded and intervening in this. Rather it is a case identifying how educational exclusions are produced through the mundane and day-to-day processes and practices of educational institutions. Thinking about educational exclusion in this way also insists that it cannot simply be used to describe the student who is out of school or deemed to be disengaged inside school. Instead, it demands that the micro exclusions that take place in the most mundane moments everyday inside schools cannot be understood as simply being experienced by students. Rather these must be understood as constitutive of the student, constitutions whose cumulative effects coagulate to limit 'who' a student can be, or even if s/he can be a student at all.

Social exclusion as it is deployed in policy discourse avoids 'who' the student is. Social and educational inequalities, however, pivot around identity categories. This book demands that these inequalities are recognised and engaged and that better understandings of the processes through which identity categories come to be entangled with social and educational exclusions are sought.

EDUCATIONAL INEQUALITIES

Insisting that concerns for educational inclusion engage with educational inequalities insists simultaneously that particular population groups, and the identity categories through which these are recognised, be placed at the centre of the analysis. This has been at the heart of activism and research by community organisations, teachers, and education scholars that aims in a variety of ways to demonstrate where injustices in education are located and/or challenge and change these.

It is perhaps most useful to conceive of this activity as a series of debates and struggles, each focused around a particular interest or population group identified through their particular positioning in terms of race, ethnicity, social class, poverty, gender, sexuality, and (dis)ability. All of these, it is argued by proponents of the particular cause, are axes around which educational inequalities and/or exclusions operate and struggles for equality or inclusion take place. In this way, these can be seen as forms of *identity politics in education* because it is the identities of the particular group of students that are fore-grounded and where the exclusion/inequality is believed to operate.

For example, Black boys, in this model, might be understood as being excluded from schooling (literally through being ejected from school or from participating in school life) because they are Black and boys. As I will show below, how these inequalities operate is subject to significant debate, both within and across national contexts. These are debates that draw on experience, politics, and theory in a multitude of ways. What seems to be agreed (although by no means universally) is that the *identity* of the excluded group is fundamental to their exclusion. This is not to suggest that the reason for such exclusions rest inside excluded persons – far from it. While suggesting a 'deficit' approach continues to have some advocates, it has been widely discredited on theoretical and substantive ground as well as for being party to the inequality and exclusion it attempts to explain. Rather, the fact that identity or group membership appears central to the operations of educational inequality and exclusion suggests that these are *social* processes – they take place in society at large and in society's institutions, including schools.

Elucidating the identity markers around which educational inequalities and exclusions appear to orbit, and around which identity politics have organised during the past three or four decades, is not as straight forward as it may initially seem. Demands for equality for girls and women, the working class, minority ethnic communities and disabled students are familiar and embedding in a history widely recognised in the educational community and beyond. The emerging demands for equality of educational experience for lesbian, gay, bisexual, queer, transgender and intersex (LGBQTI) students or 'gifted and talented' students, however, are less familiar and may not be accorded the same legitimacy as more familiar race, class and gender based claims. This demonstrates the proliferation of identity categories and identity politics and the impossibility, when attempting to take account of all specific needs and experiences, of being certain to have accounted for all populations and groups.

The population and identity groups named above are frequently the central organizing categories in scholarly considerations of educational exclusions and inequalities. Indeed, it is difficult to imagine how we might think about educational inequalities without these categories. A decade ago the educational literature would have been likely to focus on a single key category, and a review of relevant work in the sociology of education shows a historically located movement through concerns with these categories. It is clearly not possible to detail all of this work, particularly across the range of identity categories that this book aims to engage. Nevertheless, it is important to identify key arguments that have come out of this body of work and to offer some illustrations of this.

Social class

Since the introduction of the 1988 Education Reform Act in England and Wales, which formalised the rejection of progressivism in education and cemented schooling as a neo-liberal endeavour, social class has been off the political and policy agenda. This is not to suggest, however, an absence of either social class effects or scholarly attention to these. The last decade has seen significant work concerned with social class, including debate over what class is, how social class might be defined, how class differences might be measured, and how far social classes might be shifting and diversifying. Ball (2003) offers a useful account of three key strands of research concerned with social class which he identifies as: class theory, concerned with the definition of class; class analysis, concerned with the mapping of class differences, in particular inequalities; and class practices, concerned with the ways that class is produced through social practices.

A concern with class practices understands class to be the product of ongoing social processes that take place at the level of the everyday but which have wider social and material implications: Ball (2003:6) defines such an understanding of class in the following way:

> 'Class here is an identity and a lifestyle, and a set of perspectives on the social world and relationships in it, marked by varying degrees of reflexivity...We think and are thought by class. It is about being something and not being something else. It is relational.'

A key debate in this contemporary body of work concerns the differences within class categories, especially the expanding middle classes (Power 2001), and the dangers of a middle class/working class binary that may fail to access these intra-class differences (Ball 2003). Nevertheless, a distinction between middle classes and working classes remains pertinent in class analyses of education. The classed nature of parental engagement with schools and educational choices, in particular the anti-egalitarian impact of middle class choices, has been a key area of such work. (See, for example, Ball 1993, Ball and Vincent 2001, Gewirtz, *et al* 1995, Reay 1998, and Reay and Lucey 2000). And inequalities in educational outcomes have been shown to be greatest in relation to a middle class/working class divide (Gillborn and Mirza 2001). Furthermore, contemporary research exploring educational experiences has demonstrated continued differentiation along class lines (Ball, Maguire, and Macrae 2000, Reay 2001) and has shown how micro-level school processes are implicated in producing iniquitous outcomes marked by social class (Gillborn and Youdell 2000). Social class, and the distinctions between middle and working classes, then, remains a pertinent lens for analyses of education. And Ball's (2003) notion of class practices offers a useful tool for making sense of the practices of both parents and students in relation to schooling.

Social class practices inside school

The notion of class practices resonates with the tradition of school ethnography concerned with educational inequality, school experiences, and student identities. It is worth pausing to consider this in more detail as it has provided analytical tools and approaches to researching school experience that remain pertinent.

Ethnographic studies concerned with the processes and practices that make up daily life inside school have repeatedly shown social class, and class practices, to be key axes of educational inequality. There is no defining moment of research into social class and schooling, however, classic studies by Hargreaves (1967), Lacey (1970), and Willis (1977) share a concern with the relationship between school practices and the relatively low educational outcomes of working class boys. As well as establishing classed processes and practices inside schooling as a legitimate area of research, these studies also developed and elaborated important analytical tools. Specifically, the notions of differentiation and polarisation developed within these studies and subsequently refined retain a utility for understanding class practices and their impacts in schools today.

The studies by Hargreaves (1967) and Lacey (1970) share a concern with the ways that school values and norms impact on student cultures and, ultimately, educational outcomes. Both see these norms and values as embedded in the school's organisational practices of streaming and reflected in the minutiae of teachers' perceptions of and interactions with students. Both of these studies examine students as members of groups or cliques within the school suggesting that school practices of *differentiation* contribute to the *polarisation* of the student population and the formation of student sub-cultures, with their own norms and values, and which are characterised as 'pro-school' and 'anti-school'. Lacey (1970) defines differentiation as:

'the separation and ranking of students according to a multiple set of criteria which makes up the normative, academically orientated, value system of the grammar school. Differentiation is defined here as being largely carried out by teachers in the course of the their normal duties' (Lacey 1970:57).

He goes on to say that polarisation:

'takes place within the student body, partly as a result of differentiation, but influenced by external factors and with an autonomy of its own. It is a process of sub-cultural formation in which the school-dominated, normative culture is opposed by an alternative culture' (Lacey 1970:57).

Using a similar understanding of differentiation and polarisation, Hargreaves (1967) discusses how the formal and overt consequences of differentiation – streaming – impact in subtle and less visible ways. He suggests that streaming positions influence teachers' perceptions of and interactions with students and that these in turn contribute to processes of polarisation:

'These inferences which the teacher draws in such a highly selective way from students' behaviour, and the 'categorisation process' to which it leads, act as a definition of the situation in which teachers and students find themselves . ... Because the inferences are selected from limited aspects of the child's behaviour and are interpreted in terms of the teacher's role expectations, there is a constant danger of misinterpretation' (Hargreaves 1967:105).

The concern with the relatively low educational outcomes of working class students persisted after moves towards comprehensive education. Over a decade later, Ball (1981) took up the notions of differentiation and polarisation in a co-educational, comprehensive setting. Like Hargreaves and Lacey, Ball focuses on students as groups and is concerned with the roles of organisational and teacher practices in the processes of differentiation and polarisation. Ball suggests that students adopt a range of 'lines of adaptation' (Ball 1981:53) that cannot be fully understood in terms of pro- and anti-school sub-cultures. He takes up a refined understanding of pro- and anti-school positions offered by Lambert (1976) which suggests that pro-school groups might be either 'supportive' or 'manipulative' of school values and norms and anti-school groups might be either 'passive' or 'rejecting' of these norms and values (Ball 1981:121). Furthermore, he suggests that these adaptations and positions are *'flexible'* (Ball 1981:121 my emphasis). While Ball argues that the mixed ability organisational context inhibits the 'emergence of a coherent anti-school culture', he asserts that variant pockets remain (Ball, 1981:254). A key factor in this is the persistence of differentiation through teachers' perceptions of and interactions with students that are 'filtered' through teachers' preconceived notions of students' behaviour and ability (Ball 1981:39).

Willis (1977) is also concerned with the educational outcomes and employment trajectories of working class boys. Unlike Hargreaves, Lacey, and Ball, Willis' analysis is informed by an explicit neo-marxist theoretical framework that bounds the inferences and analyses made. While Willis is centrally concerned with differentiation and the processes of sub-cultural formation, his understanding of differentiation differs markedly from that of the studies already discussed. He suggests that differentiation is: 'the process whereby the typical exchanges expected in the formal institutional paradigm are reinterpreted, separated and discriminated with respect to working class interests, feelings and meanings' (Willis 1977:62). As such it is 'the intrusion of the informal into the formal' (Willis 1977:63). Working with this definition, it seems that Willis leaps over the organisational and teacher practices that concerned Hargreaves and Lacey. However, it enables Willis to focus in on the meanings and practices of the students themselves. For Willis, it is the agency of the students, in particular their resistance to the norms and values of the school, which is of interest. Yet within his neo-marxist framework, this group of students is seen to gain only limited insights into the operations of the organisation they resist – what Willis refers to as 'partial penetration' (Willis 1977:119). Willis maintains that 'there are deep disjunctions and desperate tensions within social and cultural reproduction' (Willis: 1977:175) which create possibilities for alternative outcomes. Yet ultimately, Willis argues, the structural inequalities of capitalist production are reproduced through the students' specific practices of cultural reproduction, that is, through their practices of self.

Hammersley and Turner (1984) challenge the dichotomies of pro- and anti-school and conformity and deviancy that they see as intrinsic to the notions of differentiation and polarisation. They also challenge the coherence and consistency of the school values and norms posited by the theory of differentiation and polarisation and assert that students' engagements with these will be multiple:

> '*The assumption that 'official' values/goals are the primary feature of the school environment for pupils.* This assumption seems rather implausible. Pupils have various latent identities and cultures which they bring with them to school...Furthermore, these different latent cultures may be interrelated in various ways producing multiple sub-cultures. ... We can even playfully speculate that conformity to 'official' goals might sometimes be the product of failure to succeed in other sub-cultures.' (Hammersley and Turner 1984:165 emphasis in original as sub-title).

This assertion of the multiplicity of student cultures and suggestion that school may be secondary or even incidental to students, works to disrupt the linearity of those models offered by both Hargreaves and Lacey. Furthermore, the suggestion that schools might accommodate and, therefore, divert students' adaptations is helpful for making sense of the varying efficacy and impacts of students' resistant practices.

While focusing on social class, the work of Hargreaves, Lacey, Willis, and Ball touches on the significance of race and gender and the intersection of these with social class. Of particular utility is Ball's observation of the increased currency of out-of-school youth cultures and fashions inside the co-educational school – an observation that foreshadows analyses of the school's role in the production of normative (hetero-)sexualities and begins to recognise the particular ways that constellations of identity categories function in particular moments and contexts. Similarly, Willis' juxtapositioning of the working class employment trajectories of 'the lads' with the potential future 'wagelessness' (Willis 1971:154) of Caribbean (sic) young men points towards the specific ways that class is raced and illustrates how discourses of the present (in this case Willis' 'present') are implicated in producing those 'futures' that we are concerned for (Hart 1998).

Gender

As I have discussed elsewhere (Youdell 2005), feminist studies in education have made a substantial contribution to ensuring that gendered school experiences are recognised and the role of the school in producing gendered selves is understood. While the critical school ethnographies of the 1970s tended to be concerned with the schooling of boys, Lambert (1976) undertook a study of social relations in girls' grammar school and substantial research into girls and schooling was undertaken during the following decade. Reflecting the understandings of gender inequalities and the reproduction of gender roles that were seen to underpin these that were dominant during the period, these studies demonstrated the impact of capitalism and/or patriarchy on girls' schooling as these were played out within the micro-processes of the school. See for example, Arnot and Weiner (1987), Askew and Ross (1988), Davies (1984), Griffin (1985), Holly (1989), Lees (1986), Mahony (1985), Stanley (1989) and Weiner (1985), This body of work offered a number of significant insights that are particularly pertinent here. First, it extended to studies of education the broader move within feminism that dislocated sex (male and female) from gender (man and woman). In doing this it endeavoured to challenge the causal relationship between biological sex and gender roles that was the staple of both commonsense and scientific discourse. Second, it suggested that schools not only reinforce dominant gender roles but also 'enforc[e] a set of sex and gender roles which are more rigid than those current in the wider society.' (Delamont 1990:5). Third, it was argued that girls' responses to school could not be understood in terms of pro- or anti-school sub-cultural formation. Rather, girls' gender practice in the context of the school was interpreted as an 'active response to social contradic- tions' through 'a simultaneous process of accommodation and resistance' (Anyon 1983:19). Finally, it established issues of gender on the education policy landscape and identified and secured reforms to policy and practice aimed at ameliorating girls' educational disadvantage.

Work concerned with the schooling of Black girls identified the complexities of girls' experiences of and responses to schooling and highlighted the limits of notions of differentiation and polarisation developed through critical studies of boys' schooling. For instance, Fuller (1984) argued that Black girls' adaptations to schooling are simultaneously (and consciously) pro-education and anti-school. And Mirza (1992) highlighted the inadequacy of understandings of Black boys' experiences of schooling – in particular notions of resistance – for making sense of Black girls' relationship to education and schooling.

Valerie Walkerdine has made a crucial contribution to understanding how the school is implicated in constructing gendered subjects. Walkerdine (1990) argues that a dichotomy of rationality/pathology underpins the production of self-regulating subjects in schools and suggests that girls and women teachers are positioned through an array of discourses, including discourses of femininity, passivity, and irrationality. Hey (1997) exposes the myth of such feminine passivity by showing how girls' relationships with each other are 'invested in the production of certain forms of power and subjectivity' (23) through her analyses of the intricacies of the differences between girls and the discursive frames through which their relationships are mediated. More recent studies, such as those by Benjamin (2002), Kehily (2002) and Renold (2005) have refined these tools still further and have demonstrated these processes across a range of specific contexts and in relation to the construction of particular 'sorts' of girls inside schools. My own work has sought to show how school life is suffused with gender discourses which, through the minutiae of day-to-day practices, inscribe sexed, gendered and sexualised identities (Youdell 2005). These are processes that will be interrogated further in this book.

Race

Educationalists' concerns over the unjust experiences in and outcome from schooling of minority ethnic students did not begin with the evidencing of growing gaps between ethnic groups in the context of the marketisation of education and high stakes tests that I have discussed earlier (Gillborn and Gipps 1996, Gillborn and Mirza 2000). Rather, sociology of education began to engage with these issues during the 1980s as concerns with differential experiences of working class students and girls were being explored. Much of this initial work in the UK focused on African Caribbean students and sought to challenge prevailing 'deficit' notions of African Caribbean students, their families and communities. In place of these deficit models, researchers attempted to understand experiences of schooling from the perspective of African Caribbean students and develop new explanations for African Caribbean students' disproportionately low educational outcomes. Researchers explored the impact of multiple axes of disadvantage, such as race, class and gender, and posited notions of double and triple subordination (Fuller 1984, Mac an Ghaill 1988) and considered particular groups of students orientation to education and schooling. For instance, African Caribbean girls' pro-education and anti-school positions (Fuller 1984) and 'resistance within accommodation' (Mac an Ghaill 1988:9), and African Caribbean boys' resistance of 'institutional incorporation' (Mac an Ghaill 1988:110) and creation of 'anti-school male sub-cultures' (1988:9). A tension exists in such work between a desire to acknowledge cultural difference and a need to avoid this difference being cast as deficit. In the struggle to navigate these tensions, educationalist turned from multiculturalism on the grounds that it was frequently tokenistic, had the potential to reinforce racist stereotypes, and was unable to attend to the differential power relationships that exist between the multiple cultures it claimed to include (Gillborn 2004). While the term multiculturalism remains in both policy and mainstream educational discourse, educators concerned to challenge race inequality have tended to look to other strategies, including anti-racist education in the UK (Gillborn 1995) and political multiculturalism in Australia (Rizvi 1997).

A key contribution of this work has been the development of the concept of institutional racism which has identified how racism is enacted through both routine institutional processes and individual everyday practices which, while not intended to have racist consequences are, indeed, racist in their effects. Mac an Ghaill (1988) and Gillborn (1990) led the application of this line of analysis to research on race and racism in UK schooling to show how African Caribbean boys in particular come to be positioned as in conflict with the school institution and excluded from the processes of education.

The Stephen Lawrence Enquiry, which followed the murder of Stephen Lawrence, an African Caribbean young man, by a group of White young men in London in 1993, reported in 1999 accepting that social institutions, from the police to schools, were institutionally racist and enshrined the acceptance of this and the requirement to address it in UK law. The Enquiry defined institutional racism as follows:

> 'The collective failure of an organization to provide an appropriate and professional service to people because of their colour, culture or ethnic origin. It can be seen or detected in processes, attitudes and behaviour which amount to discrimination through unwitting prejudice, ignorance, thoughtlessness and racist stereotyping which disadvantage minority ethnic people.' (Macpherson 1999: 28).

The notion of institutional racism, then, offers important insights into how minority ethnic students can attend schools that appear to have developed and be implementing equal opportunities policies and still be significantly *more* likely to be excluded (suspended or expelled) and *less* likely to attain benchmark educational outcomes than their White counter-parts.

The notion of institutional racism underpins Gillborn's (1990) take up of Becker's concept of the 'ideal client' (Gillborn 1990:26 after Becker 1970) which offers an important tool for understanding how the school context is framed by teachers' formal and informal constructions of students incorporating classed, gendered, and raced notions of appropriate behaviour. This ideal client of schooling is seen by Gillborn to have particular implications for African Caribbean boys, the minutia of whose practices – from ways of walking, styles of speech and (real or imagined) engagements in the classroom – are interpreted by teachers as a challenge to the school, interpretations that coalesce to sustained a *'myth of an Afro-Caribbean challenge to authority'* (Gillborn 1990:19 emphasis in original as title).

Not all contemporary research concerned with race and education accepts that lower differential attainment is the product of institutional racism. Work such as that by Herrnstein and Murray (1994) argues that intrinsic differences exist between race groups and that these are the cause of differential educational outcomes and subsequent life trajectories. This is clearly a return to a deficit approach embedded in a claim to innate race difference that contains echoes of formally rejected eugenicist discourses.

On the surface less controversial, but I suggest an equally deficit account, is contemporary research that places African Caribbean/African American popular and street culture, including hip-hop and rap music and its association (again real or imagined) with gang membership, drug use and violence, at the core of Black educational failure. In both the US and the UK it is argued that aspirations informed by street culture encourages African Caribbean/African American boys in particular to reject education and turn instead to forms of masculinity that are self-defeating (see Sewell (1998) and Ogbu and David (2003) for UK and US accounts respectively). This is an analysis that is vigorously contested by anti-racist activists who continue to point to the social, economic and educational exclusions experienced by African Caribbean/African American people and is demonstrated by a recent public exchange between Lee Jasper and Tony Sewell (Jasper and Sewell 2003).

In the US educators and activists concerned to offer radical challenge to the continued acceptance of African American students' differential school experience and outcomes have taken up the tools offered by Critical Race Theory (See Ladson-Billings 2004). Developed in US Legal Studies but now taken up in other areas, Critical Race Theory argues that racism is an everyday part of US society, so much so that it is often taken not as racism but as commonsense. In this sense it resonates strongly with the arguments offered about institutional racism that I outlined above. Critical Race Theory goes further, however, by identifying the benefits that White society and White individuals reap from this. In this sense it draws Critical White Studies, which interrogates the privileging of Whiteness, into concerns with race and social justice in education (Leonardo 2004). It also insists that while institutional racism, or the day-to-day practices that produce raced outcomes, might not be intentional on the part of the individual, the individual is, as least tacitly, invested in these. Furthermore, as research evidence that demonstrates the detrimental effects of particular policy trajectories on minority ethnic communities continues to be overlooked by policy makers, the state can no longer claim that these outcomes are unintentional or unanticipated (Gillborn 2005). Indeed, Gillborn has suggested that this demands that rather than consider the processes through which privileging of Whiteness is secured and enacted; we should examine how White supremacy is reproduced.

In the paper *Identity Traps* (Youdell 2003) I take up these debates in a post-structural framework in an attempt to better understand the interaction between institutional racism and African Caribbean student subjectivities, and demonstrate the constitution of African Caribbean students as unacceptable learners through the minutia of everyday life in school. Post-structural engagements with race are increasingly common (see Jacobson 1998; Mac an Ghaill 1996; Miron 1999; and Zack 1997), however, these tools have not been taken up widely in studies of race and education. In *Identity Traps* I map a series of analyses that are taken up and developed later in this book. I identify students' take up of and investment in race as a feature of the self that, while perhaps not wholly biological, is actual and immutable. From this I demonstrate how, while a White/Black binary prevails in mainstream discourse in the school, a strong counter discourse which constitutes a 'hierarchy within the Other' (Youdell 2003:9) circulates within the school's student milieu. I show how this hierarchy within the Other – which positions Black above mixed race, mixed race above Indian, and Indian above Pakistani – is cited and inscribed through students practices, including the narration and policing of intra- and inter-racial heterosexual coupling, the 'schema of raced hetero-sex' (Youdell 2003:11). While this counter-discourse secures significant status for African Caribbean students in the school, success in terms of the hierarchy within the Other sits in an inverse relationship with school discourses of the ideal, or even the acceptable student. Indeed, it seem that it is the very cultural capital valued in the student milieu that is deployed in school discourses that cite and inscribe a 'Black challenge to White hegemony' (Youdell 2003:18). The potential for such post-structural readings of the deployment of raced discourses in school settings and the ways that these are implicated in constituting particular sorts of raced students to be informed by and inform Critical Race Theory is evidenced through the analyses that follow.

Educational experiences and outcomes, then, are marked by social class, gender, and race. Multiple accounts exist, however, of *how* school experiences and outcomes come to be marked in these ways. And whether, and if so how, schooling is implicated in producing class, race and gender in particular ways is subject to significant debate. In addition, class, race and gender do not exist in isolation from each other and additive models do not adequately account for these interrelations. Furthermore, race, class and gender are not the only categories whose terms in which students are frequently classified.

Beyond race, class and gender: including disabled, SEN and GLBQTI students

Special Education Needs (SEN) and sexuality are two further axes that are receiving significant attention in contemporary education studies. These seem on the surface to be quite different orders of categorisation, and they do have quite different places in educational discourse. Special Educational Needs or, in previous incarnations, ineducability, retardation and maladjustment have long been the concern of education. Indeed, as I will suggest more fully later, it is arguable that while Special Educational Needs are often located on the fringes of education, it is in this location at the boundary that Special Educational Needs acts to define and ensure the continuity of education's normative centre. On the other hand, sexuality, and especially sexualities, are new educational terrain and remain outside mainstream concerns. Indeed, it is not widely accepted that sexuality, or sexualities, are the legitimate concern of education or educationalist. These two fields are of particular significance to this book in two ways. At the most straightforward level they are markers of identity that circulate inside schools and are as inescapable as race, class and gender. Second, they offer important insights for the analyses offered in this book. Sexualities, especially queer theory, offers insight into the relationships between sex, gender, femininity/masculinity and sexuality and is a key area in which the contribution of post-structural theory to understanding the subject positions of students inside schools has been explored. And by interrogating the constitution of the 'special needs student', emerging literature in the area also provides tools for interrogating normative constructions of the good student and the ideal learner.

Disability, Special Educational Needs, inclusive education and inclusion
As my earlier discussion indicated, social and educational exclusions are key contemporary policy concerns in the UK and elsewhere. Yet the governmental conceptualisation of inclusion that I have already discussed builds on or, indeed, is one appropriation of a longer-standing notion of inclusion advocated by educators and activists. The critical educators from whose model of inclusion this government manoeuvre marks a shift, have long been concerned about the educational experiences of students identified as having 'special educational needs' (SEN). This work has interrogated the segregated education of students deemed to be outside the normal range of intellectual, social, behavioural, or physical capacities; argued that all students should be included fully in mainstream schools; demanded that mainstream schools engage in radical change in order to allow this inclusion, and

questioned the categorisation and nomenclature of what Felicity Armstrong (2003:23) has called that 'differentiating super-category': SEN. I shall return to this shortly.

Inclusion and inclusive education in relation to students identified as having special educational needs are by no means straightforward concepts. I have noted the transformatory agenda of activists and educators (see for instance Allen 2002, Armstrong 2003, Barton 2001, Booth 2004, Norwich 2002, Slee 1995) and the recuperation into and repackaging of inclusion and inclusive education in policy discourse concerned with drawing the 'socially excluded' into particular (normative) forms of economic, political and social participation/production (Armstrong 2002, 2003). In addition, inclusion and inclusive education have been absorbed into the lexicon of mainstream/generalist education where these have been incorporated into the language of SEN and used interchangeably with, or instead of, the much-criticised notion of integration (Allen 2002, Armstrong 2003). The extent of this integration-style inclusion is in practice often constrained by the everyday institutional processes of mainstream schools that, in the absence of a transformatory effort, inevitably exclude supposedly included students (see Benjamin 2002, Beretan forthcoming).

Critical educators concerned with and for inclusion and inclusive education have been highly critical of the incorporation of a depoliticised version of inclusion into integrationist models, as well as of the concept of special educational needs that is invariably retained, either by default, purposively or strategically, in such a model. In her ground-breaking book *Bad Mouthing*, Jenny Corbett (1996:5) argues that the language of special educational needs must be understood in social and cultural contexts and that in contemporary UK culture '"special needs" is the language of sentimentality and prejudice'.

Corbett (1996), along with others, has suggested that the notion of 'special' is regularly detached from the educational needs to which it is purported to apply and comes to signify the abnormality, deficit, deviancy, and repugnance of the student her/himself. In so doing, the notion of special educational needs remains at least implicitly tethered to medical and psychological accounts (see below). In such a context, Allen (2003) suggests, teachers enact cultural performances of concern over the SEN student at the same time as they insist that they are not equipped professionally to deal with the supposed pathology. In so doing, Allen goes on, teachers evade responsibility for providing education to students so identified and instead pass this responsibility on to an imagined more 'competent' practitioner. Furthermore, the proliferation of diagnostic categories that sub-divide the 'super-category' of special educational needs does not render this less problematic. Rather, as Roger Slee (1995) insists, this acts only to provide further mechanisms to delineate the normal and the abnormal. And the echoes of formally discredited diagnoses of ineducability and maladjustment remain.

The significance of special educational needs, then, and debates concerning the inclusion, or not, of students so designated in mainstream schools, their classrooms and activities reaches well beyond the school as it constitutes and regulates normality. Armstrong argues:

> 'The processes of identification and categorization used in the statementing procedures for learners perceived as experiencing difficulties [...] are examples of wider mechanisms of social ordering and regulation. The routine use of labels such as 'special

educational needs', 'learning difficulties', 'disabled' [...] are examples of social
responses to perceived differences from 'the norm' or deviance from the dominant
values and behaviours in society.' (Armstrong 2003:24).

This claim ties debates over the implications of the continued reach of a
discourse of special educational needs and the policy and professional erasure of the
transformatory goals of inclusive education to wider debates in disability studies
concerning the meanings and status' of disability and impairment.

As Barnes *et al* (2001) note, the impact of the ascription of disability on the
lives of the people so ascribed has been the concern of disability studies for some
time (see, for instance, Blaxter 1976 and Scott 1969). More recently, however, the
medical, psychological and tragic moorings of the concept of disability have
themselves begun to be called into question, as have the notions of individual deficit
and abnormality that are implicit to these. In place of these medical/psychological
accounts a 'social model' of disability has been suggested (Barnes *et al* 2001:5)
which insists that disablement resides in social practice. Studies such as those by
Finkelstein (1980), Sutherland (1982) and Oliver 1983, identified as key examples
of the turn to the social model in disability studies, continue to recognise the
significance of impairment but take the disabling effects of economic and social
structures and practices as their focus (Barnes *et al* 2001). Similarly, Mike Oliver
(1990:xiii) insists that disability be understood as 'social restriction' and not a
medical classification or 'functional limitation' (p. 3). While some critics of the
social model have argued that focusing on disability in a frame that understands
impairment/disability in a biological/social relationship can silence the private
realm, including the bodily experience of impairment, Oliver (1990) suggests that
the term 'disabled people' best reflects lived experience. Oliver (1990) is highly
critical of World Health Organisation definitions of disability and impairment:

> 'It remains close to the medical classifications of disease – disability – handicap. In so
> doing it contains the notion of impairment as abnormality of function, disability as not
> being able to perform an activity considered normal for a human being and handicap as
> the inability to perform a social role. This reification of the idea of normality ignores the
> issue of what normality actually is, but even if the idea of normality is conceded, the
> failure to recognise the situational and cultural relativity of normality is a serious
> omission.' (Oliver, 1990:4).

Engagements with the social model of disability informed by post-structuralism
emphasise the discursive production of disability at the same time as identifying
some limits to the 'conceptual severing of impairment and disability' that is at the
centre of this politics of disability (Thomas 2001:50). For instance, Thomas (2001,
citing Price and Shildrick 1999) insists that impairment is itself a construct that can
only make sense in the context of disability and disablism. Furthermore, this
severing does not free either impairment or disability from Same/Other hierarchies.

Critical and post-structural engagements with notions of disability and
impairment and the social model have provided fruitful ground for considerations of
inclusive education and special educational needs. Particular contributions include
the identification of the significance of students' 'identity work' (Benjamin 2002)
and the way that this is constrained by particular types of SEN (Benjamin 2002);
practices of institutional ableism (Beretan forthcoming); and the intersections of and

interactions between particular sorts of SEN or disability and further categorical identities such as race, class, gender, sexuality (Allen 1999, Benjamin 2002, Beratan forthcoming, Saltmarsh and Youdell 2004).

Amongst this growing body of work, of particular interest are considerations of the implications of the ways that discourses – both those specific to SEN/disability and broader educational discourses – constitute and constrain students and teachers. (See Allen 2002, Benjamin 2002, Laws and Davies 2000, Saltmarsh and Youdell 2004).

These begin to indicate the processes through which students come to be locked into constructions of "bad" or "disturbed" and suggest how efforts to shift existing discourses (Benjamin 2002), transgress subject positions (Allen 1999), and deploy alternative discourses to open up alternative subjectivities (Laws and Davies 2000) might offer radical new agendas for inclusive educators. These ideas not only offer further insight into the processes through which students come to be "special", they also provide tools for thinking about how all students come to be constituted as learners.

Sexualities

The challenge posed to health education by HIV and AIDS prevention has seen educators face the prospect of including issues of sexuality in the school curriculum. Of course, with schools and sexuality constructed as fundamentally discrete, and the people who populate schools – students and teachers – constructed as intrinsically non-sexual (Epstein & Johnson 1998) this has been a site of significant struggle. In many instances engagement with sexuality within the school curriculum has remained restricted to a model of monogamous heterosexual coupling, if not marriage. And moral discourses of abstinence have been assumed and promoted irrespective of whether these speak to many young peoples lives. Unsurprisingly, such curricular have reflected wider gender discourses that produce girls' hetero-sexual responsibility and boys' heterosexual incontinence (Lees 1986, Holland *et al* 1998). That HIV and AIDS has, in the industrialised world, impacted gay communities particularly severely has meant that sexual health education has also looked to address issues of homosexuality. Bringing this about in schools has met with resistance from teachers and students invested in heteronormativity (Rich 1980). And has been impeded in the UK by school concerns over legislation that prohibits local government 'promotion' of homosexuality (Stonewall 2003). Despite these barriers, renewed concern for effective sexual health education has seen sexualities enter official school discourses.

This period has also seen a new wave of Gay and Lesbian activism that has identified the experiences of homophobic discrimination of gay and lesbian students and teachers in schools and demanded that schools take up anti-discrimination policies. Parallel to this reforming agenda queer theory and politics have marked a diverse set of concerns, activisms and ideas that identify the limits of liberal reform and instead call into question the hetero-/homo- hierarchy itself. This has offered tools and impetus to critical and post-structural educationalists concerned to better understand how schooling is implicated in producing particular sexualities and disavowing others (see, for instance, Talburt 2000, Britzman 1995).

Research in schools influenced by queer theory has problematised the figure of the pathologised GLB victim of homophobic bullying; the acceptance of sexuality as an innate of given personal quality; and the treatment of sexuality as either discrete from or a natural expression of gender. Instead, queer research in schools has sought to tease out how sexualities, masculinities, and femininities are constituted together and how heterosexuality is dependent on homosexuality for its ongoing construction. For instance,

Nayak & Kehily (1996) show how homophobic practices in schools are central to the ongoing constitution of heterosexual masculinities; Wayne Martino's (1999) explores the policing of hegemonic masculinity in school; and Martin Mills (1999) shows how heterosexual identities are constructed as normal while lesbian, gay and bisexual identities are constructed outside acceptability. In my paper *Sex-gender-sexuality* (Youdell 2005) I identify the discursive practices that inscribe compulsory heterosexuality and constitute girls and boys in tightly constrained forms of femininity and masculinity. Girls are constituted in an enduring virgin/whore binary, a binary to which boys are immune, while boys are subject to another constraining binary: that of boy/man, in which the man is authoritative, entitled, sexually active and masculine, and the boy is weak, passive, virginal and, so feminine. Girls attempt to negotiate the possibility of sexual activity that does not constitute them 'slag' or 'slapper' (whore), but these adult, moral, and responsible hetero-femininities are fragile and open to recuperation.

Queer research in school has also sought to identify possibilities for queer troubling of heteronormativity and the hetero-/homo- binary inside schools (see Rasmussen and Crowley 2004). For instance, Mairtin Mac an Ghaill (1994) has demonstrated the fluidity of young men's identity and sexual practices. David McInnes and Murray Couch (2001) have analysed the intersections of masculinities and sexualities *and* social class identities as 'working class sissy boys' take pleasure in queering school. And in Youdell (2004b and 2004c) I have shown how students' who are routinely vilified for 'being gay' take up gay and lesbian subjectivities through their bodily and linguistic practices and deploy popular gay discourses in school settings in ways that trouble heteronormativity, refuse homophobic incorporation, and insist on the legitimacy and desirability of the queer subject.

An aside on boys and masculinities

While queer theory and research has been troubling static notions of sexuality and gender, the education mainstream, government, and the media has paid significant attention to boys' schooling. As noted earlier, the constant comparisons of performance in standardised tests has exposed differential outcomes between boys and girls, with girls seen to out-perform boys at the end of compulsory schooling in both the UK and Australia (Arnot *et al* 1998, Collins *et al* 2000, Gillborn and Mirza 2000). As also indicated, this gap is notably smaller than the gaps between the highest and lowest performing race and social class groups. Nevertheless, it is the phenomena of boys' 'under-achievement' that has held media and policy attention in recent years (Epstein *et al* 1998). The reasons for this gap, and whether it is new or simply newly recorded, continue to be debated. Given feminist educators longstanding concerns over the experiences of girls in school this apparent advantage has at times been difficult to respond to, particularly when it has been mobilised to argue that feminism has gone too far and that its gains need to be rolled back. One feminist intervention into this debate has been to ask 'Which boys?' and 'Which girls?' (Collins *et al* 2000) – questions that expose the raced and classed nature of the gender gap and the enduring educational advantages enjoyed by White girls *and* boys from the professional middle classes. Another intervention has been to examine post school trajectories and destination, examinations that show that girls' advantages do not continue into higher education and the labour market and are again, tied up with race and social class (Collins *et al* 2000).

Nevertheless, it remains that boys of all ethnic and class backgrounds are not doing as well as girls during the compulsory school years. Of the varied accounts of the processes involved in creating these patterns, perhaps the most useful to the analyses offered in this book are those that foreground masculinities and the school as a site in which these are constituted and struggled over. Bob Connell's (1995) groundbreaking study of forms of masculinity and his identification of contextually specific hegemonic masculinities has been followed up by research informed by post-structural understandings the subject. Emma Renold's (2005) work has shown how masculinities are constituted in school settings. And Anoop Nayak's (2003) work has been particularly useful in demonstrating how masculinities that are culturally and sub-culturally specific masculinities that reach beyond the school may not sit well with the requirements of schools. My own work has identified the incommensurability of school requirements of boys' practices and the practices of particular groups of boys themselves (Youdell 2003). The question of how particular constitutions of masculinity intersect with, or foreclose, being a good student and learner will form one central thread of this book.

IDENTITY INTERSECTIONS

As the preceding discussion has shown, as work concerned with a particular identity has developed, the significance of intersections and interactions with further categories has both pressed itself upon analysis and been taken up as an important line of enquiry. From relatively simple additive models of double and triple subordination, notions of intersections that have fundamental implications for the identities in question have been posited and the exploration of these intersections have become a key endeavour amongst education researchers. Nevertheless, much research continues to take the nature and source of these multiple identity categories for granted and/or it explores these identity categories but does not fully interrogate the relationships between them. Furthermore, in policymaking, lobbying, media commentary, and research, it is still frequently the case that a single category is placed at the centre of analysis, in the current context this is particularly the case in relation to boys' 'under-achievement' where there is a reluctance to ask 'Which boys and which girls?'.

The successes of identity-based claims for legislative reform and the demonstration of the usefulness of interrogating categories and their intersections has seen the proliferation of 'identity politics' and of identity categories around which these politics organise and on whose behalf these claims are made.

The women's movement has been called upon to recognise the specificities of the experiences of, for instance, women of colour, non-heterosexual women and working class women as well as to justify the continued salience of 'woman' as an overarching organizing category. And the once gay and lesbian movement has reconfigured itself first as Gay, Lesbian, Bisexual, and more recently as Gay, Lesbian, Bisexual Queer, Transgender, Intersex. And the race equality movements have been asked to respond to minority ethnic communities demands to be recognised and to name themselves – Black, Africa, African American, African Caribbean. Aboriginal, Indigenous, First Nations. Asian sub-divided into South Asian and South East Asian, and again into Indian, Bangladeshi, Pakistani, Chinese (mainland and Hong Kong), Japanese, Indonesian, Phillipino. Latin subdivided by the linguistic gendering of Spanish into Latina/Latino. And the disability movement's debates over impairment, disability and the disabled person. And so on.

But these categorisations are not the sole domain of the political movements that take them up, cite them, and proliferate them. These categories of the person also circulate in mainstream and hegemonic discourses and, in so doing, may well act against the interests of the individual and groups so named. For instance: Islamic interchanged with Middle Eastern and Arabic and Asian. Asian interchanged with Oriental. Black and African interchanged with West-Indian, Negro. Women substituted by ladies, girls. Men substituted by boys. Men substituted by girls.

Further, recent years have seen a re-emergence of common-sense notions of unevenly distributed intelligence – high ability, average ability, low ability, gifted, talented, special needs – and the deeply problematic tendency for these to be associate with particular race and social class groups (Gillborn and Youdell 2000). There has also been a proliferation of diagnostic categories: special educational needs, learning difficulty – mild, moderate, severe; emotional and behavioural difficulties (EBD), Emotional Difficulties/Behavioural Disorder (EDBD), Attention Deficit Hyperactivity Disorder (ADHD); autistic, autistic spectrum, Asbergers syndrome; disabled, impaired – sensory, physical, intellectual. Special. And so on. While these classifications are often essential to access resources, services, even recognition of existence, they also constrain and injure (Slee 1996). And my discussion has not touched on other educational sub-categories such as English as a second language or non-native English speakers or Language other than English spoken at home, refugees and asylum seekers, or travellers, or the homeless. Nor have I named any of the many explicitly injurious names – sometimes defunct, formal classification, sometimes slang and expletives – that continue to circulate.

To come to yet another 'and so on' indicates the limits of both my vocabulary and my stomach for categorisation. It also indicates the impossibility of enumerating fully every category by which a person might be classified, and the 'illimitable *et cetera'* that Judith Butler insists offers new possibilities for thinking about politics (Butler 1990:143). As I show in the next chapter, some of these proliferations have been and continue to be the result of, and tools for, political, economic and social claims made by subordinate groups. These proliferations also have the potential to box us into tighter and tighter spaces, to open us up to closer and more precise scrutiny, to render some bodies and selves possible and others impossible. They are the occasion and vehicle of our subjection. And so they are the occasion and vehicle for our action.

MOVING ON

This book offers an intervention across the terrain of educational inequalities, political claims of and for identity, and concerns with the limits of categorical identities and the politics built around these. In offering this intervention this book holds onto the language and concerns of this terrain, while at the same time insisting on shifts in both its questions and understandings. At the centre of this book is an ambition for a just education system, in which justice is understood not just as equality of opportunity but experience and outcomes alike. As such it follows a clear trajectory from critical education theory and research. Yet at the same time the book recognises the limits of this ambition in that it has not been achieved by the efforts of transformatory education and has been rendered almost incomprehensible by decades of market reforms. As well as understanding how enduring educational inequalities are created and sustained, the book considers how the identity categories that these inequalities orbit around are produced and how these identity categories come to be central to both how we understand ourselves and others as well as how we understand educational processes and educational inequalities.

As such, the book asks: *Why are these categories so important, and why do they seem inescapable? Would social inclusion, and educational equity, be better served by jettisoning these categorisations? Might this be a viable possibility and how else might we think about the subjects of schooling? Why are these categories so readily recognisable in schools, not just from English school to English school, but in schools across the English speaking world and beyond?*

In making this intervention and responding to these questions the book offer three key lines of argument.

First, it suggests that categorical identities might be conceived of and interrogated as shifting, non-necessary *constellations* of categorisations, constellations that are themselves shifting and non-necessary. This is not to suggest that each category that is embroiled in such a constellation is discreet or sealed. Rather, it is to ask how these categories might come to be meaningful through their relationships to other categories within particular constellations and whether constellations might be necessary for apparently singular categories to be meaningful. This line of analysis suggests that each marker is informed by its intersections and interactions with further markers to form a 'constellation' that comes to 'be' the apparently 'whole' person. I say apparently whole because I am extremely sceptical about either the lived experience or the theoretical viability of the unitary subject, developing, rational, self knowing, the sum of his/her parts.

Suggesting that the interactions of identity categories be conceptualised as constellations is not intended to suggest a construction that infers prior raw materials or essences (Fuss 1990, Grosz 1995). The constellation of stars is meaningless until we join the dots, until we draw in the sky and impose meaning. If a point goes unconnected, the constellation fails – we cannot see the Bear and the constellation remains meaningless. Yet we join the dots in particular, abiding but *non-necessary* ways. We join the dots to make the Bear as we have done for centuries, but we need not join them in these ways. There are surely other pictures that could be drawn in the sky. It is these other ways of seeing, and being, that this book pursues and hopes to illustrate. Nevertheless, despite my positing and use of the notion of constellations of identities, I remain dissatisfied with it. This is because, while the light of the star that we see is not the star itself, the star remains (with or without the constellation) and a return to both a singularity and a truth of identity is threatened. Despite this reservation, I make use of the notion here in an attempt to push forward additive accounts of multiple identities and demonstrate the nature – albeit contextually specific and potentially fleeting – of the intersection and interactions of identity categories that are the concern of much contemporary literature in the field.

Second, the book argues that it is through these constellations of identity categories that particular types of students and learners are constituted. In doing this, the book demonstrates how these school identities are constituted in the day-to-day practices of schools through dichotomies of *good/bad students* and *acceptable/unacceptable* and even *ideal/impossible learners*. The book suggests that discourses of ability and intelligence are crucial for the constitution of these student and learner identities, yet they are not the sole constituents of these. Learner identities are also closely linked with notions of school orientation. Within organisational discourses, the sociological distinction between school and educational orientation is elided and school orientation subsumes and/or denies educational orientation. In turn, this school orientation becomes synonymous with degrees of effort. Furthermore, organisational discourses of school orientation also interact with discourses of behaviour and discipline. Indeed, effort is often inseparable from compliance with school rules and values such that positive school orientation becomes synonymous with acceptance of the school hegemony.

As this multiplicity of discourses interacts, learners are constituted along axes of ability, effort, conduct – axes that themselves interact with biographical identities through discourses of class, race, religion, gender, sexuality, disability, special educational needs and so on. Privileged sub-cultural and/or biographical identities are recuperated and deployed within organizational discourse to constitute bad students, unacceptable learners. Indeed, within these constitutions there appears at times to be an inverse relationship between status in the mainstream student subculture and the organizational discourse of bad students and unacceptable, even impossible, learners. That is, biographical and sub-cultural identities come together in identity constellations in ways that create possibilities and set constraints for various student and learner identities and practices that constitute high status in one of these discursive fields are the very practices that constitute low status in the other.

Finally, through these analyses the book suggests that *inclusions and exclusions are inextricably linked to the everyday school practices* that constitute students through dichotomies of good or bad, and learners as acceptable or unacceptable, ideal or impossible. While such constitutions are necessarily provisional and can have unexpected effects, the endurance of particular official and popular discourses within school contexts suggests that being made a subject in particular ways has far reaching implications for educational inclusion and exclusion. The book shows how inclusion in one domain might suggest, risk or require exclusion from another. That is, inclusion in formal school cultures might hinge upon acceptable learner identities that are bound, albeit invisibly, with particular biographical and sub-cultural identities. Conversely, inclusion in particular student sub-cultures might come to hinge on particular biographical and learner identities such that student sub-cultures might suggest, risk or require exclusion from cultures sanctioned by the school. This analysis shows how some exclusions might come to be all but necessary and some inclusions might come to be all but given and, in turn, offers important new insight into the micro-processes involved in generating, and potentially interrupting, patterns of educational inclusion and exclusion.

The book also demonstrates how these exclusions and inclusions are predicated on an implicit but pervasive separation of the normal from the abnormal that continues to pervade educational and wider modernist discourses and inscribe an abiding normative centre. This implicit normal/abnormal dichotomy underpins the inclusion of the good student, the ideal or at least acceptable learner and the exclusion of the bad student, the unacceptable or even impossible learner. This is underscored by the contemporary reach of education understood as a *positional* good, predicated on individualism and meritocracy. This provides the taken-for-granted conceptual foundation that insists that somebody must occupy the bottom of the educational, and societal, heap.

This analysis of the discursive foundations of inclusion/exclusion begins to indicate the possible limits of a transformatory inclusion project and calls radically into question the efficacy of identity politics, equal opportunities policies and legislation, and inclusion initiatives. In response to these limits the book explores the possibilities for an alternative politics and action that undercuts those hegemonic discourses that bind students' bodies and selves to excluded subjectivities, but which recognises the impossibility of a project that seeks to effect a once and for all abolition of these discourses. This deconstructive politics is not offered as a theoretical possibility. Rather, in the chapters that follow, the book offers empirical evidence that demonstrates how students are *already* engaged in practices that reflect recent calls for a politics of hegemony – practices that challenge the terms of educational exclusions by shifting the meanings of school discourses and insisting that previously disavowed discourses function in school contexts.

CHAPTER 2

RENDERING SUBJECTS

Theorising the Production of the Self

INTRODUCTION

In the previous chapter I suggested that student subjectivities and educational exclusions are tied together by the networks of discourse that make constellations of identity categories meaningful. Particular constellations of identity categories, I suggested, are more or less compatible with school notions of good students and ideal (or acceptable) learners. Indeed, I argued that some identity categories might be incommensurable with school notions of the learner such that some students might be rendered impossible learners within the discourses that frame the school.

This series of assertions rests on data generated through two school ethnographies and represented and analysed through a particular theoretical frame. This theoretical framework – which might be referred to as 'post-structural', or 'Foucauldian', or more precisely that of 'discursive performativity' and 'performative politics' – is detailed in this chapter in order to underpin the arguments outlined in chapter 1 and developed and demonstrated through the analyses that will follow in subsequent chapters. This allows the theoretical underpinnings of the book to be interrogated and, therefore, the plausibility of the analyses offered to be assessed. Furthermore, by bringing together a number of considerations of the subject and offering these in a form that should be accessible to those new to these ideas, the chapter aims to facilitate a wider engagement with and take up of these ideas.

The use of post-structural ideas may seem at odds with a concern with educational inequalities and exclusions. Indeed, post-structural ideas have been charged with relativism, self-indulgence, an evacuation of politics, and a failure to take account of, speak to, and be useful in the real world. Yet as Foucault illustrates strongly in his essay *Critical Theory/Intellectual History* (Foucault 1990d) post-structural ideas do not come out of a rejection of concerns with material conditions. Rather, they come out of a recognition that existing structural understandings of the world, whether these focus on economic, social, ideological, or linguistic structures, do not offer all the tools that we need. In supplementing these tools, Foucault's work reconfigures how we understand history (as marked by improvisational borrowing in the face of new and pressing demands); power (as at once productive and an effect of discourse); knowledge (as contingent and constructed and linked intimately to power); and the subject (as subjectivated through her/his constitution in and by discourse) (see Foucault 1990a and 1991). These ideas, which I examine in detail in this chapter, help us better understand how practices – located and real and constrained – make some things possible, or even likely, and other things all but impossible.

At the centre of this theoretical frame is a rejection of the subject understood as a natural, abiding, self-evident individual, and an acceptance of the *subject as a discursive constitution who appears to be abiding and natural not because s/he is so, but because ongoing discursive practices create this illusion.* The value of this claim is two fold: it offers new insight into the processes through which inequalities are produced, come to endure and might be shifted, and it includes the constant potential for subjects who appear to be fixed to be otherwise: the student taken to be 'badly behaved', 'less able', or 'disabled' need not be any of these.

ON POWER AND DISCOURSE

The assertion that the subject is performatively constituted rests on a particular conceptualisation of power and discourse. Within education sociology and social science more broadly, there has been a tendency for power to be conceptualised as something that is possessed and exerted. Whether possessed by a Sovereign, State, group or individual and whether exerted through consensus or coercion, the prevailing and 'commonsense' understanding of power is that it is held by one individual or group over another individual or group(s). This has been characterised as a 'zero-sum' conception of power (Parsons 1960 cited by Giddens 1993:212). Zero-sum suggests that power is an unevenly distributed finite resource. While attempts have been made to shift this notion of zero-sum power, for instance Parsons' assertion that power can both 'inflate' and 'deflate' (Parsons 1963 cited by Giddens, 1993:241-217), this has not altered the underlying assumption that power is a property that is (or is not) possessed.

This is not to suggest that power is understood generally to be held exclusively by a single individual or group within a given society. Emancipatory politics have detailed multiple axes of power through which inequalities are produced and reproduced. This has led to an 'additive' model of subordination (and, implicitly preceding this, an additive model of power) in which individuals or groups are seen to be 'doubly' or 'triply' subordinated along intersecting axes of, most commonly but only for instance, gender, race and social class. (See for example Fuller 1984 and Mac an Ghaill 1988).

Bourdieu (1990 & 1991) has offered a more nuanced account of the ways in which iniquitous relations of power are produced and reproduced. Dominated by a concern with social class, Bourdieu's formulation suggests that power relations are reproduced through differential relations of social, cultural, economic, and linguistic 'capital'. While this does not shift the notion of power as something possessed, it offers further insight into the mechanisms through which such power might be understood to be amassed, transmitted, and retained.

The notion of power as something that resides in and/or is held by 'the powerful', whether the powerful is a monarch, government, institution, social group, or individual, has been characterised as 'sovereign power' (Foucault 1990a and

1991). More recently, however, such understandings of power have been challenged. In particular, the work of Foucault has offered a reformulation of power that entails a simultaneous reformulation of the way in which the subject is understood. I will discuss this second point later in this chapter. Here I want to outline Foucault's understanding of power and the implications of adopting this particular concept-tualisation of power.

Foucault effects a shift from the notion of sovereign power, which is held, possessed and exercised, to the notion of 'disciplinary power', which is productive and formative (Foucault 1990a & 1991). I shall return to this shortly. The notion of disciplinary power is itself predicated on a prior shift from structural analyses of society to a concern with discourse and discursive practices. In this analysis, discourses are understood to be bodies of knowledge that are taken as 'truth' and through which we see the world. Foucault identifies science in particular as a discourse that functions as a 'regime' of truth (1980:112). We can also identify discourses of race or gender that set out what it means to be a gender or a race, but do this *as if* these were natural and/or self-evident. This is a crucial aspect of Foucault's account of discourse: while the terms of discourses may well be taken as reflecting 'truth', the way things are, for Foucault these are not reflections but the very moment and means of the *production* of these truths. For example, by conceiving of gender in a particular ay, gender comes to exist in that form.

This is not, however, a rigid or closed system; Foucault says of discourse:

> 'we must conceive discourse as a series of discontinuous segments whose tactical function is neither uniform nor stable. ... we must not imagine a world of discourse divided between accepted discourse and excluded discourse, or between the dominant discourse and the dominated one; but as a multiplicity of discursive elements that can come into play in various strategies' (Foucault 1990a:100).

Thinking in terms of discourses and their use or deployment – discursive practices – is not simply a concern with language, that is, text or speech. Text and speech are practices of discourse in that they repeat and so inscribe these systems of meaning and, in so doing, contribute to the ongoing constitution and bounding of what makes sense. Representations that are not immediately linguistic but are made sense of and so rendered accessible through language, such as images or gestures – pictures drawn on pencil cases, raising a hand in a classroom – also inscribe wider systems of meaning and constitute what is and is not knowable. As such, discourse comes to appear somewhat circular: discursive practices constitute discourse at the same time as being constituted by discourse.

In this understanding, meaning is historically located; it has historicity[ii] – what it means to be a particular gender in one moment might be different from what it means to be that gender in another moment. This historicity guides, but does not determine, the way that discursive practices constitute and are constituted in discourse. This is a guiding, rather than determining because meaning is understood to be equivocal, open to varying interpretations – recognisable, appropriate gender behaviour is not singular in a given context, let alone across contexts. Meaning is also contingent, it is non-necessary – gender does not *need* to be as it is and so it is open to contestation and change. One discourse is not intrinsically imbued with more or less power than another. Yet the historicity of particular discursive practices means that some discourses – that gender follows naturally from sex, for instance – do come to dominate and bound legitimate knowledge and, indeed, what is knowable. So while some meanings do appear to be more or less equivocal and contingent than others, the impossibility of fixing meaning once and for all mean that even the most enduring discourses are not 'master' (Cixous & Clement 1986a) discourses.

Foucault's 'archaeological'[iii] and 'genealogical'[iv] approaches perceive power as intrinsic to discourse, circulating through the minutiae of discursive practices. Foucault writes:

> 'Power is everywhere; not because it embraces everything, but because it comes from everywhere ... Power is not something that is acquired, seized, or shared, something that one holds on to or allows to slip away; power is exercised from innumerable points, in the interplay of nonegalitarian and mobile relations' (Foucault 1990a:93-94).

Power is not simply a repressive force that is wielded or enacted by a rational individual and/or State – it is deployed improvisationally through the micro-circuits of discursive practices in historically contingent circumstances, in the day-to-day interactions of people and practices of institutions. This is not to suggest, however, that power is either random or incidental. In his discussions of the genealogy of institutional forms (most notably the prison but also the school, hospital, sanatorium and military) and the discourse of sexuality, Foucault offers the concept of 'disciplinary power' (Foucault 1990a & 1991) along with a series of regulatory 'technologies' through which it operates. Disciplinary power is described by Foucault as follows:

> 'it implies an uninterrupted coercion, supervising the processes of the activity rather that its result and it is exercised according to a codification that partitions as closely as possible time, space, movement. These methods, which made possible the meticulous control of the operations of the body, which assured the constant subjection of its forces and imposed upon them a relation of docility-utility, might be called the 'disciplines'. (Foucault 1991:137).

Foucault (1991) identifies a series of 'disciplines' or 'technologies' of disciplinary power. 'Spatial distributions' are concerned with enclosure and partitioning, the establishment of functional sites, and the ranking or classification of bodies – the assembly hall, the classroom, the row of desks. 'The control of activity' is concerned with time-tabling, the elaboration of the act, body and gesture, and exhaustive use of time – the thorough compartmentalizing of the school day, the on-task student neatly underlining the title in her/his exercise book, sitting neatly behind her/his desk. 'Normalizing judgment' compares, differentiates, categorises, homogenises, corrects and excludes – the good student, the bright student, the bad student, the special student. The 'examination' documents individuals into cases – databases of student-by-student performance in standardised high stakes test. 'Hierarchical observation' or 'surveillance' underpins theses technologies – the student, teacher, and school are each subject to the gaze of the next, and all are subject to the gaze of the state. In turn, and perhaps most significantly, this gives rise to the 'self-surveillance' of the observed, examined and judged 'individual' whose activity is controlled and who is distributed across functional sites – the student acts the good student, the teacher acts the good teacher, the school acts the good school as accountability mechanisms render all visible and open to assessment and correction.

These technologies are seen as drawing from, circulating within and sustaining those established and emergent discursive frames available in particular historical circumstances in order to meet the particular exigencies faced. Industrialisation saw borrowing from the practices of the church and army in organising school and students. In the contemporary moment, post-industrial developed nations borrow the techniques of corporate management and make use of newly available information technologies in their efforts to ensure that schools and students meet the needs of the state and the economy.

The theorisation of these technologies of power in the context of emergent institutions, or 'disciplinary institutions' (Foucault 1991) does not imply that disciplinary power is seen either to be the privilege of those who plan, develop and manage these institutions or as located exclusively within these institutions. Indeed, these technologies are understood to constitute and circulate through those discourses and discursive practices that constitute social life. As such, the schools that forms the central sites of study in this book can be understood as disciplinary institutions in which the discursive practices that constitute school life are permeated by the localised effects of disciplinary power. I will return to this understanding of the school when I detail my research methodology in Chapter 3.

This reformulation of discursive and disciplinary power suggests that power and knowledge are intertwined. Knowledge does not enable power to be accessed, nor does power give access to knowledge. Discursive technologies of power constitute, disavow, and resist particular knowledges. At the same time, power is an effect of knowledge and the discursive deployment of its 'truths'. As such, Foucault refers to 'power/knowledge': 'what is said [...] must not be analyzed simply as the surface of projection of these power mechanisms. Indeed, it is in discourse that power and knowledge are joined together' (Foucault 1990a100). This notion of power is central to Foucault's understanding of the subject

THE SOCIALLY CONSTRUCTED SUBJECT AND THE LIMITS OF CONSTRUCTIONISM

The debate over whether persons are natural and abiding or created through some sort of social or linguistic process has been underway for some time. Commonly referred to as the nature-nurture debate, this struggle over essences and constructs gained significant momentum through the political activism of identity politics. Nevertheless, there remains a tendency in social science and education research that is not specifically concerned with the nature of the individual to accept (at least implicitly) the rational, knowing subject – or Cartesian man (sic) – inherited from Enlightenment thought.

In educational and social scientific research that is centrally concerned with making sense of the subjects of whom it speaks, understandings of identities as socially/culturally constructed have largely supplanted essentialist models of identities within the social sciences. These have countered the apparent determinism of biological explanations and open up space in which possibilities for change could be conceptualised. Such theorisations suggest that identities are shaped through social and cultural institutions located within particular historical contexts and constraints.

Yet despite the initial promise and ongoing attractiveness of identity politics based on socially constructed and potentially elective common identities, the usefulness of this understanding has been called into question for two apparently contrasting reasons. On the one hand, opposition to essentialist theorisations have led it to reject determinism to the extent that identities have come to be configured as a matter of choice: 'the point that needs underlining is that *identity* is a choice' (Weeks 1991:80 original emphasis). In so doing, they appear to side-step the historical contextualisation they call for and simultaneously retain, either implicitly or explicitly, a notion of the rational subject who makes this 'choice'. On the other hand, while constructionist understandings have sought to overcome the determinism of biological explanations of identities, the social/cultural institutions through which identities are said to be constructed have been positioned (and in some senses demonstrated) to be so powerful and far reaching that biological 'determinism' has been replaced by a 'social/cultural determinism'.

The appropriateness of positioning 'essence' and 'construct' as oppositional and, indeed, the utility of pursuing this debate has been called into question. Fuss (1990) queries both the logic and the utility of establishing a good/bad dichotomy between constructionism and essentialism. Fuss argues that, while set up in opposition to one another, essentialism and constructionism are deeply entwined. Essentialism, she argues, is not inherently materialist or reactionary. And constructionism, while concerned with refuting essentialism, is itself deeply essentialist, relying heavily upon essentialist notions while simultaneously renouncing essence. Fuss illustrates the essentialism upon which constructionism is set with recourse to the categories man and woman: while constructionist arguments foreground the discursive production of these categories, the categories themselves are sustained. Hence she argues that '[s]ome minimal point of commonality and continuity necessitates at least the linguistic retention of these particular terms' (Fuss 1990:4). Fuss does not accept the constructionist pluralisation of terms – femininities, sexualities, for instance – as an adequate negotiation of this contradiction. This is because plurality within a category retains the category itself: '[t]he essentialism at stake is not countered so much as *displaced*' (Fuss 1990:4 original emphasis). Similarly, the constructionist assertion of the body as "always already' culturally mapped' – bodily sex is meaningless without a cultural understanding of this body – does not obliterate the possibility of an essence beneath the surfaces of this cultural mapping. Rather, it too 'defer[s] the encounter with essence, displacing it, in this case, onto the concept of sociality' (Fuss 1990:6).

Fuss is not alone in identifying these implicit reliances upon essence within a constructionism that has the express intention of undermining all recourse to essence. Elizabeth Grosz highlights the internal contradiction within constructionism when she queries how constructionism might account for the 'raw materials' from which it constructs – if not through recourse to essences:

> 'In my understanding, a mistaken bifurcation or division is created between so-called
> essentialist and constructionists insofar as constructionism is inherently bound up with
> notions of essence. Constructionism, in order to be consistent, must explain what the
> "raw materials" of the construction consist in; these raw materials must, by definition,

be essential insofar as they precondition and make possible the process of social construction' (Grosz 1995:245 footnote 1).

The implicit dependence of constructionism on essentialism creates, therefore, an impasse within its own terms. And alternative ways of understanding the processes through which subjects come to appear self-evident have been sought.

DECONSTRUCTION AND THE SUBJECT

The work of Jacques Derrida makes an important intervention into this terrain. Underpinning Derrida's argument is a critical engagement with language – both written and spoken – and his preferred notion of communication (Derrida 1988). Derrida interrogates these in the context of a broader analysis of the limits of metaphysics and the foundations of Western thought.

Derrida identifies hierarchical binary pairs at the heart of meaning making and the inscription of power relations: mind/body; reason/nature; nature/culture; writing/speech; man/woman; masculine/feminine; white/black; heterosexual/homosexual; capitalism/socialism; Same/Other. These binaries demarcate presence and absence, domination and subordination, intelligibility and unintelligibility, *the Same and the Other*. Furthermore, the terms of these binaries are bound in an inextricable dependency. This is because the dominant presence is always defined against the absent Other, that is, *in terms of what it is not*: Black is extrapolated to define what is not White; disabled is extrapolated to define what is not able-bodied; the Other is extrapolated to define what is not the Same, what is not normal and taken for granted. The Same depends on the Other, even as it disavows it.

These binary concepts are frequently entangled in webs of associations, for instance, mind-reason-man-masculine opposed to, and disavowing, body-nature-woman-feminine. This entanglement is often so deeply set that concepts from one or other side of the binary become almost synonymous, for example, man-masculine/woman-feminine. As such:

'an opposition of metaphysical concepts ...is never the confrontation of two terms, but a hierarchy and the order of a subordination [...] every concept, moreover, belongs to a systematic chain and constitutes itself in a system of predicates.' (Derrida 1988:21).

These systemic chains can be understood as discourses in which 'the central signified, the original or transcendental signified, is never absolutely present outside a system of differences' (Derrida 1978:354). That is, the privileged term – able-bodied – is only meaningful through in relation to a subordinate partner – disabled, impaired. This means that the residue of the subordinate term remains as an insistent absent presence. It also insists that the meaning of the privileged term does not reside in itself but is deferred through its relationship with further terms – this simultaneous difference and deferral is Derrida's *difference* (Derrida 1978).

Recognising this, Derrida's deconstruction offers an intervention that moves past opposing the hierarchical nature of the conceptual pairs and championing the subordinate partner – gay rights, disability rights, women's rights. Instead, he suggests strategies of deconstruction that involve:

'conserving all these old concepts within the domain of empirical discovery while here and there denouncing their limits, treating them as tools which can still be used. No longer is any truth value attributed to them; there is a readiness to abandon them, if necessary, should other instruments appear more useful. In the meantime, their relative efficacy is exploited, and they are employed to destroy the old machinery to which they belong and of which they are themselves pieces. (Derrida 1978:358-9)

'Normal' is opened up to interrogation and exposed as being full of contradiction, provisional, and dependent on the 'abnormal' which it is posited as notbeing. For Derrida, then, possibility lies not in attempting to jettison either or both term of a hierarchical pair, but instead a strategic and provisional retention of old names:

'Deconstruction cannot be restricted or immediately pass to a neutralization: it must, through a double gesture, a double science, a double writing—put into practice a *reversal* of the classical opposition *and* a general *displacement* of the system. It is on that condition alone that deconstruction will provide the means of *intervening* in the field of oppositions it criticizes ... deconstruction does not consist in moving from one concept to another, but in reversing and displacing a conceptual order' (Derrida 1988:21, original emphasis).

Same/Other hierarchies cannot simply be erased or equalised and so opposing discourses of the Same from the position of/by the Other is intrinsically limited as a politics. Instead discourses of the Same should be interrogated in order to expose both their intrinsic reliance on the Other and their internal tensions and contradictions. Practices of deconstruction, then, supplant oppositional modes of resistance.

Such a deconstructive analysis is well illustrated in relation to sex/gender by the *ecriture feminine*⁷ of Helene Cixous (1986:68) who asks:

'Where is she?
Activity / Passivity
Sun / Moon
Culture / Nature
Day / Night
Father / Mother
Head / Heart
Intelligible / Palpable
Logos / Pathos.

Form, convex, step, advance, semen, progress
Matter, concave, ground—where steps are taken, holding- and dumping- ground
Man
———
Woman

Always the same metaphor: we follow it, it carries us, beneath all its figures, wherever discourse is organised.'

Cixous' text illustrates the way in which the feminine is at once constituted as and tied to the subordinate side of these gendered hierarchical binaries. It also shows how this tethering is implicated in the ongoing constitution of the masculine on the as the privileged part of the pair *and* dependent on the feminine for its continued meaningful constitution in these terms.

Over time the apparently universal concept of 'woman' has come to be seen as increasingly problematic: the differences between women, in particular their differential power positions[vi], have led to a questioning of this concept and the shared (while potentially still distinct) subordination of particular groups of men and women has been highlighted, in turn challenging the proposition of universal patriarchy. Perhaps most significantly here, it has been suggested that the category 'woman' implicitly rests upon those assertions of 'natural' or 'essential' difference which feminism has sought to challenge. A key strategy for countering this has been the drawing of a distinction drawn between the categories of biological 'sex' – male/female – and the socially and historically constructed and inequitous categories of 'gender' – man/woman.

However, feminists such as Cixous have problematised the strategic severing of sex and gender as well as these very notions. This is because an assertion of oppositional categories of sex inadvertently inscribes, or is at least open to recuperation by, dominant discourses that assert a natural and essential difference between man and woman. Likewise, it has been argued that as Woman explicates what Man is not, to organise around gender (rather than sex) categories does not avoid this implicit inscription of the Same. That is, the very discursive practices through which women's subordination has been effected. Indeed, it has been suggested that any reliance on the subordinate term of a binary hierarchy intrinsically inscribes the dominant term that is being opposed – 'woman' and 'man' are meaningless except through their mutual (but unequal) exclusion. As such, an increasing number of feminist scholars have been concerned with the possibility of identifying a 'third term' which exceeds and is irreducible to the binary (see, for instance, Cixous and Clement's discussion of 'bisexual' (Cixous & Clement 1986) and Wittig's discussion of 'lesbian' (Wittig 1981)

These debates have been mirrored in relation to theorisations of race and the politics of anti-racism. The assertion of biologically distinct racial groups has been widely discredited (see, for instance, Lang 1997) and the strategy of deconstruction has been deployed in order to expose the dependence of the (unspoken) category of 'Whiteness' on disavowed 'Black' and 'Other' racial categories (see Lamont 1999, Leonardo 2004 and Jacobson 1998).

THE DISCURSIVELY CONSTITUTED SUBJECT

My earlier discussion of discourse and power touched upon a Foucauldian understanding of the subject. For Foucault, the subject is constituted through the productive power of discursive practices. Foucault borrows Althusser's (1971) notion of subjection to suggest that *the person is at once rendered a subject and subjected to relations of power through discourse*, in Foucault's terms, s/he is subjectivated.

Processes of subjectivation are demonstrated throughout Foucault's work. In *Discipline and Punish* (1991) and the *History of Sexuality Vol.1* (1990a) Foucault shows how the person is subjected to relations of power as s/he is individualised, categorised, classified, hierarchized, normalised, surveilled and provoked to self-surveillance. As I have already noted, these are technologies of subjectivation brought into play within institutions such as schools that improvise, cite and circulate discursive frames and disciplinary technologies that render subjects in relations of power. Foucault says of the relation between productive power and the subject, and the subject's location in productive power:

> 'This form of power applies itself to immediate everyday life which categorizes the individual, marks him [sic] by his own individuality, attaches him to his own identity, imposes a law of truth on him which he must recognise and which others have to recognise in him. It is a form of power which makes individuals subjects. There are two meanings of the word subject: subject to someone else by control and dependence, and tied to his own identity by a conscious self-knowledge. Both meanings suggest a form of power which subjugates and makes subject to.' (Foucault 1990a: 212).

In Foucault's *History of Sexuality Vol. 2* (1992) and *Vol. 3* (1990b) his focus shifts to the potential for subjectivated subjects to be otherwise. Here aesthetics, self-care, and technologies of self suggest possibilities of being otherwise through the self-conscious practices of subjects, even if these subjects come into being through the condition of subjectivation. Foucault says:

> 'the subject is constituted through practices of subjection, or, in a more autonomous way, through practices of liberation, or liberty, as in Antiquity, on the basis, of course, of a number of rules, styles, inventions to be found in the cultural environment.' (1990c: 51)

Here, the self-conscious practices of the subject, and her/his involvement in her/his own constitution, are indicated as (potentially) 'practices of liberation' *at the same time as* the constrained context in which this subject acts is indicated by 'practices of subjection'.

Foucault's work suggests, then, that the person is made subject by and subject to discursive relations of disciplinary power, but being such a subject s/he can also engage self-consciously in practices that might make her/him differently. The subject acts, but s/he acts within/at the limits of subjectivation.

Performatively constituting subjects

Judith Butler begins by adopting Foucault's notion of discourse. In exploring the productive power of discourse in relation to the production of subjects, in particular sexed and gendered subjects, Butler makes use of Foucault's notion of subjectivation as well as the notion of the performative. This performative is borrowed from Derrida's work concerning the nature of language and its relationship to the world in which a performative is: 'that discursive practice that enacts or produces that which it names' (Butler 1993:13). Butler argues that:

> 'Discursive performativity appears to produce that which it names, to enact its own referent, to name and to do, to name and to make. ... [g]enerally speaking, a performative functions to produce that which it declares' (Butler 1993:107).

This is a significant, if perhaps, counter-intuitive claim. With this understanding of the performative, the schoolgirl and boy, the gifted and talented student, the student with emotional and behavioural difficulties, even the teacher, is so because he/she is designated as such. Indeed, while these designations appear to describe pre-existing subjects, it is the very act of designation that constitutes the subject as if they were already student, teacher, gifted and so on. Indeed, Butler argues that the subject must be performativity constituted in order to make sense *as* a subject. While these subjects of schools appear, at least at the level of the everyday or commonsense to precede their designation, this apparent prior subject is an artefact of its performative constitution. This has massive implications for education because it insists that nobody is necessarily anything and so what it means to be a teacher, a student, a learner might be opened up to radical rethinking.

This performative constitution of gender is not understood to be a singular or definitive enactment – we call a girl 'girl' and she is a girl. Working with a Foucauldian notion of discourse, the performative constitution of gender is understood to be productive only in so far as it is 'derivative' (Butler 1993:107) – calling a girl 'girl' works because what girl means is derived from existing knowledges, or discourses. Butler draws on Derrida's discussion of the contextual and citational nature of the performative and his insistence that those 'infelicities' identified by Austin (1968) are, in fact, contextual 'breaks' intrinsic to performatives (Derrida 1998). She asserts that the performative 'is an inherited set of voices, an echo of others who speak as the "I"' (Butler 1997a:25) and is, therefore, always citational. That is, they are contextual, spoken within a chain of signification, imbued with prior and future uses in which meanings are open to change and dispute. As such, Butler suggests that 'speech is always in some ways out of control' (Butler 1997a:15).Butler (1990) also suggests that gender performatives are 'compulsive' and 'compulsory', the condition upon which the subject is effected – people do not make sense if they are not 'he' or 'she', to call a person 'it' either an injury or does not make sense. Butler also suggests that gender performatives demand 'repetition' (Butler 1990) – we must call up gender time and again for it to continue to have meaning.

Discursive performatives are often considered as they are used in spoken and written language. This might be through *direct* naming of social and biographical categories (like girl, boy, student, teacher) or supposed characteristics (like clever, or gifted, or disruptive or badly behaved), which in some discursive frames relate back to social and biographical categories (like Herrnstein and Murray's (1994) now infamous claims for the links between intelligence and race). Discursive performatives, however, might also be deployed *obliquely*. This might be through *association* to a discourse that is drawn on directly in speech or text or through representations that *implicitly* cite particular discourses. For instance, the sorts of photos of students found on government department websites and the covers of glossy school prospectuses. Discursive performatives may be deployed through bodily gestures, adornments, acts – the way students sit at their desks, how they wear (or do not wear) their school uniform, how they link arms in the corridor. Finally, performatives might be deployed through silence, through what is unspoken and what is not done – when a student is ignored by the teacher or other students, when her/his different (behaviour, culture, skin) is perceived but unacknowledged, when s/he is denigrated by playground abuse and nobody intervenes these silences and omissions have effects because they are still citing discourses.

Also of particular use in Butler's work is her rearticulation of Althusser's (1971) understanding of interpellation, or the hail of authority, as a crucial component of subject formation. Butler suggests that '[b]eing called a name is ... one of the conditions by which a subject is constituted in language' (Butler 1997a:2). Butler is not arguing here that a pre-existing subject is given a name, rather that this naming is a prerequisite for being '*recognizable*' (Butler 1997a:5, original emphasis) as a subject. As such, '[o]ne comes to "exist" by virtue of this fundamental dependency on the address of the Other' (Butler 1997a:5). This does not infer that the address conveys a 'truth' about the one addressed. Such interpellations are not understood as being descriptive; rather they are understood as being 'inaugurative': '[i]t seeks to introduce a reality rather than reporting an existing one' (Butler 1997a:33).

In illustrating the constitutive power of the address Butler considers what she describes as 'an impossible scene': a 'body' that, having not been named, is without 'social definition' and is, therefore, not accessible to us. It is only through being interpellated, she argues, that this 'body' acquires the social definition that makes it accessible. Butler understands this interpellation not as a discovery but as a 'fundamental constitution' (Butler 1997a:5). Butler offers as an example the scene of birth in which the medic makes a pronouncement of 'sex': 'it is a girl' or 'it is a boy' (Butler 1990, 1993 and 1997a).

Intelligibility and performative constraints

Performatives have to make sense to work – they have to be recognisable in the discourses that are circulating in the settings and moments in which they are deployed. In school contexts being a schoolgirl or boy, being gifted, having emotional or behaviour difficulties makes sense. These subjects cite enduring institutional discourses about who students are and what schools are about. School discourses are suffused with girls and boys, teachers and students. We cannot 'think' schools without them.

That the discursive performative has to make sense in its context in order to make sense also suggests that performatives might *constrain* the sorts of subject students might be *at the same time* as they constitute students. Here Butler's ideas about performativity intersect with Foucault's ideas about subjectivation that I explored earlier. The notion of simultaneous production and constraint that 'subjectivation' conveys is usefully elaborated by Judith Butler as follows:

> ' "subjectivation" ...denotes both the becoming of the subject and the process of subjection – one inhabits the figure of autonomy only by becoming subjected to a power, a subjection which implies a radical dependency. [...] Subjection is, literally, the *making* of a subject, the principle of regulation according to which a subject is formulated or produced. Such subjection is a kind of power that not only unilaterally *acts on* a given individual as a form of domination, but also *activates* or forms the subject. Hence, subjection is neither simply the domination of a subject nor its production, but designates a certain kind of restriction *in* production' (Butler 1997b: 83-4 original emphasis).

The girl is inaugurated into subjecthood through gender discourse – she at once becomes a girl and subject to the rules of being a girl. She must continually cite (be it tacitly or knowingly) these rules if she is to remain intelligible as a girl, and so as a subject. And behaving well in school according to school discourses of the good female student – being cooperative, empathetic, and industrious – is one of the discursive threads through which this is made possible. In this sense the subject who comes to be a subject through thee processes of subjectivation is necessarily 'self-incarcerating' (Butler 1997b:32).

Performatives that do not make sense in the discourses that frame schooling, or that are counter to prevailing institutional discourses may fail or may act to constitute a subject outside the bounds of acceptability as a student. The boy is also inaugurated into subjecthood through gender discourse. Yet the discursive practices that constitute certain heterosexual masculinities – entitlement, aggression, active sexuality – can constitute subjects that are incommensurate with school discourses of acceptable learners who are restrained, malleable, asexual. This understanding of the ongoing subjectivation of subjects through discursive performativity enables us to see how schools come to be suffused with exclusions, with what the student-subject cannot be, with who cannot be the student-subject. These ideas demonstrate that subjecthood – and studenthood – comes with costs.

Bodies

In illustrating the use to which these ideas are being put in this book I have drawn on categories that, at a commonsense level at least – might be taken as *bodily* as well as, or rather than, social or discursive. The moves in feminism to separate sex and gender that I discussed previously, and similar moves to separate impairment and disability, have deflected attention away from the body. Yet the body, sexed, raced, able, impaired, remains a significant field of concern here. Thinking about the person as subjectivated through performatives can seem to suggest that even though the person is embodied, flesh and blood, this person does not 'exist' unless s/he is subjectivated. Clearly, the bodies of subjects cannot be passed over that easily. And neither Foucault nor Butler attempt to do so. Rather, considering the body and its relationship to the subject is a key feature of their work.

In his discussion of disciplinary power, Foucault identifies the centrality of the relationship between 'productive' (Foucault 1990c:118) power and the body. He suggests that this relationship is marked by two key deployments of discursive power. First, the 'anatomo-politics of the human body' in which the sorts of disciplinary technologies that I explored earlier address the optimisation and utility of the body (Foucault 1990a:139). Second, the 'bio-politics of the population' in which biological processes (such as, health, reproduction and mortality) of the population as a whole are regulated (Foucault 1990a:139). For Foucault, the proliferation of discourses of sexuality, and the concomitant proliferation of sexualities, has been a central locus of this activity (Foucault 1980, 1990a, 1990b, 1992). This focus on sexuality is not arbitrary – sex is a key locus of disciplinary power because it encompasses the body both of the individual and the population: it is 'a means of access both to the life of the body and the life of the species' (Foucault, 1990a:149). Yet for Foucault the biological sex and sexual practices of the body do not precede or precipitate these discourses of sexuality. Rather, these discourses are understood to have produced *as an effect* the sex which comes to be seen as a prior, biological fact:

'We must not make the mistake of thinking that sex is an autonomous agency which
secondarily produces manifold effects of sexuality over the entire surface of its contact
with power. On the contrary, sex is the most speculative, most ideal, and most internal
element of a deployment of sexuality organised by power in its grip on bodies and their
materiality, their forces, sensations and pleasures.' (Foucault 1990a:155).

Sex and sexuality are we know than are inseparable from the disciplinary
technologies and discourses to and by which they (we) are subjected.

In *Bodies   that   Matter*, Butler takes up Foucault's understanding of the
centrality of the body to both the formation of subjects and the operations of
disciplinary power. Butler challenges the idea that the material body is somehow
absolute, saying that the body is 'bound up with signification from the start' (Butler
1993:30). This is not to argue that bodies do not 'exist' prior to signification, but to
say that material bodies need meaning to be attached to them in order to be
accessible and intelligible – a female body, a Black body, a homosexual body, an
impaired body is meaningful as such because it has been signified in these terms,
signification that works because it is part of an enduring chain of meaning. Butler
writes:

'The body posited as prior to the sign, is always *posited* or *signified* as prior. This
signification produces as an *effect* of its own procedure the very body that it
nevertheless simultaneously claims to discover as that which *precedes* its own action'
(Butler 1993:30 original emphasis).

The body understood as beneath or before its representation in discourse, comes
to inhabit this beneath or before *through   this   discourse.* Butler offers the figure
of the 'girl' as an example of this insistent relationship between the body and
representation and the way in which the meanings of bodies, just like social
categories of self, are discursively constituted:

'To the extent that the naming of the "girl" ... initiates the process by which a certain
"girling" is compelled, the term or, rather, its symbolic power, governs the formation of
a corporeally enacted femininity that never fully approximates the norm. This is a
"girl", however, who is compelled to "cite" the norm in order to qualify and remain a
viable subject' (Butler 1993:232).

This ideal cannot be fully approximated because, even suspending grammatical
limitations and accepting the impossible scene of the body 'before' discourse, the
pre-discursive body cannot *already* be 'girl' precisely because it is before those
discourses in which the meaning of girl resides and is reproduced. This does not
render the body of the girl a matter of choice or something that can be easily
discarded. The girl must 'cite' or *do* girl in linguistic and bodily practice in order to
retain an embodied subjectivity that is intelligible and accessible – an intelligibility
and accessibility that is necessarily discursive. The demand for an intelligible and
accessible body, in the case of this example the sexed body, is predicated on it being
at once a condition and effect of subjecthood.

Bourdieu's notion of bodily *habitus* makes a significant contribution to
understanding the body. This is concerned with the ways in which bodily practices
are normalised and naturalised and, in turn, contribute to the reproduction of class
relations. Bourdieu focuses on those bodily practices that make up 'the most
apparently insignificant aspects of the things, situations and practices of everyday
life' (Bourdieu 1991:51). He refers to ways of standing, walking, feeling, eating,

drinking, laughing and speaking. These ways of being and doing are not understood as being natural, arbitrary, chosen or consciously learnt. Rather, they are seen as being inculcated and 'internalized as a second nature' (Bourdieu 1990:56) without the awareness or conscious effort of the subject. The practices, or dispositions, inculcated through the *habitus* are sedimented in what Bourdieu calls the 'bodily hexis'; 'a life-style made flesh' (Bourdieu 1991:86).

Familial and cultural contexts are seen as being central to the inculcation of *habitus*. While this inculcation is ongoing, it is the inculcation of *habitus* within young children to which Bourdieu give particular emphasis. This is not understood as the imitation of a model (the child imitating the parent, sibling, etc. who sets him/herself up as an example to be emulated), rather, it is seen as a 'practical *mimesis* ... which implies an overall relation of identification' (Bourdieu 1990:73 original emphasis). The family as the primary site of inculcation means that the *habitus*' of subjects within a particular context or milieu is reproduced. Having been inculcated without the awareness of the subject and sedimented as a second nature, these bodily practices take on a natural appearance that is so enduring and mundane as to be barely noteworthy within everyday life – girls sit with knees together, boys sit with knees apart. In this way, bodily practices are seen to 'naturalise the decisive breaks that constitute an arbitrary cultural limit' (Bourdieu 1991:123). The *habitus* then, imbues the body with a '*sense of limits*' (Bourdieu 1991:123 original emphasis); a set of truths and ways of being which the subject tacitly believes in and owns yet is unaware of in either inculcation or practice. The naturalisation of these dispositions means that the subject is unlikely to have a sense of subjugation through them –the *habitus* obviates any sense of being or doing otherwise.

Bourdieu's account of the accidental and unnoticed inculcation of the *habitus* articulates strongly with Butler's claim, after Foucault, that the body is inseparable from discourse. Butler takes up Bourdieu's notion of *habitus* stressing that, as a 'bodily understanding' (Butler 1997a:134), *habitus* is not reducible to the following of rules or norms in a self-conscious way, but is a 'tacit normativity' (Butler 1997a:154). The tacit nature of these processes produces the 'obviousness' of a given culture (Butler 1997a:153). Butler suggests that the body does not simply obey bodily rules or reflect bodily norms, rather, she asserts that the body *is* these rules and norms and can be understood as 'a kind of incorporated memory' (Butler 1997a:154) – a girl's body does not concede that knees must be together, rather a girl's body *is* a girl's body *because* its (her) knees are together. Over time, then, ritual and convention forms the body. Simultaneously, and in an extension of Bourdieu's notion, Butler suggests that bodily activity is formative of this ritual and convention. She suggests that 'it is in this sense that the bodily *habitus* constitutes a tacit form of performativity, a citational chain lived an believed at the level of the body' (Butler 1997a:155 original emphasis).

The material body, then, elbows its way into any discussion of the speaking, discursively constituted subject. At the same time, this speaking subject shouts over any discussion of the material body. The subject is inseparable from his/her embodiment.

Subjects, subjectivity, and identity

As I explore these subjectivating processes inside school I work with the notions subject, subjectivity and identity. This subject is understood as the person made in relations of productive power as examined in detail here. Subjectivity, then, is taken as this subjectivated subject's particular subject position; her/his sense and experience of her/himself; as well as her/his audiences' understanding of 'who' s/he is and can be. Identity is understood here in a similar way. While the usefulness of the notion of identity has been questioned on the grounds of its various, and incompatible, disciplinary and common sense[vii] meanings (Connell, no date), it is retained here. This is because language escapes me and insists on the term in order to discuss in an accessible and straightforward way the subjectivating effects of the everyday categorisations through which subjects are made knowable, inequities emerge, and identity politics are formed. My retention of the term here is ultimately unsatisfactory to me, but it is a necessary compromise. As Butler (1999) notes in relation to sex and desire, the discursive tools that make subjects meaningful are not easily jettisoned. I continue to look for language that breaks with old meanings while remaining meaningful.

AGENCY AND POLITICS

Understanding students as subjectivated through ongoing performative constitutions suggests that the political challenge is to intercept these performatives in order to constitute students differently. Foucault, Derrida and Butler offer tools for thinking how this might be done.

A key contribution to thinking about how particular subjectivities might be shifted or undone is Derrida's (1988) assertion that any performative is open to misfire and so might fail or doing something unintended or unexpected. And Foucault's (1990a) insistence that, while particular discourses prevail in some contexts and endure, no discourse is guaranteed also insists on the potential for the meanings of discourses to shift and be unsettled. Butler draws on both of these ideas to detail how discourse and its performative effects offer political potential. Imagining politics, however, also imagines the subject as an agent who acts with intent in an effort to make particular things happen. Often such an agent is taken to be that Cartesian man who is a rational, self-realising being and who this discussion has called into question. In contrast, the decentred subject who is the product of discourse and is in constant assemblage is often taken to lack agency, specifically because of her/his ongoing constitution in discourse.

Yet in Butler's account of subjection the possibility for a specific understanding of intent and agency remain. The subject who is interpellated can, in turn, interpellate others, that is, the performatively constituted subject has 'linguistic agency' (Butler 1997a:15). *This is not the agency of a sovereign subject who exerts its will. Rather, this agency is derivative, an effect of discursive power.*

'Because the agency of the subject is not a property of the subject, an inherent will or freedom, but an effect of power, it is *constrained but not determined* in advance. ... As the agency of a postsovereign subject, its discursive operation is delimited in advance but also open to a further unexpected delimitation' (Butler 1997a:139-140, my emphasis).

The linguistic agency of this performatively interpellated subject is, therefore, simultaneously enabled and constrained through discourse. This subject retains intention and can seek to realise this intent through the deployment of discursive practices. The efficacy of this deployment, however, is never guaranteed due to the citationality and historicity of discursive practices.

Further, Butler suggests that while the subject needs to be named in ways that make sense in discourse in order to be '*recognizable*' (Butler 1997a:5, original emphasis), by being performatively constituted the subject can performatively constitute another. Butler writes:

'the one who names, who works within language to find a name for another, is presumed to be already named, positioned within language as one who is already subject to the founding or inaugurating address. This suggests that such a subject in language is positioned as both addressed and addressing, and that the very possibility of naming another requires that one first be named. The subject of speech who is named becomes, potentially, one who might well name another in time' (Butler 1997a:29).

Butler also calls the capacity to name and so constitute that result from subjectivation 'discursive agency' (Butler 1997a:127). By thinking of agency as discursive – as being the product of being inaugurated in discourse and so able to join citational chains of discourse – Butler moves past an understanding of intent and agency that is the property of a rational self-knowing subject. Yet she does this while accounting for how the subject continues to act with intent. Discourse and its effects exceed the intent or free will of an agent, but the performatively constituted subject can still deploy discursive performatives that have the potential to be constitutive. As such, challenges to prevailing constitutions of subjects can be deployed self-consciously through the discursive practices of subjects who are themselves subjectivated.

The 'disabled' student cannot simply jettison this performative and erase the discourse that gives it meaning, but s/he can resist it, act outside the terms of this discourse, call her/himself 'crip' and in so doing rest this ordinarily injurious performative out of its usual place in discourse as the aberrant, abnormal, outside and insist instead that 'crip' might not be a source of shame, pity and exclusion but something to be enjoyed, revelled in, or nothing at all.

Butler suggests that these insurrectionary practices would involve:

'decontextualizing and recontextualizing ... terms through radical acts of public misappropriation such that the conventional relation between [interpellation and meaning] might become tenuous and even broken over time' (Butler 1997a:100).

She insists, after Foucault, that the sedimented meanings of enduring and prevailing discourses might be unsettled and resignified or reinscribed. And that subordinate, disavowed, or silenced discourses might be deployed in, and made meaningful in, contexts from which they have been barred. In this sense *re*signification or *re*inscription is not simply a doing again, but a reversal or a doing again *differently*. So the enduring inequalities that are produced through the performative practices of institutions, teachers and, indeed, students, might be unsettled. Gay, lesbian, bisexual and transgender politics' reinscription of 'queer'; disability studies' reinscription of 'crip'; and, undoubtedly more problematically, hip hop's reinscription of 'nigga' might all be understood as examples of such performative politics in action.

This is not to suggest, however, that such a performative politics is simply a matter of asserting a new or altered meaning. The regulatory operations of authorised discourses and the historicity of terms render normative meanings resistant to reinscription. Yet while normative meanings may be resistant to reinscription, they are never immune from it. The possibility of reinscription is intrinsic to the perlocutionary performative interpellation. Butler writes:

> 'contexts inhere in certain speech acts in ways that are very difficult to shake. ... [but] contexts are never fully determined in advance ... the possibility for the speech act to take on a non-ordinary meaning, to function in contexts where it has not belonged, is precisely the political promise of the performative, one that positions the performative at the center of a politics of hegemony, one that offers an unanticipated political future for deconstructive thinking' (Butler 1997:161).

Such performative politics might be effected through the practices of an individual or a group (whose organisation, coherence and longevity may well vary). It may be a single subject who engages in practices of reinscription – a student drums on the table in class– and whose performatives may, or may not, achieve (be received another subject as having) a 'non-ordinary' – is this simply a 'bad' student or does has what it means to be a student and a teacher been unsettled?. The reinscription of a single subject, however, cannot transform normative meanings. Such a transformation requires the non-ordinary meaning of the performative to work to the point that this non-ordinary meaning alters the normative meaning of the name or practice – an expanding community of speakers use 'queer' so persistently as an affirmative name that it is unlikely to work as injurious name. Such an alteration can only be effected through repetition and *re*-citation. This *re*-citation might imbue the performative interpellation with an altered historicity, a *re*-historicity that then acts to govern its normative meaning. As such, the proposition of a politics of performative reinscription is not a renunciation of organised and/or collective resistance. Rather, reflecting Butler's utilisation of deconstruction and understanding of productive power, it indicates a recognition of the necessary limits of State focused and oppositional politics.

Inside school, gifted students, clever students, challenging students, disabled students, special students, hardworking girls, naughty boys, boffins, swots, dumb kids, retards, rude girls, homeboys, gypsies, faggots, and dykes all remain, but they might all be made to mean differently. And made to position the student in new relationships with school institutions and with learning. Such a 'performative politics,' Butler claims, offers 'an unanticipated political future for deconstructive thinking' (Butler 1997a:161). This is a politics that, after Derrida, seeks to open up normative, privileged subjectivities to interrogation; unpick their inconsistencies, and expose their radical dependence on the subjectivities they disavow.

Understanding the subject as discursively constituted, as subjectivated but with discursive agency promises to expose how subjects come to 'be' particular sort of students and learners in school. It promises to enable us to see how it is in the minutiae of school life, its routine practices, mundane occurrences, and everyday interactions that students come to be preformatively constituted – not just along social, biographical and sub-cultural axes, but also as students and learners. And by understanding these constitutions as the effects of matrices of intersecting discourses and, indeed, planes of incommensurable discourses, we can see how markers such as race, gender, ability, sexuality, disability, social class come to be entangled with the sorts of learners that it is discursively possible, intelligible, for students to be. And how some students come to be impossible learners. It is these tools, then, that I take up in the analyses that follow.

PART TWO: RESEARCHING SUBJECTS

In Part One I outlined the concerns and arguments of this book and located these in the context of both existing scholarship in the field and the theoretical ideas that underpin them. In this part of the book I explore the processes of researching these issues and demonstrate the analytical approaches that I employ. This provides a basis for engaging with and interrogating the empirical data analyses that I offer.

Chapter 3, then, is concerned with how the principles, practices, data, and analyses of school ethnography can be understood, and indeed reconciled with, a post-structural framework that is concerned with calling fundamentally into question both the subject and 'truth'. The chapter explores these tensions and offers a framework for moving to the representation and analysis of data whose status is radically unsettled.

Chapter 4 goes on to undertake these representations and analyses, demonstrating how multiple types of data are constructed for representation and how a deconstructive and Foucauldian discourse analysis of these takes shape. In doing this, the chapter applies those theories of the subject explored in chapter 2 and works through some of the key conceptual ideas of the book. These analyses engage raced, gendered, sexed and classed subjectivities and demonstrate how spoken, textual, and bodily practices are implicated in the discursive constitution of subjects inside schools. As this analysis progresses, the significance of the constitution of student and learner identities presses upon the analysis and so prepares the ground for the exploration of the relationship between subjectivities and educational exclusions that is the focus of Parts 3 and 4 of this book.

CHAPTER 3

RESEARCHING SUBJECTIVITY AND EDUCATIONAL EXCLUSIONS

INTRODUCTION

In the preceding chapters I have suggested that subjectivities are not the stable, interior possessions of a self-knowing subject, but are instead artefacts of discourses that produce these subjects as though they were pre-existing. I have also suggested that these constituting processes are deeply implicated in social and educational exclusions. In this chapter I consider the implications of these starting points for doing ethnographic research in schools asking how we might know this, how we might research this, and what sort of evidence we might offer to support this.

As I have indicated, there are a series of concerns and contexts at the heart of this book. First, the book is concerned with the discursive constitution of subjects and the way that schools are implicated in both these constituting processes and the reproduction of inequalities along axes of particular identity categories. These concerns drove the first ethnography drawn on in this book – an ethnography undertaken as part of my doctoral research during 1998 in a south London secondary school, Taylor Comprehensive[viii]. Given the simultaneous concern with subjecthood, categorical identities, inequality, and school processes, I sought a school that was co-educational, multi-ethnic, served a mixed social class population and included students identified as having special educational needs.

Second, the book is concerned with the discursive constitution of the young people who populated the school as students and as learners. This concern developed as the interests of the ethnography of Taylor Comprehensive were addressed and as the processes of 'educational triage' (Gillborn and Youdell 2000) explored in chapter 1 came to appear as not just selective but also as constitutive. This second set of concerns came to the fore while I was lecturing in Sydney, Australia. This location offered me the opportunity to pursue these issues at the same time as exploring the usefulness of my theoretical tools in another national and local context. In order to examine the constitutive practices that make students and learners, and to consider the contextual specificities of these processes, I undertook a second ethnography during 2001 in Plains High[ix], an outer Western Sydney high school. Once again I sought a school that was co-educational, multi-ethnic, and included students identified as having special educational needs. Unlike Taylor Comprehensive, however, Plains High did not have a mixed social class profile. Instead, in a national context dominated by a discourse of socio-economic status and where a myth of classlessness prevails, Plains was located in a low socio-economic status outer suburb where the promise of social or geographical mobility was extremely limited.

My third concern is with understanding educational exclusion in terms of exclusions from the project of schooling and not simply the school, and the way that such exclusions and inclusions might be constituted through the day-to-day processes of schooling. This concern crystallised as I undertook the Plains ethnography and repeatedly set the data I was generating there, as well as the Taylor data, against the theoretical ideas I was working with. While the Plains ethnography set out to make sense of the constitution of learners, then, the concern with constitutive processes of educational exclusion has been mapped retrospectively onto, and theorised through, both of these sets of data.

In doing ethnography in school framed by these concerns, then, I am looking for discourses and their effects. I am hoping to see discourse in action. I am looking for moments in which subjects; students and learners; and inclusions and exclusions are constituted. I am looking for discourse and its deployment. I am asking after the discourses that circulate inside and/or across school contexts, how these are deployed, and what their effects might be. *Ultimately, I want to know whether thinking in terms of discourse and performative constitutions can help us to understand student subjectivities, students and learners, processes of inclusion and exclusion, and the interactions across these.*

In order to see discourse in action, I go into school and do ethnography. In doing school ethnography I make use of the usual methods of interview, observation, collection of artefacts and texts but I am not asking the research participants to take me through their understanding or perception of the setting (although sometimes I do this) nor am I asking them to or to identify discourses that circulate there (although sometimes they do this). Rather, as I talk to students and teachers, and participate (as neither a teacher nor a student) in lessons, assemblies and break-times, I am seeking to identify, unpack, and untangle the effects of the discourses that are deployed. While at times discourses and their effects are clearly evident, more often these are subtle and oblique, needing to be teased out, inferred. This is not the collection of 'real' or 'actual' discourses but is wholly constrained by my own discursive repertoire – the discourse that I see and name – and my capacity to represent these. I am, then, absolutely entangled in my research data, data that are inevitably my own construction. In this way the research process itself becomes deeply implicated in the very constitutive processes that it is trying to understand. It also means the research is inevitably inferential, with the data generated and theory deployed bearing a heavy interpretive burden. This is, then, a theoretically driven, theory testing and theory generating approach. I am not seeking to describe the nuances of the context and tease out what is happening within it. Rather, I am seeking to construct compelling representations of moments inside schools in order to untangle the discursive frames that guide meaning there.

THE SCHOOL CONTEXT

There is not one or best way of investigating educational exclusions as they relate to and create particular 'sorts' of subjects inside schools. But going inside the school to explore its everyday practices and the discourse that frame these has the potential to offer particular insight into and understanding of the way that schooling subjectivates students. In industrialised nations at least, schooling provides both a formal educational context and an informal social context that, in principle, all children are obliged to enter and spend a substantial part of their early lives in. Yet schools, and the education they undertake, are not simply neutral institutions whose processes are universally beneficial. Whitty and Menter (1989:60) have suggested that 'education is a key route to the thoughts and values of people within nations'. In the theoretical frame I am using, education does not just provide this access, it is constitutive of both people and nations.

In understanding the nature of school contexts it is useful to begin by looking briefly at earlier debates within the Sociology of Education. An increasing focus on in-school socialisation processes rejected the idea that education is intrinsically 'good' and that educational 'failure' can be explained in terms of student 'deficit'. Rather, it was proposed that educational institutions and processes should themselves be problematised and subjected to critical scrutiny. This work saw social and cultural relations implicated in, and reproduced through, the designation of appropriate knowledges within the school curriculum (see Whitty 1985; Maclaren 1998; Apple 1990). Understandings of the role of the school in the reproduction of cultural, social and economic relations was also extended by Bowles and Gintis' (1976) work concerning the 'official' and 'hidden' curriculum. Inspired by the transformatory education of Paulo Friere in Brazil (1970), concerns over schooling's reproduction of inequitous social relations led to the development of critical pedagogies and these have formed a key feature of progressivist educational efforts. While the limits of critical pedagogies' endeavours to develop strategies for emancipatory schooling have been highlighted (Luke and Gore 1992), critical educators continue to explore the possibilities for transformatory education and seek out examples of critical pedagogic work on which other educators might draw (Apple 2003, Apple and Beane 1999, Giroux 2001, Nieto 2004, Maclaren 1998).

As some of the more recent school ethnographies discussed in Chapter 1 demonstrate, developing theorisations have offered the Sociology of Education further tools with which to make sense of schooling. Perhaps most notable amongst these theorisations is Foucault's work on discourse and disciplinary power. Hunter (1996) suggests that the work of Foucault offers two key opportunities; first, to examine the school's possible role in shaping the subject, and second, to explore the relationship between educational theory and education itself (Hunter 1996). Post-structural theory has been drawn upon within education sociology and policy analysis to develop new understandings of the school and school processes, the differential educational experiences of outcomes of students, and the identities of both students and teachers inside schools. See, for instance, Ball (1990), Brine (1999), Britzman (2003), Epstein and Johnson (1998); Gewirtz *et al* (1995), Gillborn and Youdell (2000), Gore (1995), Hey (1997), Luke and Gore (1992), Mac an Ghaill (1994), St Pierre (2000), Walkerdine (1987), Wolpe (1988).

Reflecting this broader move within the Sociology of Education, my school research is underpinned by Foucault's understanding of the school as a disciplinary institution in which the sorts of disciplinary technologies that I explored in chapter 1 define the institution and constitute the 'students' and 'teachers' who populate it (Foucault 1991). Hunter (1996) has usefully considered the school in a Foucauldian framework to identify the inevitable limits of both liberal and Marxist conceptions of the school and agendas for schooling. Adopting a genealogical approach, Hunter suggests that mass public schooling was established to serve neither a democratising nor repressive project. Rather, schooling is seen as being shaped by the ongoing deployment of available discursive strategies. After Foucault, these deployments are seen as attempts to meet the demands of particular circumstances, and their effects are understood as the effects of power/knowledges. As such, schooling inevitably fails to realise either the progressive or repressive goals that it is frequently perceived to have been established to achieve. Hunter writes:

> '[T]he modern school system is not the historical creation of democratic politics or of popular political struggle. Neither, on the other hand, can it be understood as the instrument through which the aspirations of rational individuals or self-realizing classes have been defeated, through the cold calculations of the State acting on behalf of an inhuman economic system. ... the school system can be neither as good as its critics wish it were, nor as bad as they think it is' (Hunter 1996:147).

Hunter is not denying the centrality in contemporary schooling of democratic politics, political struggle, and the realisation of individual and societal potentials. He is suggesting, however, that these at times contradictory efforts are not the objectives of schooling but *effects* of those discursive practices mobilised in the establishment and continued reform and reinvention of schooling. For instance, while the intention of mass public schooling was not, at its inception, the continued betterment of individuals, the deployment and adaptation of pastoral discourses has produced this as an unintended effect and embedded these practices within the school institution. Such an understanding moves away from a concern with schooling as the good or bad design and/or intervention of the powerful State. It considers instead the discourses through which schooling has been established in particular contexts and in the light of particular demands:

> 'The school system, I suggest, is not bureaucratic and disciplinary by default, having betrayed its mission of human self-realization to a repressive State or a rapacious economy. It is positively and irrevocably bureaucratic and disciplinary, emerging as it does from the exigencies of social governance and from the pastoral disciplines with which the administrative State attempted to meet these exigencies' (Hunter 1996:149).

The school is also a material location. Setting aside the increasing interest in virtual classrooms offered by information technologies, the school's buildings and grounds are comprised of a series of locations – classrooms, halls, canteens, kitchens, corridors, toilets – with a variety of possibly mobile official and unofficial purposes and uses. The significance of location, in terms of material spaces and their imagined meanings, is increasingly being recognised and explored (see Keith and Pile 1993, Massey 1994 and 2004). This work suggests that, along with mobile purposes and uses, the meanings of these spaces may well be multiple, contested and shifting. This is across time and across those individuals or groups who occupy, pass through, avoid, boycott or are barred from these spaces and whose subjectivities are mediated by them. These ideas are increasingly being taken up in education sociology and have been used to demonstrate the significance of spatial meanings, their contestation, and inclusion and exclusion from them. See for instance Armstrong (2003), Devine (1996), Gulson (2005), Lipman (2004), and Symes and Preston (1997). While the precise architecture of the panopticon (Foucault 1991) might be absent from the school, the disciplinary technologies of hierarchical observation, classification, examination, normalization, surveillance and self-surveillance are evident.

Coming to sociology of education from a commitment to social justice and a hope that schools can be an equalizing or emancipatory force, thinking about the school in this way was at first difficult for me. Yet that this is not what schooling has been establishes *for* does not mean that schools cannot be recruited to this project. Taking a Foucauldian approach, the school can be seen as a disciplinary institution in which particular power/knowledges are inscribed and contested. These are not only related to those knowledges identified as being legitimate components of the school curriculum, but entail the multiple power/knowledges which are deployed throughout the school day by teachers and students. This does not automatically infer that students (and teachers) are successfully or permanently rendered docile bodies – resistances, dissonances and ambiguities (however momentary, quickly recuperated, mundane) can also be found. Thinking about schools in this way does not mean that practices of schooling cannot be liberatory, but it does shift what might be understood by liberation and how practices of schooling might be seen as contributing to this. Ethnography promises a multitude of opportunities for exploring these possibilities.

ETHNOGRAPHY

Accounts that treat ethnography as method tend to posit it as a straight forward set of activities that progress in linear fashion from data collection, to analysis and, ultimately, description and/or interpretation. Understanding ethnography as method, however, overlooks the theoretical and methodological debates over the meanings it uncovers or creates, the claims it can make, and the promises made on its behalf. As Ball (1993:32) notes '[T]he choice of ethnography carries with it implications about theory, epistemology and ontology'. (Ball 1993:32). Here ethnography might be a method, but if it is a method it is one suffused with both theory and the broader philosophical questions of knowing and being.

While ethnography cannot be reduced to a set of research methods, the use of certain methods is an enduring feature of such studies. 'Unstructured' and/or 'semi-structured' interviews along with various modes of observation are commonly found within accounts of both how to *do* ethnographic research and ethnographic studies themselves. Case studies and, to a lesser extent, life histories are also regularly present. The place of documentary evidence and statistical data in ethnographic research is debated more frequently. However, these methods were utilised by the Chicago School of the early twentieth century that is widely credited as the founding school of ethnographic research (Hammersley 1989). Furthermore, early research within the new sociology of education drew on quantitative methods as part of broader ethnographic studies (see, for instance, Ball 1981, Hargreaves 1967 and Lacey 1970). More recently, surveys and their subsequent statistical analyses have been the terrain on which an epistemological battle between qualitative and quantitative research has been fought. Nevertheless, these methods retain a place in ethnography (Hammersley and Atkinson 1983 and 1995) and continue to be drawn upon – albeit for sometimes radically transformed reasons (see Prior 1997; Watson 1997; Maclure 2002).

This does not mean that ethnography is synonymous with qualitative research. Ethnography is situated, it is concerned for the mediating effects of specific settings and extended periods of time are spent in these settings. These features mean that ethnography can offer nuanced accounts of settings and the practices that take place within them as well test and develop theory in the light of these accounts.

The place of theory

Theory provides a crucial underpinning and is a substantive concern of the ethnographies that I discuss in this book. Ethnography is a useful vehicle for testing and developing theory. This is not achieved through the scientific mode of falsification, but through interpretation. Such theorisation aims to understand the 'mechanisms or processes' (Hammersley and Atkinson 1983:20) underpinning social relations and practices and offers 'confidence' rather than 'proof' (Hammersley and Atkinson 1983:25).

Hammersley (1990) criticised contemporary ethnography of the time on the basis that it was descriptive: depicting diversity without attempting to explain the patterns that it observed. He argued that interpretive ethnography had failed to test theory or contribute to theoretical knowledge and was, as such, 'condemned to rely upon theoretical ideas which are vague and untested' (Hammersley 1990:102) and called for a 'reassessment and reconstruction of ethnographic practice' to allow for the 'cumulative development of theory' (Hammersley 1990:136).

More recently, however, Hammersley and Atkinson (1995:236-7) assert that descriptive ethnography is itself concerned with selection and interpretation and so all ethnography is engaged either explicitly or implicitly with the 'refinement and testing of theories'. Miller (1997) has suggested that ethnographic work should take up its 'distinctive opportunities to develop analytic perspectives that speak directly to the practical circumstances of everyday life' (Miller 1997: 24). The theoretical opportunities offered by ethnography are considered to be distinctive precisely because ethnographic data is generated in and concerned with context(s). Miller suggests, therefore, that theoretical developments derived from ethnographic study are able to 'speak to issues of everyday life and practice' (Miller 1997:24).

Drawing on a Foucauldian notion of discourse (Foucault 1991), a distinction between descriptive and theoretical ethnography appears both false and unhelpful. The notion of a purely descriptive ethnography is itself underpinned by particular theoretical frames – descriptive ethnography does not stand outside discourse, it is engaged in the citation and inscription of theory as Miller (1997) and Hammersley and Atkinson (1995) note. The question becomes, then, not whether ethnography is theoretical, *but how far its theoretical framework is made explicit and worked through research questions, data generation, analysis and writing.* As I undertook the ethnographies reported here, and as I continue to write about them, I am at once endeavouring to test and develop theories that I anticipate will make a valuable contribution to my work and to studies of education *and* be mindful of how these theories close down what I might look for and see *and* make these processes transparent to the readers of the accounts I produce.

Research objects, subjects and reflexivity

Understanding the person as constituted through the ongoing deployment of discursive performatives has implications for how I think about and do research. The image of a neutral but self-knowing researcher and research subject, who in practice is taken (or sampled) to be a White, middle class, male and leaves Black and minority ethnic, women's, and working class perspectives out of the research account, has been roundly discredited in education and social science research. And in reverse, research that takes these minoritised groups as its objects has been challenged as objectifying, voyeuristic, and blunt. The strength of criticism of these approaches has been such that they are all but unsustainable in contemporary educational and social science research. Yet rejecting the neutral researcher and homogenous respondent, exposing the objectifying impact of some research, and acknowledging the inescapability of theory in research does not resolve the dilemmas raised by constituted and located subjects doing research on or with other subjects who are also constituted and located.

A series of key tools have been offered in responses to these dilemmas. These might be identified as reflexivity, standpoint, researcher-researcher match, and collaboration.

The broadly accepted response to the recognition of the theory-ladenness of research has been the turn to *reflexivity*. It has been argued that the researcher shapes the contexts in which data are gathered (Hammersley and Atkinson 1995); the theories tested, generated in, or brought to the field (Ball 1993, Hammersley 1990); and the ethnographic text produced (Atkinson 1990, Delamont and Atkinson 1995, Hammersley and Atkinson 1995, Miller 1997). Rather than either ignoring or attempting, hopelessly, to erase these effects, reflexive research practices enable the ethnographer to interrogate her/his effects. Hammersley and Atkinson state:

> 'By including our own role within the research focus, and perhaps even systematically exploiting our participation in the settings under study as researchers, we can produce accounts of the social world and justify them without placing reliance on futile appeals to empiricism, of either positivist or naturalist varieties' (Hammersley and Atkinson 1995:21-22).

The call to reflexivity within ethnography, however, raises the question of the 'subject'. The notion of the reflexive researcher infers a knowing subject, a subject who can assess rationally the actions, words, thoughts, meanings of both her/himself and the researched. And if the researcher is such a subject, then so is the researched. Many sociologists and social theorists have worked vigorously against Enlightenment modes of 'truth-through-science'. Yet another artifact of the Enlightenment – the rational, knowing Cartesian subject that I have critiqued and supplanted in chapter 2 – is allowed to remain unchallenged in this account of the reflexive researcher. This rational subject appears to be implicit within much ethnography (and other empirical social research), although explicit cognitive, psychological, psychoanalytical or philosophical models for such a subject are rarely offered. While reflexivity elides the subjectivity/objectivity dichotomy, it by no means solves or resolves the binary. As Silverman (1997b) notes 'perhaps the reflexivity card is now being played too regularly in the social sciences' (Silverman 1997b:239).

The agency and rationality of both the researcher and the researched is frequently implicit in discussions of relations within the field. Discussions of the role of the researcher frequently cover the need for 'impression management' (Hammersley and Atkinson 1995:83), through dress, speech and demeanour, as well as the presentation of 'different 'selves'' (Hammersley and Atkinson 1995:87) appropriate to different research contexts. This clearly embraces a notion of an active, rational researcher managing her/his identity/ies within the field. The notion of 'ascribed characteristics' (Hammersley and Atkinson 1995:92) closes down the possibilities for impression management. Here, the researched makes assumptions and mobilises stereotypes on the basis of ascribed characteristics – such as gender, race and age – that the researcher cannot 'manage' or present 'differently'. At a practical level this is reasonable – commonsense tells us that, short of drag, passing or cosmetic surgery, and irrespective of the status of these categories, they will be evident to the researched. But if characteristics are understood as ascribed then they are, to some degree, *determined* (whether socially or biologically).

Feminist research and research methodology have played a significant role in promoting discussion of a problematised researcher and researched. While it is important to note the extent of diversity and debate amongst feminist scholars and researchers, not least in relation to the question of whether a feminist methodology exists (Clegg 1985), feminist writers have made specific and recognisable contributions to understandings of the researcher and the researched.

Notably, feminism has demanded that attention be paid to the power relations implicit in the researcher-researched relationship (as well as within the academy itself) (Oakley 1974 and 1980; Skeggs 1994) and the possibility for empowerment/ emancipation through collaborative research agendas and processes (Lather 1991). As such, feminist research methodologies are characterised by their underpinning political commitments and histories.

It is possible to draw a distinction between feminist research that understands gender identities in terms of material relations and feminist research that understands gender identities in terms of discursive relations. Across this distinction, however, feminist research methodologies foreground the significance of the identities of both the researcher and the researched. Among materialist/structuralist feminists this is most strongly illustrated by feminist standpoint or feminist ontology (Skeggs 1994; Stanley and Wise 1990) and feminist epistemology (Stanley and Wise 1993). While there are differences within and between these strands of feminist research, they all position ontology as prior to, and in a deterministic relationship with, epistemology – what we *are* determines what/how we will/can *know*. This intersects strongly with, and arguably has stimulated, much discussion concerning the social locations of the researcher and researched found outside 'feminist' research. What most strongly distinguishes standpoint epistemology is its insistence on making standpoint visible and interrogating its impact on both the research process and findings. To some extent, then, this is akin to reflexivity. Calls to reflexivity, and 'reciprocal reflexivity' (Lather 1991:59) are common within feminist research and it has been argued that feminist interrogations of these issues have prompted the widespread adoption of reflexive research practices more broadly (Stanley and Wise 1990).

Given the fundamental influence that ontology is seen to have on knowing, and the potential for multiple power imbalances within the research process, the benefits of an ontological match between the researcher and the researched have been explored within feminist movements. Similar arguments have been put strongly by other strands of identity politics, for instance anti-racist movements have suggested that the experiences of Black communities should be researched by Black researchers, and disability rights movements have suggested that the experiences of disabled people should be researched from inside the disabled community. Such approaches have the potential to eschew the potentially objectifying effects of research criticised earlier, and people inside a community may well see things differently from those outside it. Yet to call for ontological match between the researcher and the researched also premises a 'true' experience which is accessible, if only to the 'right' researcher, and assumes a subject whose being, or ontology, is 'authentic' and 'essential' even where this authenticity and essence is understood to be socially constructed (Fuss 1990).

Calls for reflexivity, standpoint and reciprocity all position the researcher and the researched as knowing subjects who are engaged in an ongoing reading-off of identity categories – some malleable, others fixed. But none of these responses call radically into question the nature of the subject – the *ways* in which these subjects are constituted is not engaged. The researching and research subject is specified – their class, race, gender, sexuality, disability etc is identified, considered and the possible influence of these factored into the research process and analysis. Yet this does not unsettle the ascribed or given (whether biologically, socially or otherwise) status of these characteristics. The researcher and the researched in these accounts remains a rational, knowing subject who appears to be imbued with essence(s) (Fuss 1990). Such accounts sit uncomfortably with the constituted subject I explored in chapter 2. For me these are not just methodological concerns, but crucial methodological and substantive questions – it is not so much a question of *who* the researcher and researched are but *how* they are produced in these terms. This is where the ethnographies drawn on in this book and other like it diverge methodologically from much existing work.

Feminist research engaged with post-structural/post-modern notions of the subject has acknowledged and explored the tensions and contradictions between the ontological basis of feminism and the contingent and constructed subject of post-structuralism (Bordo 1992; Britzman 2000; Harwood 2001; Lather 2000; Maclure 2002; McCoy 2000; St. Pierre 2000). This contradiction has been responded to by repositioning gendered identities as discursively produced, thereby refocusing the research agenda from a concern with disadvantage to a concern with multiple and shifting (while constrained) discursively produced power relations (Jones 1993; Middleton 1993; St Pierre 2000, Lather 2000, Britzman 2000). In attempting to retain the central categorisation of 'women' in this context, Jones (1993) suggests that '[o]ne option is simultaneously to use *and* reject it' (Jones 1993). As such, preceding notions of feminist standpoint, ontology and epistemology have been reworked through ''feminist postmodernist' epistemology' (Stanley and Wise 1990:27) and 'feminist stand*points*' (Stanley and Wise 1990:47). Nevertheless, the overriding ontological basis of feminism has not been reconciled fully with the constituted and contingent subjectivities of post-structuralism.

Ethnographic studies informed by the work of Michel Foucault express the researched in a different way. Here discourse provides the 'conditions of possibility' (Miller 1997:33) within which 'setting members' (Miller 1997:38) make (limited and constrained) use of particular 'discursive practices' and 'interpretive frameworks' (Miller 1997:32). For Holstein and Gubrium (1997), the researched as 'subject' is a passive vessel (to be tapped for facts and experiences by the researcher) and needs to be re-situated as 'active maker of meaning' (Holstein and Gubrium 1997:117). Yet as my discussion in chapter 2 shows, these are not unconstrained meaning makers, nor are the meanings made necessarily self-conscious or coherent. The shift from the usually unproblematic reference to research 'subjects'/'participants' to 'setting members' or 'maker of meaning' belies the tension inherent to empirical research framed by theory which is uncomfortable with, or even rejects, the notion of the rational subject. Yet this self-conscious shift in language is not sufficient to erase the underlying sovereign subject.

Understanding the researching and researched subject to be perpetually but provisionally constituted through discourse means that research practice (as well as analysis and writing) is also an occasion for constituting subjects and so is wholly implicated in processes of ongoing subjectivation (of both the researcher and the researched). This recognition is all the more significant, and discomforting, when, as in the case of my work, these subjectivities form the focus of my studies.

This cannot be factored out, overcome or otherwise neutralised. Instead, it means that the research and the researcher must proceed from a recognition of how it (s/he) is implicated in constituting subject and an acceptance that analysis can only ever be a set of interpretations of the discourses the researcher imagines s/he can identify. This does not mean, or course, that the researched is simply a passive vessel waiting for the researcher to constitute her/him. Replacing sovereign agency with the notion of discursive agency (Butler 1997a) offers an ethnography that recognises the agency and intent of the researched in the context of discursive constraint.

This sort of agency suggests that the discourses deployed by students and teachers (and researchers) may be both intentional and unintentional: discourses intentionally deployed may escape or exceed the intent of the subject who talks or acts and/or the subject may unwittingly deploy discourses whose historicities and/or intersections assert unanticipated meanings. Indeed, discursive practices may entail the deployment of complex combinations of intentional and unintentional discourses and their discursive effects. Taking up the notion of discursive agency, this analysis assumes multiple degrees of both intent and understanding amongst subjects in terms of the embedded meanings and effects of discourses. On the one hand, it suggests that subjects do not necessarily regurgitate discourse unwittingly. On the other hand, however, it suggests that discourses are not necessarily used knowingly and that discourses are not necessarily known explicitly to the subjects and/or audiences who use them. As such, subjects need not be self-consciously alert to the discourses used in order for their familiar and embedded meanings to be inscribed. Furthermore, discourses do not need to be cited in order to be deployed. Rather, multiple discourses are references through the meanings and associations embedded in the historicity of apparently simple and benign utterances and bodily practices. For example, a student may call another 'dumb' and know that this suggests lack of intelligence/intellectual capacity and is an injury. This student may have no conscious sense of the historicity of discourses of innate intelligence, retardation and educability that this 'dumb' calls up (although s/he may well have a practical sense (Bourdieu 1990) of this). In calling up this particular example, and the other examples I have used to illustrate my theory and methodology, I as researcher and writer cite these names and give them further performative force. It also means that if I ask after such characteristics in discussion with the researched, I am not only asking after these but constituting them as real and meaningful.

As I have explored elsewhere (Youdell 2005), these discussions render indeterminable the question of whether I should offer an account of myself as the researcher. The risk of slipping into an inadvertent essentialism tempts me to avoid such an account, however, the risk of assuming a disembodied authorial authority by not doing so seems much greater. Given the centrality of visual economies to prevailing discourses of gender and race (see Jacobson 1998, Seshadri-Crooks 2000), my own location within these discourses (woman, White) is undoubtedly 'visible' to, and taken as immutable by, the students involved in my research. Yet my social class, sexuality, sub-cultural, and age locations are perhaps less singular or 'obvious' and, therefore, less tightly constrained. In line with the wider theorisation of discourse and subjectivation that frame this book, identity categorisations are seen to be as mobile as the discursive circuits through which they are performatively constituted. For instance, in the context of prevailing hetero-normative discourse, it is likely that students locate (constitute) me as heterosexual – the unspoken Same of the heterosexual/homosexual Same/Other binary – as long as an alternative sexual identity is not asserted. However, once such Other positions are suggested (as they were during the Taylor ethnography in some circumstances and with some students), the circulation of previously absent, marginalised, or unrecognised discourses becomes evident, as do the possibilities and limits for Other subjectivities that these discourses offer. Introducing such discourses into a research setting has the potential to subjectivate the researcher and the researched in ways that may well be unfamiliar, at least in the school context, even as these are recognised as being contingent, provisional and fragile – these moment in the field might themselves be moments of performative politics. These moments also have the potential to 'disrupt' relations in the field: as the researcher I decided to explicitly 'out' myself in a particular way to (some) students in Taylor (but not in Plains), but what happened next was not down to respondents responses in this particular discursive frame. Similarly, while my national identity was perhaps taken as self-evident in the Taylor ethnography, as a British ('English') woman doing school ethnography in Australia, nationality was an explicit axis of my subjectivation and a key facilitator of field relationships. Students who had speculated privately that I might be "very posh" or "from England" (but not both) were reassured by my Englishness (in ways that posh-ness may not have been reassuring in this low-income locale). This became constitutive of my position as an outsider whose lack of knowledge of the context was acceptable and whose interest in it was comprehensible (or just about).

There is, then, a growing body of literature exploring the promise for new understandings offered by empirical research informed by post-structural ideas. (See Maclure 2002; St Pierre 2000; Stronach and Maclure 1997) Such research shifts the focus beyond individuals' experiences and perspectives to an examination of discursive practices and their effects, including how these constitute subjects. As such, ethnographic study becomes the exploration of the ways in which the researched create their local realities through those discourses available to them (Miller 1997) and data is understood and utilised as a 'venue' (Miller 1997:39) for exploring discourse. Such an analysis is not positioned as interpretive but as the interrogation of discourse as 'monument' (Prior 1997:77).

Doing post-structural ethnography

When I do ethnography I try to spend a significant amount of time (perhaps two days a week) over an extended period (perhaps a school year) in the setting (one school) with the subjects who form the focus of the study (perhaps a single class). As I do this I at once recognise my common sense, familiarity with the school settings I research *and* seek to fight this familiarity and make this apparently self-evident institution 'strange' (Delamont 1990). At the same time, and perhaps paradoxically, I recognise myself as an outsider in this setting and seek to become familiar with it and the subjects who inhabit it. And further, in a post-structural frame, I recognise the impossibility of ever 'knowing' the context and its subjects and so of pinning down the meanings of it/their practices once and for all. With this (illusory and partial) familiarity, the initial semi-formality and awkwardness of interactions between me and the researched lessens and, with some of the researched at least, a strange pseudo-friendship develops that allows me to watch, listen-in, ask questions, and join in even as I remain a peculiarity and an outsider.

This pseudo-friendship that lets me watch, listen-in, join in and ask questions is the researcher 'state' in which I feel most comfortable and which I most enjoy (and in which I take the most risks). What I want to do is 'simply' 'hang out' in lessons and break-time. But this is not a simple thing at all: hanging out requires a significant degree of acceptance and active inclusion by the researched. And this means constituting myself and my research in ways that make sense to and are approved of across different students sub-cultures – pushing the acceptable limits of the social chameleon (without being seen to be fake) by self-consciously engaging the very practices of self that my research is concerned with. And all the time, this sense of fitting in, of becoming more at ease in the setting rubs up against my efforts for strangeness and my interrogation of the very notion of the subject.

To prevent this account falling into the trap of romaticising the researcher-researched relationship and inferring fieldwork skills that are surely unobtainable, it is important to also point out that almost all secondary (high) school-aged students that I have met are happy to talk to someone who has demonstrated what seems a legitimate purpose and who shows a genuine interest in them and their world. Many students are pleased when this coincides with the opportunity to miss all or part of a lesson (in the case of interviews) or when it introduces a novel twist, and perhaps an assistant, to a lesson (in the case of classroom observations). When 'hanging out' means getting a group of friends out of a lesson for an interview or sitting with a group of friends during a lesson, it is reasonably achievable. When 'hanging out' means spending break-time in informal school spaces it is less straightforward. Who I spend break-time with might be taken by other students as wholly elective and so allegiances might be assumed that close down other relationships. Spaces might be strictly invitation-only, impossible to 'happen through' hoping for a 'hello' – the territory of a particular sub-culture or group; favoured out-of-bounds areas, the local shops, smokers' corner, the girls' cloakroom – and these invitations are often absent or, too risky to take up when they do come. At these moments the pseudo-friendship falls away exposing a strange, adult(?) woman who comes regularly to school and attends lessons because she appears to find schools, classrooms and especially school students interesting.

After giving a class of students an account of myself and my research (with heart-thudding, there seems to be so much at stake on day one in the field), I spend several visits doing formal interviews (guided by a topic list) with groups of friends until everyone in the class has taken part in at least one interview. At the same time, I start observing lessons, sitting at the back of the class or at an empty desk, smiling when students catch me watching and explaining what I am doing, what I am watching, what I am putting in my notebook as clearly as I can when I am asked, as I invariably am. This simultaneous early formal interviewing and lone- (rather than 'non') participant observation lets students (and teachers) find out about me and my research; sound me out on issues (what do I think about the toilets being locked during lesson times); test me out (what do I do if someone calls another student a slag in front of me). Quite quickly I find myself being asked if I want to do another interview (during lesson time, naturally), chatted to in corridors, offered suggestions of lessons I might observe, and invited to sit at a table of friends during a lesson.

When I am interviewing, or leading a group discussion, or gossiping with a group of friends, or accepting information that students have decided it is important for me to know, I am concerned with how knowledges are constituted and how these constitute subjects. I try to set aside the notion of accounts that provide insight into participants' knowledge of phenomena and participants' perspectives (although we live this model of the world and our place in it so wholly that it is difficult to give up). Instead, borrowing from (Holstein and Gubrium 1997:114), I try to approach such moments as the 'site of, and occasion for, producing reportable knowledge itself', sites and occasions in which discourses circulate, performatives are deployed, and subjects are constituted. With my focus on the discourses that students use, and the ways that students are constituted as subjects, my considerations over topic lists, interview questions and opportunistic 'chats' are twofold: first, I want to make the interaction one that makes sense to students and in which they can talk about their school, themselves and their lives; and second I want to make it a space where I can explore what might (or might not) happen if I introduce particular discourses or open up particular subject positions for discussion.

As my previous discussion started to suggest, observation is perhaps the central tool that I use to in my exploration of teachers' and students' discursive practices and the discourses that frame these. As such, my ethnographic work includes substantial observation of formal and informal aspects of school life. Whether I am sitting alone at the side of a classroom watching or wandering through corridors at break-time with a group of friend, I am never either non-participant or fully participant. There is always observer-effect. Perhaps more significantly though, as I observe I interpret. It is impossible for me to observe (and thereby access) any external 'reality' that is devoid of interpretation. Miller (1997:27) argues that 'social realities are always under construction' and suggests that observation is crucial to ethnography that is concerned with discursive practices. Observation, then, is a route to discerning the discursive constitution the world and the subject who inhabit it. But observation is itself simultaneously constitutive of and constituted by the world and the subjects that it seeks to observe. As such, the observation – as contained within the text of the researcher's fieldnotes – cannot be (even a partial) neutral account of a seen, heard, felt exteriority. Instead it is a representation that is itself wholly mediated by the discursive frames brought by the observer and constitutive of the setting it observes and so represents. This might make observation feel impossible, unable to capture anything 'real' or 'true'. But for me this 'problematic' of the method is emblematic of the conception of the social world and the subjects that guides my research – the only way to access the world and the subject is through discourse.

Similar understandings underpin my approach to documentary data and the documents (including this book) that I produce. Prior (1997) suggests that '[t]extually ordered knowledge packages and stabilises the order of things as they appear within a wider realm of discourse' (Prior 1997:67). As such, documentary data can be understood as 'a representation of what is assumed to exist' (Prior 1997:69). Subsequently, analysis of documentary data is concerned with 'the origins, nature and structure of the discursive themes by means of which the text has been produced' (Prior 1997:66). Such an understanding has implications for the ultimate product of ethnographic study – the ethnographic text. This text is not a 'true' representation of 'real' schools' and 'real' students. Rather, it is a recon-struction of schools and students who do not exist in singular, complete form, but always through their constitution, their making and remaking, in shifting fields of discourse. And it is created within (or, perhaps, against) the bounds of the ethnographic genre (Atkinson 1990; Stronach and Maclure 1997). The text is, as Prior (1997) suggests, 'a simulacrum rather than a reflection' (Prior 1997:69).

Within my two ethnographies, then, interviews, across a spectrum of occasions of/for discourse, were pursued on the basis of theory and opportunity. The selection of observational sites and 'moments' within my study was driven by theory, hunches, opportunism, students' suggestions and entreaties as well as the demands, and perhaps more significantly limitations, of field relationships. A multiplicity of textual sources circulated within the two schools, from the public and publicity orientated prospectus to student-produced fanzines and notes passed in classrooms. A small selection of these data appears in this book, most remain in box files and shoes boxes itching to be read for an audience. This does not suggest that these remain unanalyzed. As the theoretical framework I have detailed suggests, for me analysis is intrinsic to and separable from data generation.

In drawing on such approaches I am suturing established features of school ethnography with more recent understandings of the nature of discourse and power/knowledge. In this way, my selection of particular methods is not predicated on an assessment of their relative abilities to access 'truth' or even 'experience'.

Rather, selection is based on considerations of how best to access the discursive practices through which subjects are constituted, sustained, contested and reinscribed. As such, I utilise those key methods of ethnographic data generation – interviews and observations alongside relevant documentary data – but do so with a somewhat transformed understanding of their nature:

> 'no method of research can stand outside the cultural and material world ... this involvement of methodologies in the world suggests that we should be a little cautious about the claims we make about our preferred research techniques. The appeals to 'authenticity' and of the direct contact with human 'experience' are, I believe, part of the messages of the world we live in. As such, they are to be explained rather than to be relied upon' (Silverman 1997b:249).

For me the central value of a shift from structural or cultural analyses to Foucauldian discourse analysis is the *reconfiguration of power and subjectivity* which it entails. What my ethnographies of school practices 'sees' might be similar to (earlier) studies underpinned by (typically, but only for example) neo-marxist, feminist or symbolic interactionist theorisations. For example: girls still apply lipstick during maths lessons, boys are still aggressive and sexist; the precise items of clothing, shoes and accessories necessary to demarcate membership may have changed, but sub-cultures are still in evidence; the expectations of teachers remain reflected in the educational experiences and outcomes of individuals and groups; hierarchies in which race, class, gender, sexuality and (dis)ability are pivotal indicators of position remain.

It is at the levels of data generation and analysis where the difference, something new, a set of further insights, a proposition of new possibilities and limitations becomes evident. By taking a different approach to what constitutes data and its 'proper' collection (generation), my Foucauldian school ethnographies might (or might not) 'see' something different, the stories on the tape recorder and the notes scribbled in the field-book might (or might not) change. What *does* change is the status ascribed to those stories and notes and the sense made of them. It is at the level of analysis, of meaning making – in the moment in the field, while scribbling in my field-book, rambling into my tape recorder on the drive home, in my day dreams and fractured ideas about my data and later in formal analysis and writing – that these theorisations 'change' school ethnography. What this change 'looks' like is perhaps best demonstrated in practice through data analysis.

Aside – a fragment of data

> A girl gets out of her seat, walks to the front of the classroom, takes a sheet of paper from the teacher's desk, turns, begins walking back to her seat, meets the eyes of a boy and, still walking, smiles at him, reaches her desk and sits down.

What is *in* the fragment and what is *omitted* from it speaks of my substantive area of concern, theoretical underpinnings and analytical frame. So what might this fragment tell the reader?

Perhaps the reader sees participation in designated classroom activity and implicit understanding/playing out of classroom norms established between the teacher and student(s) – suggesting the girl is 'pro-school' or 'pro-education'. But I have not provided the contextual background to allow any certainty of this. I have not indicated what task the class has been given and omitted (until now) the teacher's earlier announcement that paper was available on her desk for any students needing it. Taking paper from the teacher's desk and moving around the classroom making social contacts with a (male) student might just have easily been evidence of the girls 'bad' behaviour and 'anti-school' or 'anti-education' position. Alternatively, the reader may see gender, (hetero)sexuality, desire, desirability which might be understood in terms of (for instance) patriarchal gender relations or the shared meanings and contextual practices of social actors.

But what interested me was the *way* the girl walked, the *way* she held the paper, the *way* she smiled. The untroubled, steadily paced sashay (did she get that from TV make-over and red-carpet award shows?), the paper held at the edge by relaxed thumb and forefinger, other fingers fanned, elbow bent and hand rocking as it hangs from the wrist, the affirmation in the smile (the star acknowledging the attention of her audience?) ... For me, a constellation of gendered and sexualised discourses coalesced to produce a (necessarily embodied?) performative moment. One that I captured, or was captured by. Was it compulsion that activated this collection of citations? What sort of subject or subjects does it assert, avow, allow? Was it a considered performance? Was it all for her audience? What meaning would these performative practices have without audience? Does the mediation of discourse insist that she always already has an audience? Would her body have been the same in an empty classroom? Would she still smile? Has she practiced this in private in front of her bedroom mirror?

Formal analysis does not include (impossibly) wholesale, exhaustive coding of interview and observation transcripts and documentary data. Instead it involves the detailed unpicking of the minutiae of discursive practices. The level of analytical detail that I need to go into in order to demonstrate subjectivation-in-practice is such that only a fraction of the data generated can be subject to such readings. Ongoing 'first level' and 'informal' analysis in and out of the field does, however, allow a sense of theoretical saturation to build. It also leads particular pieces of data, sometimes mundane or typical, sometimes exceptional, to stand out for the sort of detailed, written analysis that I offer here. Just as data is generated both purposively and opportunistically, so a given piece of data is analysed in-depth because a particular question presses upon me or the opportunity to talk or write about particular concerns presents itself.

REPRESENTATIONS

Representing linguistic practices

Over the course of the chapters that follow I represent and deconstruct a number of examples of potentially performative linguistic practices. Students' talk and interaction is suffused by constituting names. The examples offered are inevitably a partial representation of an inexhaustible field of both names and constitutions. Examples have been selected on the basis of their reflection of recurrent and enduring discursive practices. Furthermore, presenting and analysing naming practices is itself a process of performative constitution. These factors do not place subjectivities and the discourses through which these are constituted beyond the realm of appropriate inquiry and/or utterance. Rather, they illustrate the importance of exposing such naming practices to vigorous scrutiny (Butler 1997a).

The presented examples draw on students' talk, talk that took place in contexts of small, self-selected group discussions (informal interviews) or during observations of lessons and time spent informally around the school. Listening to audio-cassettes made of these discussions and reading my fieldnotes of observations underlines that there is much more to speech than the words spoken. The text of speech, that is, the transcribed verbatim does not in itself 'contain' or 'convey' meanings. Particularly striking are the ways in which the intonations, sounds, bodily movements, and gestures that accompany/stand in for speech open up, close down, and add layers of possible meanings. It is impossible, both theoretically and practically, to present to the reader 'everything' that has contributed to the moments offered as examples. Nevertheless, I endeavour to present detail in excess of the utterances themselves. Furthermore, such speech and gestures are contextually situated, with meanings being mediated by these contexts. I attempt to offer extended extracts of data that enable assessments of the mediating effects of context to be made. I recognise, however, the impossibility of either presenting data in its 'entirety' or determining 'how much' context is 'enough'.

The subjectivities that these data and analyses are concerned are not discrete, nor do they progress from one to another in a linear fashion. Rather, these subjectivities are multiple and entwined and the performative interpellation of one categorisation of the subject is often implicitly implicated in the simultaneous constitution and disavowal of others. For this reason the book works constantly with constellations familiar categories. In doing this, it facilitates an analytical movement across authorised and alternative discourses; reflects the complexity of the discursive practices through which subjectivities are constituted; and enables the constitution of students and learners, and their entanglement in educational exclusions, to be demonstrated.

Representing bodily practices

The inseparability of the body and the subject is evident in my dilemmas and wrangling over which bodily data to represent, how to represent them and where these representations should appear in this book.

The school is populated by *embodied* students and teachers. Each moment in a classroom, corridor or assembly hall offers a plethora of apparently mundane and self-evident bodily stylisations, adornments, postures, gestures, movements and deeds. Understanding bodily practices was a key question for these ethnographies. Yet when I returned to those data I had generated these bodily practices were difficult to 'see'. While my data were full of bodily practices, the primacy of language coupled with the taken for grantedness of bodily practices meant that I had to force myself to silence the 'talk' of the data in order to attend to the apparently mundane and self-evident body. As such, while it may seem counter-intuitive for a discussion of bodily practices to appear *after* linguistic practices of naming, this is indicative of the resilience of the hierarchical binary of the biological/social in which the biological is taken to precede (and inform or even determine) the social.

My analysis demonstrates that such a causal and oppositional conception is spurious: without the discursive, the bodily is inaccessible and, therefore, without meaning. Bodily practices, in the *moment* of practice, may be outside language (the spoken and written), but they remain *inside* discourse. This renders the question of whether the biological precedes the social obsolete – if the biological cannot be accessed without the social, then to ask after it is social.

In deciding how to represent students' bodily practices I began by looking for modes of representation that were non-linguistic. I considered using photographs, drawings storyboards, accompanying videotaped re-enactments. These possibilities raised technical difficulties – such as the limits of my artistic competence – as well as concerns over the anonymity of students and schools. The separation also seemed to be an artificial one: students' bodily practices contribute to the meanings made and identities potentially constituted through their linguistic practices; their bodily practices are frequently coupled with linguistic practices; and certain bodily practices, most notably students' sexual practices, are only accessible through linguistic representations of them.

More importantly, it seemed to me that attempting to represent students' bodily practices non-linguistically acted to inscribe the body/mind, biological/social dichotomies that I problematise. In Chapter 1 I suggested that it is through discourse (and often language) that bodies become intelligible and accessible. Bodies are meaningful and have the potential to inscribe meaning only within discourse. In this theoretical framework, the discursive is already present when attempting to detail the body, indeed, representing the body is impossible without discourse. Even if I were to represent students' bodily practice in non-linguistic ways, these representations would be steeped in discursive historicity and I would have to turn to language in order to make sense of these representations within this text. Bodily practices, then, are described textually, despite my misgivings over reducing the bodily, once again, to language.

Representing data episodes

In presenting data, I attempt to combine sociological transcription conventions with the conventions of a dramatic script. This borrowing from theatrical conventions does not infer that I understand these data as accounts of students (and myself) putting on an act, as a series self-conscious performances. (Although at times this is clearly the case; I endeavour to indicate these performances within my presentation.) These examples are presented as a series of 'episodes'. In some instances these 'episodes' are made up of a number of 'scenes'. I adopt this presentational style for a number of reasons. First, to underline and expose the complex, contextual, interactive and ongoing nature of discursive practices. Second, to facilitate detailed analysis of the deployment of multiple discourses, as well as their intersections and contradictions. Third, to demonstrate the analytical approach being taken. Fourth, to explore the possibilities and limits of the ethnographic genre. Finally, to leave the data open, as far as possible, to facilitate further, alternative analysis`.

I hope that this approach will allow the reader to access the minutiae and complexity of the apparently mundane and everyday practices of schooling and appreciate the significance of the way that these practices constitute subjects in very particular ways – including as subjects included in or excluded from the project of schooling. Finally, I hope this book will offer readers a method of looking at other classrooms, perhaps their own, and unpicking how these other classrooms might also include and exclude.

CHAPTER 4

NAMES AND PRACTICES

Making Subjects in/of School

To name and to make, to name and to do (Judith Butler 1993:107)

There is no ... "doer" behind the deed (Judith Butler 1990:25)

INTRODUCTION

In the previous chapters I have identified what I consider to be the key issues at stake in thinking about educational inclusions and exclusions, detailed the conceptual tools that I use to make sense of these processes, and discussed how I researched these. In this chapter I turn from existing literatures and theoretical frames to the empirical data I generated recently inside Taylor Comprehensive in London, UK and Plains High in Sydney, Australia. In examining these data I demonstrate the analytical process that I am engaged in and illustrate the sorts of readings of data that this approach can produce. The readings of empirical data offered in this chapter demonstrate first, how subjectivities marked by categorical biographical and sub-cultural identities are constituted through talk, action, and representation and second, how the intersections between both categorical identities and discursive frames have the potential to impact 'who' it is possible for a subject to be. In the terms of the theoretical understanding of the subject that underpins the analysis offered in this book, this chapter shows *how* performative constitutions occur in school contexts.

I open this chapter with two ideas from the work of Judith Butler that I discussed in detail in chapter 2. These are that in our talk, understood here as a form of discursive practice, we can be seen 'to name and to make, to name and to do' and that when we act 'there is no doer behind the deed'. What is being suggested here is that when we name, or interpellate, another we in fact do not describe that person but, rather, contribute to the making of them in the terms of the name we have used. And in so far as to name is to make, it is also an action, a doing, that is, speech and action come together in discursive practice. Furthermore, that 'there is no doer behind the deed' insists that there is no pre-existing subject who, in her/his rationality, chooses a course of action and embarks upon it. Instead, it suggests that while there may be intention behind actions, it is the discourses in which these actions are embedded that gives them meaning and which need to be considered in understanding their effects. It is not good or bad intention, then, that determines the outcome of action, but the discursive frame in which the action is located. It also suggests that some actions exceed the intent of the subject – deeds that are practiced without self-reference or recognition continue to have constitutive potential. Finally, it suggests that making and doing is not a one-way production, but that the doer is her/himself also produced by the acts that s/he performs. This doer is constituted again and again through her/his own practices – not because of her/his desire to be so, but because of the discourses that are called up by his/her deeds.

These ideas are extremely helpful because they offer us tools for making sense of educational inclusions and exclusions. Specifically, they can help us to untangle how particular students come to occupy particular subject positions; how particular inequalities come about; and how these come to appear so abiding, or even natural. In this chapter, then, I demonstrate these conceptual tools in action as I use them to analyse how categorical and given names, actions, and representations are caught up in the ongoing production of particular sorts of subjects.

NAMING AND MAKING:
THE EXAMPLE OF RACE, ETHNICITY, AND NATION IN THE UK

The first illustration of these processes that I offer is concerned with categories of race. My analysis of the episode that follows shows how the naming of race and national categories contributes to the production of these, even as, in apparent contradiction, they are produced as self-evident, distinct, and natural. This is not straightforward, however, and my analysis draws out the contextual specificities of these seemingly natural raced and nationed selves and the various discourses that are embedded in the apparently mundane discursive practices of the teacher and students represented here.

Episode 1: Races, nations, exotic Others

Taylor Comprehensive School, London, UK. Personal and Social Education classroom, students aged 15-16).

DY (*the researcher, aged 28, woman, White*)
MISS BAXTER (*group tutor, late thirties/early forties, woman, White*)
STEVE (*student, boy, White*)
MARCELLA (*student, girl, Black*)
MRIDULA (*student, girl, Indian*)
THE REST OF THE TUTOR GROUP (*boys and girls, predominantly White*)

The students are completing questionnaires for the Careers Service that have been distributed by MISS BAXTER. DY *is observing. On previous occasions several students, most notably* MARCELLA, *have discussed racism inside the school with* DY.

STEVE: (*calls out*) Miss, I still want to know why there isn't a White British here if there's a Black British.
MARCELLA: (*rolling her eyes, slightly annoyed/weary*) OK Steve, just fill it in.
MISS BAXTER: (*to Steve*) Why? you want something more exotic?
MARCELLA: (*flashes Miss Baxter an intense stare, then looks at* DY)
STEVE: Yeah, I'll be White Pakistani.
MRIDULA: (*turns around in her seat to look at* Steve)
MISS BAXTER: (*to Steve*) Just close your eyes and put a cross in it.

STEVE: (*makes a dramatic display of following* Miss Baxter's *suggestion*) [It is not known how Steve eventually identified his race on the questionnaire.]

Later in the lesson, DY *tells the students that all names will be changed when writing about the research and invites students to offer their own pseudonyms.* Miss Baxter *responds to* DY's *invitation:*

MISS BAXTER: There you are Steve, you can think of something really exotic.
STEVE: (*does not respond/responds by appearing to ignore this comment*)
MARCELLA: (*flashes* Miss Baxter *another intense stare, and then looks at* DY)

(Fieldnotes)

A struggle over the proper race and national identities of students within a UK classroom is evident here. The significance of national context is immediate: it is raced *Britishness* that is at stake in this exchange. Furthermore, the specificities of local context in terms of the nature of race/ethnic/national composition is clear: this is a locale that includes Black, Indian, Pakistani and White populations. The slippage between race phenotypes and national markers is crucial to the struggle represented here and the raced and nationed identities that are 'possible' in this context. Yet while these identities are specific to this local and national context, students' and teachers' recognition, policing, and production of the limits of intelligible raced and nationed identities is not. While in this setting it is combinations of Black, White, British, and Pakistani that are at stake, I will show later how in an outer Western Sydney comprehensive school an alternative set of names and categorisations circulate but are recognised, policed, and produced through very similar sets of processes.

Steve's questioning of the absence of a particular ethnic/national categorisation might simply be understood as an example of a counter-school practice (see Ball 1981, Hargreaves 1967, Lacey 1970 and Willis 1977), with the questionnaire being completed taken as an instance of official school processes and Steve's question taken as a mundane and momentary challenge to these processes. In such an analysis, Steve's challenge would be read as a manifestation of his negative educational orientation, with the reference to race and national identities read as incidental.

However, Steve's question cites familiar race discourses. His assertion of a "White British" identity draws on and inscribes a discourse of (authentic, pure, and superior) Whiteness that is entangled with discourses of colonialism, nationalism, and eugenics (Leonardo 2004). Across national contexts these discourses of Whiteness have been mobilised within far-right nationalist and racist discourses at the same time as the claimed 'excesses' of equity and anti-racism programmes and a concomitant threat to White people and lifestyles have been asserted (Apple 2001). This is not just evident in extreme and overtly racist political forms such the UK's British National Party, or Australia's One Nation party; rather, it can be identified in widely legitimated conservative restorationist movements (Apple 2001). Ethnic monitoring practices, equal opportunities and anti-discrimination legislation, and affirmative action policies have become sites on which these discursive battles are fought (Butler 1997a).

In this set of discursive conditions, Steve's question might be taken as indicative of, at least, an implicit racism and, intent aside, seen to cite a web of raced and racist discourses. At the level of the school institution, ethnic monitoring is positioned within equity and anti-racist discourses as a tool against discrimination. If Steve's question is taken as a challenge to ethnic monitoring and, by extension, a tacit challenge to anti-racist practices, and if equity and anti-racist discourses are, at a policy level at least, part of the school organisational ethos, then Steve's question can be taken as both racist and a counter-school challenge. The teacher's invitation to Steve to "Just close your eyes and put a cross in it" might itself be understood as a negation of the importance and validity of ethnic monitoring and, by extension, a tacit citation of the racist discourses and conservativism explored above. It may also be understood as a moment in the ongoing constitution of Steve's negative school orientation (and Steve is offered by a group of popular girls as an example of a "known" boy – a boy known for his disciplinary run-ins with the school and his high status in the student sub-culture).

Yet Steve's assertion of a White British identity might have other, quite different discursive effects. Steve question can be taken as an attempt to performatively constitute himself as White British. The 'British' implicit in the 'White' of UK ethnic monitoring categories, however, interrupts this naming. In this context White *is* White British and as such the latter specification is superfluous. Indeed, it is absurd; *of course* White means White British. Yet the responses to Steve's question seem to illustrate that it is also unsettling. The question exposes the implicit 'Britishness' of White and, in so doing, exposes the 'not-quite-Britishness' of racial categories that are not White, where the Britishness must be specified. In this context White is *already* British. Other race identities may well not be. So while Steve's question can be read as citing racist discourses, his questioning of the absence of a White British category exposes the prevailing authorised discursive frame and indicates the silence through which Whiteness operates within it.

Understood in this way, ethnic monitoring practices are exposed as being implicated in the inscription of White hegemony through the citation of categorisations that constitute non-White students as Other. In this sense, it is the school/career service's discourse that is imbued with very particular and potentially constraining constitutions of race and nationality – constitutions that are exposed by Steve's apparently counter-school/racist challenge. The apparent racism of Steve's namings might be understood as discursive by-products of the exposure of the non-neutral categorisations used within ethnic monitoring and the constituting force of these categorisations. Ultimately, however, the anti-racist discourse of ethnic monitoring is not destabilised: the exposure is recuperated by being positioned as racist. The anti-racism of ethnic monitoring and its embedded discursive practices are sustained through the elision of its own racialised, and implicitly racist, performatives.

The teacher's response introduces a further racialised and implicitly racist discourse into the discursive frame; that is, the discourse of the exotic Other or what Edward Said (2003) has call Orientalism. Steve does not suggest that non-White identities are exotic, or that he wishes to identify himself as something other than that which he considers himself to be. He questions why the nationality/national affiliation of White remains unspecified while the nationality/national affiliation of other 'races' is specified. The teacher does not respond to this. Rather, she effects a discursive shift away from discourses of nationality/nationalism, White hegemony, equity and anti-racism. These discourses are replaced with the discourse of the exotic Other, itself entangled with discourses of the pastoral colonial and the colonised savage; a savage who is hyper-sexual, untamed, and ungodly (and certainly not British) (Brah 1996, Said 2003).

Steve recuperates and mobilises this discursive shift away from the question of nation and nationality by asserting himself as "White Pakistani". Whether understood as a performative interpellation or a description of a pre-existing ethnicity this name is unintelligible: despite being an ethnic category in which questions of race are elided, a key discursive marker of Pakistani is its not-Whiteness. White Pakistani is, therefore, outside the bounds of possibility. Once again, the name is absurd; *of course* Steve is not White *and* Pakistani. And, once again, the performative fails. This assertion also refers back to the previous questioning of the presence of "Black British" in the (textual but not discursive) absence of White British. The intimation may be that if Black can be British then, following the same formulation, White can be Pakistani. And as White Pakistani is clearly unintelligible, then, by extension, all non-White Britishness is simultaneously disavowed.

Marcella's and Mridula's differing contributions to the episode are informative. Marcella's early response to Steve may indicate that she is aware, at least tacitly, that his question/comment raises a number of troubling challenges to the enduring understanding of 'real' and distinct races, ethnicities, and nationalities. Yet, while Steve's question might be troubling, it is Miss Baxter's "exotic" that prompts Marcella's stare. Having spoken to me about racism in the school and the difficulty of specifying its mundane and everyday appearances, Marcella look at me appears to seek confirmation that I understand that what is happening here – the casual deployment of the discourse of the exotic Other – is an example of this.

Conversely, while Mridula does not appear to respond to Miss Baxter's citation of the exotic Other, her turn in her seat might censure Steve's White Pakistani. Mridula is undoubtedly alert to the historicity of 'Paki'; the abbreviation of Pakistani that is so frequently deployed in the UK as a generic injurious name against all South Asian people (Brah 1996). Indeed, this meaning may be so congealed that the injurious name itself need not be uttered in order for it to be interpellated: in this context the injurious 'Paki' may be already 'present' in Steve's treatment of the (not-so-neutral) term Pakistani. Steve's unintelligible coupling of Pakistani with White, while not *the* injury, cites *the* injury and Pakistani is implicitly denigrated and rendered injurious by the coupling. Indeed, the very unintelligibility of this coupling may well contribute to its denigrating/injurious force. That it is a Black student who responds to Steve's White British/Black British, and an Indian (not Pakistani) student who responds to his White Pakistani, is also of note. In the discursive frame of 'real' phenotypical races and corresponding national affiliations that dominates this scene, it is students who identify as/with these races/nationalities who defend them against possible challenge. That Steve's challenge exposes the constituted and constituting nature of race/nationality and has the potential, therefore, to unsettle these – an unsettling that might hold out possibilities for race and nation to be constituted differently –goes un-noted.

The teacher's later shift from exotic races to exotic given names could be taken as an intentional discursive movement designed to dissociate the exotic from the racial Other. Yet, the historicity of the discourse of the exotic Other means that is not vulnerable to such easy reinscription. Rather than effecting a dissociation, the exotic name is colonised by, and confirms, the racial Otherness of the exotic – any 'exotic' name is (potentially) racially Other. The Other is potentially constituted as such through each utterance of the given name, not simply in those moments when a racial identity is uttered. Indeed, the exotic given name comes to stand in for the name of the racial group in these performative constitutions – processes that I will turn to later in this chapter. The teacher's implicit assertion that non-White races, whether designated by group or individual given name, are exotic, is not addressed directly at the non-White students in the class. Nevertheless, in this moment it not only constitutes these students as such, but, in joining a chain of citation, it also contributes to such constitutions beyond the walls of this classroom. The teacher does not recognise and describe already exotic students, rather, she constitutes them as Other through her discursive practice.

This context, then, is dominated by a discourse of natural and distinct races. From the race identities assumed by and constituted through the questionnaire; through to students identifying (constituting) themselves in these terms; and the exchange that surrounds Steve's question, races are understood as real and biologically given. These essential races are defined first through a visual economy of phenotypes, in particular skin colour, that is taken to precede social designation. This visual economy of race intersects a further discourse that turns away from the body, albeit a body whose difference continues to be seen, to foreground regional and national associations. This can be understood as a discursive shift from race to ethnicity. This changed marker does not render 'Pakistani' any less constrained, or any less bodily, than 'Black' or 'White', it simply foregrounds an alternative, prevailing discourse and deflects the encounter with the Pakistani body and leaves unstated the race phenotypes (imagined as) constitutive of Pakistani. As these discourses circulate and intersect in this context, the categories that they deploy are understood to describe pre-existing racial/ethnic groups, groups that are themselves not open to question. It seems that Steve's namings of himself must ultimately fail: in the context of a London classroom, could a White boy *really* be White Pakistani? And could a Black or Pakistani student *really* be British?

NAMING AND MAKING:
RACE, ETHNICITY, AND NATION IN AUSTRALIA

Similar processes can be seen at work in the practices of students in the Sydney high school. Episode 2 is a different sort of encounter than the one examined in episode 1. While episode 1 considers the events surrounding a formal moment of race/ethnic designation inside the London school, episode 2 draws on data generated during an informal interview with a group of Sydney students asked not about race but about social groupings amongst students in the school. In responding to this enquiry, however, discourses of race/ethnicity quickly come to the fore. In both instances, such performatives are seen to constitute students as particular sorts of raced subjects and, in some moments, particular sorts of learners. While these race identities and the discourses through which they are constituted reflect the specificities of these local and national contexts, it is evident from these preliminary analyses that these theoretical tools will have resonance in further contexts, and in relation to further categorical markers of identity.

Episode 2: Fobs, Wogs, Aussies
Plains High, Sydney, Australia. Interview/discussion, in an empty classroom during lesson time.

DY (Researcher, Woman, English, 30)
JOSIE   (student, girl, Croatian, 15)
VALERIE (student, girl, unknown, 15)
TARIQ (student, boy, Turkish, 15)

DY: So what about students in the school? Are there any kind of particular social groups, or do people have like particular groups of friends, or people that they hang around with all the time?
GIRLS: Definitely.
Yeah.
There's heaps of groups.
TARIQ: Yeah, you've got all the, like the wogs and all them that hang around the quad…
JOSIE: And the fobs, in the um…
TARIQ: …grass area.
DY: What do you mean by wogs?
JOSIE: Well, European
VALERIE: Like Maltese
TARIQ: Just, yeah, all them
JOSIE: European, European
DY: OK, OK
TARIQ: And then you got your people like fobs
GIRLS: Islanders
Like, Islanders
Yeah, Islander people
VALERIE: They're all in the um, basketball court, and you have the smokers up the back…
[…]
TARIQ: Up at the tree […] But you got those groups, and then you got all the people who are you know, the goodie-goodie types, who're right up there in the shade with the teachers
JOSIE: Sitting up in the shaded area
TARIQ: Yeah
JOSIE: And some little kids still trade Barbies, that's the ones in Year 7.
DY: So, you were saying the groups, were you saying there was the wogs group and the fobs group, and a smokers group, and the
VALERIE: …and the Aussie group…there's all different groups
DY: I was gonna say, what about the White kids?
TARIQ: I don't know
JOSIE: I like, my group of friends we hang outside, well not *my* group, but …there's mixed groups, we're
VALERIE: There's some people in this school, like, you'll find that they are five that are racist. But, not many, because our school's a multicultural school.
[…]
TARIQ: We try just to, you know what I mean, all be Australians, like everyone
JOSIE: Like we all go to this school, like, it should be fair
LISA: Fair,.like, everyone's equal. It should be fair, we should get treated equally.

Like the London students, these students deploy discourses of regional and national affiliation. They do not, however, engage a discourse of phenotypical races and any visual economy of race that underpins the classifications they make use of is wholly unacknowledged. Indeed, when I ask after White students, my UK background (where, as episode 1 illustrates, discourses of phenotypical race are prevalent) and my mistake become immediately evident.

The discourses deployed by these students, then, are specific to the particular history of colonization and immigration not only of Australia, but also of this part of Sydney. Yet despite this specificity, there is also notable continuity across the London and Sydney schools. One key point of continuity is the discourse of national affiliation and identity deployed in both settings, albeit with the emphases on the different national origins of the minority ethnic communities in each locale. This continuity is unsurprising given the transnational and international acceptance of discourses of ethnicity (see for instance Brah 1996), despite the shifting and sometimes incoherent nature of these. These discursive continuities also reflect the particular colonial and post-colonial relationship between Britain and Australia. Indeed, they might themselves be understood, in part, as the continued echoes of British colonialism in contemporary Australia (ref). Finally, the applicability and utility across contexts of theorisations that understand practices of naming as moments not of description, but of performative constitution is evident.

The exchange offers further insight into the ways that race and ethnic identities are at once constituted and elided, and begins to suggest how these might intersect with particular types of learner identity. When asked about *social* groups the students turn first to groups defined through ethnic and national affiliations: the 'fobs' and the 'wogs'.

'Fob', the abbreviation of 'fresh off the boat', is a well known slang term in Australia used to refer to (constitute) new migrants (those who are fresh off the boat) and which frequently includes an implicit injury in that it alludes to the new migrant's supposed incompetencies both in terms of (Australian-)English language as well as skills for living and working in the particular social, political, economic, geographical, and climatic contexts of Australia. That 'fob' is a somewhat outmoded term is suggested by the form of transport it references – it has been some years since migrants commonly arrived in Australia by ship. This is in part why I was initially surprised to hear it in everyday use in 2001. I was also initially surprised that, when the group embellished, it was 'Pacific Islanders' who were constituted 'fobs' – the Pacific Islander communities in Sydney's outer west are by no means new to the country or the locale, and in many instances are longer established that some of the eastern European and near/middle eastern communities in the school.

Rather than simply being an incorrect and unexpected usage of the term 'fob', however, it seems that 'fob' functions here to constitute Pacific Islanders as particular sorts of raced subjects. That is, this interpellation acts to constitute the Islander-'fob' as particularly new to Australia and, therefore, as particularly Other. That it is Islanders who are constituted as 'fresh off the boat' might also infer not a commercial ocean liner, but the primitive canoe of classical anthropology and contemporary holiday brochures as well as the fishing and freight vessels bearing asylum seekers/illegal immigrants that have been at the centre of Australian media and political panic (Mares, 2002). These implicit citations further effect the extreme Otherness, and, indeed, illegitimate presence, of the Islander. Naming also acts to constitute those who use it and it is students from other minority ethnic communities whose history of migration to Australia post-dates that of Pacific Islanders who do so here. In naming the Pacific Islander 'fob' the minority ethnic students involved in this conversation constitute themselves as not- 'fob' and so not-'new' or 'illegitimate', and, most importantly, not- *as* Other as the 'fobs'.

This leads me to the second ethnically based group the students identify: 'wogs'. In the UK and the US the term 'wog' refers to (constitutes) African-Caribbean and African American people respectively, and does so with such implicit injury as to render the word almost unsayable and, perhaps, beyond the recuperative efforts that have been seen in the case of 'Nigga' in particular Black sub-cultural forms. In Australia, however, 'wog' traditionally names Italian and Greek migrants and, more recently, (and as indicated by Valerie) Maltese and (by Josie) European, as well as eastern European and near/middle eastern migrants. All of the students participating in this discussion then, might understand themselves as, and be constituted as, 'wogs'.

While the injury of 'fob' is evident in my preceding discussion, the one-time injury of 'wog' in its Australian incarnation is now less certain. The appropriation of 'wog' by young people with southern and eastern European or near/middle eastern heritage echoes that of 'Nigga' by black young people. Its sub-cultural and even popular reinscription is arguably reflected in the mainstream success of the of the Australian comedy *Wog Boy* (think an Australian-Italian version of *My Big Fat Greek Wedding*) and the Australian TV alternative comedy *Fat's Pizza* (Think a lebanese-Australian *Kumars* or *Ali G*). As with the US and UK films and TV shows, however, the success and/or endurance of this reinscription is open to debate. There is continued risk of recuperation into earlier and continuing discourses that cast (constitute) the 'wog' as uneducated and of limited educability; work-shy; and steeped in her/his home culture such that s/he could never be 'Australian' – a 'fact' evidenced in this discursive frame by ethnic enclaves, the endurance of religious and cultural forms and practices, traditional gender roles, and the accented English that is a corner-stone of the irreverent humour of both *Wog Boy* and *Fat's Pizza*. Nevertheless, 'wog' is taking on new meanings and functioning in new ways, and is by no means either as injurious, or as Other, as 'fob'. As I have argued in relation to students constitutions of minority ethnic identities in the UK, then, a hierarchy within the Other (Youdell 2003), specific to this particular context, is constituted through the performative interpellations of students in this Sydney school.

The local specificity of the meaning of both 'fob' and 'wog' illustrates how a performative name might be unmoored from a meaning it has long held, an unmooring that I have explored elsewhere (Youdell 2003) in relation to the particular understanding of 'Coolie' amongst students in Taylor Comp. Of course, this apparent specificity also masks the enormous cultural and national diversity collapsed into both 'fob' and 'wog'. While this provides community and camaraderie for minority ethnic students in Anglo-Australian schools, it also risks homogenising the Other and, therefore, acting further to privilege the normative status of British, Anglo, Aussie, White.

As well as identifying 'fobs' and 'wogs', the group also talks about 'smokers', 'goodie goodies' and 'Aussies'. 'Smokers' and 'goodie goodies' are clearly of a different order to 'fobs', 'wogs', and 'Aussies'. This is not to suggest that 'smokers' and 'goodie goodies' are not raced, but these names do identify the multiple discursive frames through which students are constituted and the way that different markers come in and out of the frame.

'Smokers' (intrinsically constituted as anti-authoritarian and cool by being smokers) and goodie goodies (intrinsically pro-school and un-cool by being good and spending time with teachers) might be understood to be constituted in a hierarchical binary whose privilege/subordinate relations shift across contexts. In terms of student sub-culture, it is the 'smokers' who are privileged. In terms of the official school culture, however, it is clearly the 'goodie goodies' who are the privileged item in the pair and the 'smokers', as breakers of school rules and ignorers of health warnings, who are quite simply lesser students by far. Neither 'smoker' nor 'goodie goodie' is explicitly raced in the episode, an absence that suggests the constant absent-presence of Whiteness.

And then there is the 'Aussie'. In Australia's stories about itself the 'Aussie', or indeed the 'Aussie Battler', is the salt of the earth Anglo- or, depending on context, Anglo-Celtic- Australian whose blood, sweat, and tears built the nation and made post-penal Australia the 'land of opportunity' for the White, working class migrant. In this discursive frame, it is this foundation laid by the hard work of the Aussie that the 'fob' and the 'wog' builds on or, depending on perspective, exploits. And the 'Aussie' is White. But when I introduced race, distinct from ethnicity or culture in this tacitly multicultural frame, the students baulk. The race, and indeed racism, of the discourses circulating in the moment (and arguably the school, the community, and the nation), and the White privilege that these underpin, were unceremoniously exposed by my recourse to the until-then unspoken raced underpinning of these discourses. And the students reverted to the discourse of official pluralistic multiculturalism in which nobody is racist, everyone is to be treated fairly, and we are all 'Australian' together. While at the time, and on listening again to the tape and re-reading the transcript, I shudder at the clumsiness, amaturism, and, ironically, insensitivity to context of my comment, I am also pleased I said it. I am pleased because it made very clear the separateness, and indeed irreconcilability, of students' sub-cultural discourse of ethnicity and official multicultural discourses. Indeed, it is a moment in the failure of pluralistic multiculturalism and the endurance of discourses of race phenotypes, despite their prohibition.

Before moving away from these arguments concerning the significance of performative namings, it is worth considering how the Pacific Islander students constitute themselves. They have not appropriated the injurious 'fob' and sought to reinscribed it as in the case of 'wog'. Rather, while in one-to-one conversations some Islander students offer the specific island with which they are associated, in the school context these students tend to refer to themselves collectively as 'Islanders'. Furthermore, they spend a lot of social time in school as a group and further mark this collective identity by occasionally wearing traditional sarongs in place of school uniform trousers, skirts or shorts. Islander students report that when they only wear sarongs occasionally it is overlooked by the school (in the spirit of Multicultural pluralism?), however, when they wear sarongs persistently, as they did during one week of fieldwork, the school moves to enforce uniform requirements (in demonstration of the limits of this multiculturalism? (See Rizvi 1997). This take up traditional dress by these students can be seen as constitutive of the distinctness of the Islander even as it is also constitutive of the Islander as, in this setting (where there is not a visible Aboriginal indigenous Other to carry this mark), the most Other, the other-Other. At the same time as it can be understood as a challenge to (Anglo-Australian) school uniform regulations, and so constitutive of the Islander (paralleling the African Caribbean and African American student in UK and US contexts respectively) as anti-school and so a challenge to school authority (Gillborn 1990, Youdell 2003).

However, Islander students' wearing of sarongs is not straightforward. Both boys and girls wear their sarongs in combination with items drawn from youth fashion, in particular styles associated with hip-hop and R and B, and so constitutive of the wearer as not just into the music but also the (perceived if not actual anti-establishment) politics and lifestyle associated with it. For instance, Sonny wears an oversized white polo shirt and basketball trainers with either black hi-tech tracksuit pants, one or both legs pulled up to mid calf, or an orange patterned sarong. And, irrespective of the weather, Sonny always wears his Black knitted beanie over his jaw-length corkscrew curls. These sorts of practices of bodily adornment draw on and cite multiple discourses with distinct origins and which on initial consideration might appear incongruous. It is these incongruities, however, that are crucial to constituting these students across intersecting axes of race, gender and sub-culture simultaneously, rendering them at once Islander; desirably (hetero-) masculine/ feminine; anti-school-cool; and not only embedded in US-derived hip-hop culture, but its most 'authentic' conveyors in this context. I will consider these constitutions of self and their implications in subsequent chapters.

All of these groups of students are spatially located in the school. The 'wogs' in the quad (where the sun reflects heat off the concrete onto their dark Mediterranean skin?); the 'fobs' on the grass area (the primitive close to nature?) or the basketball courts (the Australian version of African-American sporting physicality?); the 'smokers' at the back by the tree (beyond the reach and obscured from the view of the school's authority?); and the 'goodie goodies' in the shade (where the weakness of sun-sensitive skin and heat-intolerant bodies are indulged and the intrinsically feminine school-minds of good students inevitable fail to coexist with the strength and endurance of true 'Aussie' bodies).

What I hope is by now evident is that pre-existing subjects are not described by race and other categorical names, but that these subjects are constituted by these names and the discourses that give them meaning. Furthermore, I hope that I have shown that these constitutions are ongoing; that single subjects can be constituted in differing, and apparently irreconcilable ways; that constitutions by others and self can be effected simultaneously and can endure in different moments and contexts; that these constitutions are reliant on the discourses framing contexts and not simply the intent of an actor; and that constitutions of race, ethnicity, and other categorical identity markers intersect with and may have implications for students as learners.

NAMING AND MAKING:
GIVEN NAMES AND TAKEN NAMES

I touched on the constitutive force of given names, rather than categorical names, in my analysis of Miss Baxter's deployment of the discourse of the exotic Other in episode 1. My analysis of the ways that students' deploy, manipulate, and abuse given names further demonstrates the constitutive potential of given names.

The given name may seem on first consideration to have limited constitutive potential. And, certainly, to be far less likely to be implicated in constraining the person constituted than a categorical name based on, as in the prior examples, race, ethnicity, or nationality. Indeed, it might be argued that the given name of the individual is a word that, in English, has no meaning or function other than to differentiate one individual from another. While a number of given names are shared with or taken from objects or things, this is not a literal correspondence. For instance, the given name Rose does not infer that the bearer of the name *is* a rose (although the giver of such a name might intend to suggest that the bearer is *like* a rose). In this sense, when I am called Deborah the given name is simply a devise which allows a speaker to differentiate me from a group and address me specifically.

However, when I am called Deborah, on the occasion of my first naming and subsequent addresses, this particular given name also constitutes me as female and potentially Judaeo-Christian. While, once again in English, a minority of given names are used for both girls and boys, in general the given name is implicitly gendered. It is also arguable that given names have the potential in particular historical and social contexts to constitute subjects along axes of social class and race. In addition, abbreviated, adopted, pet, and otherwise altered given names have the potential to contribute to the constitution of the subject in particular ways.

Abbreviated names

In Taylor Comprehensive, the London school I drew on in episode 1, the abbreviation of given names was common amongst a particular group of positively educationally orientated and high attaining girls (but not boys) from professional middle class backgrounds. These abbreviated names were self-selected, had specified spellings, and were actively promoted – Victoria became Vici; Suzanne became Suzi, and Penelope became Peni. It seems that these girls had a tacit sense that their given names had the potential to constitute (conservative) middle class identities in ways that their abbreviated names might not. Calling themselves and each other by these abbreviated names, then, can be seen as discursive practices by which the girls attempted to constitute themselves as radical, marginal and non-conformist – that is, *not* middle class and pro-school. The choice of possible abbreviations and the specific spellings of these, however, are such that they underline that these names are, in fact, abbreviations. As such, the given name (and it's particular constituting possibilities) is cited through the abbreviation. The abbreviation, then, is simultaneously distanced from and retains the constituting possibilities of the given name.

In contrast, a group of working class girls from Taylor Comprehensive rarely abbreviate one another's given names. Indeed, their almost exclusive use of full (often multi-syllabic) given names – Juliet, Marcella, Nicola, Molly – was notable. Like their middle class counterparts, these girls may well have had a tactic sense of the very market value of full given names that the middle class girls were attempting to eschew.

Nicknames

In both schools, a number of students had nicknames. Some of these names were given and embraced, some were given and disputed. Some of these names appear to have been given by peers in primary school, some by other students, and in once instance, by a teacher.

For instance, "Elana Banana", a nickname based on a simple rhyme, appears to have been actively carried into secondary school by the bearer of this name. When Elana is asked about this name by another student she explains "Ah, it was my name in primary school, some people still call me that". This name might be understood as citing discourses of childhood (femininity?) and exotic fruit (race? active sexuality?), while also conveying the intimacy and longevity of particular friendships. In contrast, "Little Lucy" appeared to have been given her nickname by one of her female teachers. This name contributes to the constitution of a particular relationship between Lucy and the teacher; one of intimacy and nurture, or even mother and child. Reflecting this, the wider use of this name by other students appears to have the potential to constitute Lucy as a child and the caller as an adult. Simultaneously, calling a diminutive young *woman* in this way also cites discourses of desirable, adult, heterosexual femininity.

New names

Another alteration common in Taylor Comprehensive, but not evident to the same degree in Plains High, was the anglicising of 'non-English' given names. In particular, a large number (but not all) of the south-east Asian students in the London comprehensive called themselves, and were called by teachers and other students, traditional English names. These names contrasted with the students' actual given names, logged in official school records, which potentially constitute (not-White/British) race identities. For instance Su Lin became Chloe and Liu became William.

I do not interpret this re-naming practice as a rejection or denial of race. Indeed, in a discursive frame dominated by race phenotypes such an attempt is likely to be futile and meaningless to the students concerned. Rather, this re-naming practice might be understood as an attempt on the part of these students to distance themselves from a traditional race identity and reinscribe this race identity in ways that are more acceptable and/or desirable within the dominant student sub-culture and popular culture more broadly. Indeed, it might be evidence of the provisional success, for example, of Chinese-British or Vietnamese-British – race/national identities that were contested implicitly within episode 1.

Such anglicisation of given names is not found amongst other groups of students in Taylor Comp whose given names might have the potential to constitute (not-White/British) race identities. Indeed, this practice appears to be absent amongst South Asian students. South east Asian students' distancing from traditional race identity and south Asian students' retention of a key marker of traditional race identity may be indicative of distinct experiences, negotiations and constraints of diaspora within these different ethnically and/or religiously marked communities.

Taken names

The significance of the given name to students, and the possibility that students tacitly recognise its constituting potential, is evidenced by the textual practice of "V-ing out" amongst students in Taylor Comprehensive. "V-ing out" is a practice common amongst what appears to be a number of students. As illustrated by Figure 2, below, V-ing out involves a student writing a large letter V over the top of another person's name when it appears written in an informal context, such as graffiti in/on another student's school diary.

Figure 2. 'V-ing out':
Reproduction of graffiti in/on students' school diaries

To V out another person's name is considered to be a serious challenge to the person concerned. The genesis of this practice appears to be unclear; I was told that it came "from time". The implications, however, are well understood; one student explained that V-ing out is a *"major* insult". As such, V-ing out made a significant contribution to sustaining and escalating conflicts between students. The sign would often be found where one party to a conflict had written her/his given name on the personal possession (a school diary or bag) of a third party, the V sign then being written over it in the absence of the name's bearer by the other party to the conflict. The role of the third party remained one of supposedly neutral observer and perhaps secondary 'victim' of friends' graffiti.

It appears that writing given names in/on school diaries (and other items) belonging to friends is a textual practice of self; citing graffiti 'tags' as well as the wider practices of providing signatures and collecting autographs. In turn, V-ing out is a textual challenge to this self–it is a defacement that seems to 'take' the name and, in doing so, dispute the status and even subjecthood of the person who bears it.

As the students in Taylor Comprehensive approached the end of their compulsory schooling, they took up the long-standing tradition of writing and drawing on their school sweatshirts. In an apparent extension of the textual practices of self discussed above, students' sweatshirts were covered in tags and signatures. Students did not, however, V out names appearing on these sweatshirts. It is likely that such defacement would be unacceptable to the wearer, be so public as to implicate the wearer in the injury, and demand harsh retaliation from the bearer of the name. However, several students V-ed out the school logo printed on the front of their sweatshirts. This textual practice provoked a great deal of laughter and congratulation amongst students. School staff appeared unaware or the significance of V-ing out within the student sub-culture and, therefore, did not recognise this *"major"* insult". Yet within the discursive frame of the student sub-culture the severity of the injury was not diminished by this lack of recognition. Indeed, that the school organisation was oblivious to the injury it had sustained through the defacement or 'taking' of its name appeared only to make it funnier.

The given name, then, can be understood as a potentially constitutive. By implicitly citing and inscribing a multiplicity of discourses the given name can be seen to be shot through by race, ethnicity, nationality, gender, social class, sub-cultural affiliation and status, and, by extension, perhaps also acceptability as a learner. Given names, and adaptations of and challenges to these, constitute subjects along particular axes and function to include and exclude subjects from groups and allegiances in which these axes act as boundaries of belonging and otherness. Names then, both categorical and given, come together in contextually specific discursive webs that function to constitute particular subjects and render other subjects excluded or even unintelligible. As such, names have the potential to constitute the Same and the Other, becoming sites of both linguistic and textual struggles over particular identities and even subject-hood itself.

DOING AND MAKING:
THE PRODUCTIVE CAPACITY OF ACTIONS AND DEEDS

In the previous sections I have shown how categorical and given names act to demarcate belonging and otherness and, indeed, subject-hood inside school contexts. First I demonstrated these processes as they are effected through the linguistic practices of students and teachers. And second, through my consideration of V-ing out, I showed how these processes also operate through textual practices of representation. In this section I shift my focus to explore how actions or, in Butler's terms, deeds are implicated in constituting particular sorts of subjects in schools. I analyse increasingly complex episodes that bring together bodily, linguistic, and representational practices in order to demonstrate first, the inseparability of bodily, linguistic and representational practices and, second, how school, popular, and sub-cultural discourses interact.

Episodes 3 and 4 represent a series of bodily postures, gestures, movement, and contacts that are apparently mundane and insignificant. They are mundane in as much as the bodily practices that they represent are unexceptional and everyday within the schools in which they take place. This does not mean that they are insignificant. In analysing these practices and thinking about them in terms of Butler's (1997a) performative *habitus* discussed in chapter 2, I argue that it is their ordinariness that lends them their constitutive force. The necessarily discursive intelligibility and accessibility of these bodies becomes evident within my analysis. These postures, gestures, movements and deeds are unintelligible, in either the moment of their practice or within this text, without recourse to the discursive frames that they are located in and that they cite and inscribe. These intelligible, animated bodies are both constituted by and constitutive of discourse. Heterosexual masculinities and femininities are evident across both episodes. At the level of students' intent, the sexualities cited and inscribed through these practices appear to be a key motivational force for these practices. At the level of the performative habitus, these embodied sexualities are a key feature of the bodily dispositions (Bourdieu 1990) that are unintentionally cited and constituted through these bodily practices.

Practicing Femininity

> *Episode 3: Grooming bodies*
> *Taylor Comprehensive, London, UK.* MISS BAXTER'S tutor (roll) group (aged 15-16) morning registration period, the first day of term. During the holiday NICOLA'S (girl, White) hair has been cut from mid-back length into a bob at the nape of her neck. Nicola is seated talking to other girls while brushing her newly cut hair. The arm holding the brush reaches up and back to brush the hair while the free hand reached up to follow the brush over hair in a smoothing, stroking action. Miss Baxter looks over at her and says in a clipped but friendly tone: "Nicola, it looks lovely, you can stop brushing it now!". Nicola grins and continues to brush saying: "Just a couple more Miss". Miss Baxter replies: "Really, it looks lovely". Nicola stops brushing her hair shortly after this exchange but, apparently, in her own time.
>
> (Fieldnotes)

Episode 3 illustrates one of numerous occasions inside the classrooms of both Taylor Comprehensive and Plains High when girls applied lipstick and lip gloss, checked their faces in compacts, manicured their fingernails, adjusted their clothing and groomed their own or another girl's hair. This checking of the body's appearance seems to be sometimes automatic and sometimes self-conscious. Whether automatic or self-conscious, these activities can be seen as bodily performatives that are constituted through and are constitutive of discourses of femininity.

When Nicola brushes her hair in the classroom she may well have the intention (tacit or self-conscious) of announcing and displaying her new hairstyle. The way that she brushes her hair, however, seems less likely to be consciously modelled. Rather, this combination of movements might be understood as the bodily dispositions of the performative *habitus*. The fact of Nicola publicly brushing her hair *and* the way that she brushes it are citational and constitutive of a bodily femininity concerned centrally with the achievement of physical beauty. Miss Baxter's request for Nicola to stop can be seen as a moment of the institutional surveillance and correction of bodies (Foucault 1991). Yet Miss Baxter is also complicit with these bodily performatives. First, Miss Baxter praises the femininity that Nicola's practices cite and constitute. Second, and arguably most importantly, Miss Baxter does not challenge the higher relative value of femininity in relation to school norms and teacher authority that is asserted by Nicola's postponed compliance. Through the bodily practice of brushing her hair, then, Nicola cites a particular discourse of femininity, constitutes her body and self in these terms, and underscores the possibility for such femininity to exceed the value of school rules and teacher authority even in the context of a school classroom. While Nicola does not obey immediately, her momentary refusal of the school's/teacher's authority is played out through practices that are not aggressive, confrontational, or disruptive. Instead, her non-compliance is effected through practices that, paradoxically, have the potential to constitute passive femininity. Furthermore, Nicola's postponement is momentary – she does comply with the teacher. As such Nicola's privileging of practices of femininity over the practices of the good student does not appear to constitute her at too great a remove from the good student, indeed, the good *girl* student may well be constituted, at least in part, by her successful femininity.

Brushing hair is a bodily act – lifting hands, picking up brush, pulling brush through hair, following brush with stroking hand. It is shot through with meaning. Who brushes hair, how, when? How far is an authoritative injunction to stop abided by? What are the implications of this sequence of practices? A girl brushing her hair in class is not a simple breach of rules – it is constitutive. How the body, or more precisely *bodily practices*, cite discourses and how these intersect with linguistic citations to constitute particular sorts of masculine and feminine subjectivities is demonstrated in episode 4.

Practising classed hetero-masculinity

> *Episode 4: Violent bodies*
> *Plains High, Sydney, Australia. History Lesson (students aged 14-15).* The group is described publicly by the teacher as "mixed ability" but by the students as "dumb". The class today is chaotic as usual, with limited work either being given by the teacher or undertaken by the students. There is high-level noise. Students are engaged in social activities, including chatting and listening to music on CD walkmans, as well as regular outbursts of more physical activity, including throwing/flicking paper and other missiles at one another and play fighting. Two boys, PHIL (White) and TRENT (White), are wrestling, and Phil holds Trent in an arm-lock. The teacher, MISS STARKEY (Woman, mid thirties, White) tells them to stop what they are doing and to sit down. PHIL turns to a girl sitting nearby (although everyone is listening) and says "my Dad taught me that. Security Guard Services. He showed me that. How you dislocate their shoulder and break their elbow in the one move!" Trent breaks free, and the two boys begin chasing each other around the room. They are boxing roughly, with Phil punching Trent while holding him in a headlock. They chase each other over the tops of desks, throwing chairs, punching each other and screaming out insults:
>
> TRENT: "Fucking homeless cunt!"
> PHIL: "Gutterboy!"
> TRENT (*looking over to a boy who is watching from nearby*): "Yeah, PISS on him!"
>
> At this point, the teacher intervenes, and sends Phil out of the room. She follows him out, and gives him a warning to behave, which can be overheard from inside the classroom. Phil walks back into the class smirking.
>
> (Fieldnotes)

The practices represented here, understood in the terms of a discourse of behaviour management, might be considered classroom disruption of the most extreme kind and, therefore, far from mundane. In this classroom, however, and in some but not all classrooms in Plains High, scenes of this sort were common-place. As such, while these practices appeared to raise amusement and irritation from students and anger, frustration, and resignation from teachers, members of the school community were not surprised or shocked by such events and treated them as routine and everyday occurrences. I will return to consider in detail the way that such practices, and responses to them, constitute students as learners shortly.

In the analysis I offer here I resist the urge to interrogate these practices through a concern with conduct that is deemed appropriate, or not. Instead my analysis considers these practices as one dimension of a range of practices – including playing coin-table-tennis, slapsies, and arm wrestling – through which a particular version of heterosexual masculinity marked by physicality, aggression and violence is constituted. With such an understanding, extremes of classroom disruption, while still of interest, come to appear as by-products of bodily practices that are constitutive of these students as *particular sorts of boys*. Indeed, practices that disrupt classrooms and enact anti-authoritarianism are themselves constitutive of a masculinity that is valorised in this sub-cultural setting even as it is constitutive of these boys as being beyond the bounds of acceptable student-hood.

When Phil and Trent wrestle in this history classroom, their bodies cite abiding scientific and popular discourses in which 'male' is understood as a biological given that exist in a binary relationship with 'female' and which is causative of its social expression in an equally natural masculinity. Yet these discourses do not describe a series of truths about maleness and manhood, rather they are productive of maleness and manhood in particular ways and in a series of particular, hierarchical relations with femaleness, femininity, and unmanliness. While this masculinity is not singular, certain modes of masculinity do prevail in particular contexts (see Connell 1995, Mac and Ghaill 1996). As I have indicated, and as is clearly evident from the episode, in this context maleness and its concomitant masculinity is marked by physicality, aggression and violence – a hyper-masculinity. This hyper-masculine body is intrinsically counter to official school norms and requirements for the deportment of students' bodies. These bodies are surveilled, judged and, albeit apparently halfheartedly and ineffectively, reprimanded by the teacher.

While naturalness is at the centre of these discourses of masculinity, this naturalness is by no means secure. Indeed, when Phil holds Trent in a headlock and explains to a girl seated nearby that he has been taught this by his father, he exposes the learnt, and so perhaps not-naturalness of his bodily practices of masculinity. At the same time, by directing this address to a girl (when the whole class is watching this spectacle) this girl's lack of such physical capacities and the wider female lack – femininity – are inscribed.

This also begins to suggest the classed nature of these masculine bodies. Phil asserts that his head-locking skills have been acquired from his father – a security guard. This occupation is at once classed and gendered – the semi-skilled manual work of the contemporary working class man. Indeed, this working class man is employed to be just that, the physically competent male, who is at once intimidating, capable of physical violence and in control of his aggression and his body. Class location is also called up by the boys' "gutterboy" and "fucking homeless". The classed masculine hierarchy constituted in this context, is seems, locates the employed, working class male in a position of privilege in relation to the unemployed, homeless and low class; economic and social locations that, through the inference of failure to provide as is required of the traditional working class family man, it seems, may be at odds with masculinity itself.

By practicing in these ways these boys' bodies cite and inscribe particular discourses of heterosexual masculinity and simultaneously constitute themselves as embodied subjects within these terms. These boys' practices sit well outside school expectations for behaviour inside the classroom. The 'ideal' (Gillborn 1990 after Becker 1970) student, even the tolerable student, does not wrestle, leap over desks, and swing chairs in the history classroom. In terms of official school discourse, these behaviours cite and constitute negative school orientation and a challenge to authority – orientations that are all but incompatible with being a learner inside school.

The delayed, and unconvincing intervention by the teacher, and the boys' response to this is also of interest. When the teacher first instructs them to stop, they instead escalate their play fight – constituting further their irreverent, physical masculinity, the authority of the masculine body over the (feminine) school and the female teacher, and underscoring their sub-cultural cool through their anti-school practices. It is unclear why the students do eventually concede the teacher's authority and exit the classroom as instructed. Perhaps this is a moment of appeasement in a well-worn script where students reject school authority but concede just in time to avoid serious sanctions. By leaving the room as instructed and accepting the teacher's warning to behave, the boys' remain just inside the boundary of acceptability in this classroom without undermining either the sub-cultural status or the masculinity that their practices have cited and inscribed. And by re-entering the classroom with a smirk on his face, Phil deploys once again the intersecting discourses of anti-authoritarian hyper-masculinity cited by the practices that she has been warned against.

While this particular class is designated "mixed ability" by the teacher, students' identify it as the "dumb" class, and the teacher's apparent willingness to allow students to opt out of any learning in the classroom, and her delayed and halfhearted intervention into Phil and Trent's activity are constitutive of the students in the group as "dumb" as not worth teaching, or disciplining, as unworthy, unacceptable or impossible learners.

These bodily activities cite and constitute the *habitus* and are both formed by and formative of discourses of bodily femininity and masculinity. These practices, and their effects, are understood here to be both intentional and tacit. But these bodies are not simply the neutral instruments of self-conscious subjects. They are bound up with signification and the continued viability of the subject. These boys cannot wrestle today but give this up for affectionate touching the next without catastrophic performative effects. Indeed, such practices are likely to be unimaginable to these boys, outside an injurious discourse of the reviled, un-masculine homosexual. As such, these practices are constitutive of heterosexual masculinity and of the masculine body's possibilities and limits. And this is not just boyish bad behaviour, it is also constitutive of the bad student. Who can play-fight in a classroom? How? When? With whom? With what accompanying commentary? To what audience? And, most importantly, with what performative effects?

TOOLS FOR UNDERSTANDING EXCLUSION

In this chapter I have demonstrated the analytical tools that I discussed in previous chapters, showing how linguistic, bodily and representational practices constitute subjectivities, subjectivities constituted through the coalescence of multiple categorical names that come together in various constellations and become meaningful through the multiple discourses that circulate in particular contexts.

The significance of the demonstrations of these analytical tools that I have offered in this chapter is threefold. First, they show how what we call ourselves and others, how we engage our bodies and the bodies of others, and the representation practices we engage and are engaged by *create* these selves and others. Second, they shed new light on the meanings and significances of even the most mundane and taken-for granted aspects of life inside school. Finally, they illustrate how constellations of identity categories might be entangled with the sorts of students and learners that the subjects of schooling are and can be. These connections will form the focus of the next section of the book.

PART 3: EDUCATIONAL EXCLUSIONS: BAD STUDENTS AND IMPOSSIBLE LEARNERS

INTRODUCTION

What kind of student is a girl who brushes her hair in class and, when asked to stop, continues until she decides the task is complete? What kinds of students are a group of girls and boys who tell a story of a social world made up of race-based groupings, rule breakers, and ridiculed weak and compliant friends to teachers? What kinds of learners are boys whose friendly wrestling has them leaping over desks and swinging chairs during a history lesson? And what kind of learner is a boy who, instead of filling in the ethnic monitoring form his teacher has given him, publicly calls the form and its race/ethnic categories into question?

In Chapter 4 I explored the episodes to which these questions refer in order to show how linguistic, bodily, and representational practices act to both constitute subjects and constrain them within the terms of the discourses that make these constitutive practices meaningful and effective. In doing this, I took as my focus biographically marked subjectivities and questions of race, ethnicity, nation, gender, sexuality, and social class were at the centre of my analysis. Centreing these categorical identities allowed me to move from my theoretical contestation of these identities as natural, innate, or otherwise unproblematic categories in earlier chapters, to an illustration of the ongoing constitution of these through everyday practice. Centreing these categorical identities also foreshadowed my empirical exploration of the key concern of this book – the processes through which educational exclusions and inequalities come to exist in abiding relationships with particular biographical and (sub-) cultural identities. Indeed, in offering my readings of the episodes contained in chapter 4, the question of what sort of learners the students might be pressed upon the analysis. And the dynamic interrelations between discourses concerned with what makes the 'good student' and discourses of social and biographical identities became impossible to avoid. The girl who brushes her hair in class and postpones her compliance with a teacher's instruction to stop is not an ideal learner, but her citation of femininity is not irreconcilable with learning. On the other hand, the boy who holds his friend in a headlock inside the history class and postpones his compliance with a teacher's instruction to stop, is acting beyond the bounds of those discourses that define acceptability as a learner in a school context.

In this section of the book I develop my analysis of these connections and interrelations through close readings of a further selection of episodes drawn from my research in Taylor Comprehensive and Plains High. Once again, I move between these locations in order to demonstrate the simultaneous specificity of these contexts and the discursive continuities across them. In doing this, I argue that the discourses that inform what it is to be a student (good or otherwise) and the discourses that make constellations of social, biographical and sub-cultural identity categories meaningful coalesce, intersect, and contradict in ways that open up or close down the possibilities available for the sort of student and learner a subject of schooling can be and for the sort of social, biographical and sub-cultural subject a student can be. This suggests that the discourses through which constellations of identity markers are constituted might make it all but impossible for some students to attain sub-cultural status within the student milieu, while the sub-cultural status of other students is all but guaranteed. And, in reverse, it might be all but impossible for some students to be recognised, or recognisable, as learners in school.

In making this argument I am drawing on Judith Butler's (1997a, 1997b, 2004) considerations of Althusser's (1971) notion of subjection and Foucault's subsequent notion of subjectivation (1990). These ideas that I detailed in chapter 2 suggest that to be made meaningful as a person is at the same time to be subjected to relations of power. This means that subjection is simultaneously formative and regulative – the very processes that make the subject are also the processes that regulate her/him in the terms of prevailing discourse. This is why the position of subject always entails cost. The subjects of schooling then – students, learners – are at once rendered subjects and subjected to the restrictions of the discourses that circulate in the school context.

The analyses offered in the following chapters, then, suggests that, through their dependence on the circuits, matrices, and planes of discourse that make them meaningful, identities frequently bring with them particular limits, as well as further constitutions which are unforeseen, undesirable or even counter to those identities which the subject intentionally or tacitly sought. That is, situated within, citing and inscribing discursive frames that are mobile and often unknown to the subject, there are likely to be implications for the subject who is provisionally constituted within the terms of/as a particular identity or constellation of identities – the discursive practices that constitute identities may also be traps.

These chapters hope neither to contain every moment in which students' identities appear as traps nor exhaust every identity or constellation of identity categories that might be subject to such discursive traps. Instead the chapters endeavour to indicate the ways in which a range of categorical identities entrap subjects and outline some of the implications of this for subjects constituted by and through particular discourses. Specifically, I consider how those identities constituted through the discursive practice of surveillent and self-surveillent subjects might be seen as discursive traps that make exclusion from being a student and a learner – and so from the educational process – all but certain.

GOOD STUDENTS/BAD STUDENTS:
IDEAL LEARNERS/IMPOSSIBLE LEARNERS:
INTELLIGIBLE SUBJECTS/UNINTELLIGIBLE SUBJECTS

Central to the analysis offered in the subsequent chapters is an understanding of the subject, the student and the learner constituted through citational chains of discourses. These discourses create discursive circuits, matrices, and planes that render being one sort of student, learner and subject all but inevitable and being another sort all but unthinkable. Crucial here is an appreciation of two sets of ideas that were detailed in chapter 2. First, after Derrida, the centrality of hierarchical binaries to meaning-making and the inscription of power relations in Western thinking. And second, after Foucault, relationships between discourses and their productive effects. These ideas, I suggests, allow an appreciation of how the subjects of schooling are discursively constituted as good or bad students, ideal or impossible learners and, indeed, as intelligible or unintelligible subjects.

In thinking about an 'ideal student-learner' I am taking up Howard Becker's (1970) notion of the ideal client. This notion has been drawn on in critical sociology of education to understand the way that particular students are perceived by the institutions that they attend and the teachers by whom they are taught. David Gillborn (1990), for instance, makes use of the notion of the ideal client of schooling to explore how such institutional and teacher expectations are implicated in the functioning of institutional racism inside schools. Using this as a point of departure, the notion of the ideal client of schooling allows us to begin to understand the exclusion of certain groups from educational processes in terms of their location outside the schools formal, informal, explicit, implicit and tacit assessments of who approximates this ideal. That is, it allows us to identify the proliferation of discourses of the educational Other. The constitution of this non-normative educational Other defines the parameter of the normative frame(s) that constitute the educational insider.

This ideal, it has been argued, is a white, professional middle-class (Gillborn 1990) and male (Walkerdine 1989). The notion of the ideal client is both a useful device for making sense of educational inclusion and exclusion and the qualities of the ideal identified here have been empirically investigated. The ideal client of schooling conceived as a White boy from a professional middle-class background might seem on the surface to be contradicted by popular contemporary concerns over boys' school performance. Critical interrogations of these concerns have stressed the need to disaggregate the category 'boy' in order to see 'which boys' are sharing least in educational outcomes: boys (and girls) from particular minority ethnic backgrounds, boys (and girls) from working class background and particular disadvantaged localities (see Collins 2000, Gillborn and Mirza 2000). This insights offered by such dis-aggregation go to the importance of recognizing categorical identities in constellations, not in homogenous blocks.

David Gillborn and I have sought to develop the idea of the ideal client of schooling and its implications for students judged to be outside the ideal. In doing this we have emphasised the intersections of school discourses of 'ability' and 'conduct' and suggested that these are inextricably linked such that notions of ability and appropriate conduct mediate each other in a multiplicity of ways that act to constrain the possibility for a student, or group of students, to approximate the ideal (Gillborn and Youdell 2000, Gillborn and Youdell 2004).

The notion of the *performative constitution* of the subject of schooling moves this thinking on as it shows that understandings and identifications of students in there terms are not simply teachers' perceptions or descriptions of students, but are implicated in *creating* students in these terms. Here I want to think further about the subject of schooling and consider critically the student and the learner, and the relationship between these two apparently interchangeable subject positions. All school-age children and young people, I suggest, are constituted as *students* through educational discourse; their legal requirement to attend school or alternative out-of-school provision; and their literal attendance (or non-attendance). But not all of these students are simultaneously constituted as *learners*.

The student as the subject of schooling is defined – and more importantly constituted – through discourses of ability (or intelligence) and conduct *as well as* discourses of race, class, gender, sexuality, religion, sub-culture, and so on. Derrida's identification of the operation of hierarchical binaries and the way that each terms of the binary makes the other meaningful suggests that these subjects of schooling can be understood in an good student/bad student dichotomy. This does not mean that what it is to be either a good student or a bad student is singular, indeed this is likely to shift within and across contexts. Nevertheless, schooling does remain framed by the ongoing citation of particular enduring discourses of childhood and adolescence. In such a discursive frame the good student is likely to be marked by qualities, at times in contradiction, of obedience, politeness, eagerness to learn, inquisitiveness, acquiescence to adult authority, restraint, cleanliness, asexuality, helpfulness, friendliness, good sense and common sense, childishness, maturity.

While the school regularly exhorts its students to strive for and/or display such characteristics and so constitute themselves as the good student, it is the student who does not do so who is the focus of institutional discourses of deficit. In Foucauldian terms, all students are subjected to the hierarchical observation and normalizing judgment of the disciplinary institution. But it is the bad student that simultaneously provokes and is constituted through the citation and inscription of a multitude of discourses that identify and diagnose her/his deficits, and the deployment of disciplinary technologies of correction. And as these discourses invoke the bad student, they also inscribe that which the bad student is not – the good student. This insists that the hierarchical binaries through which privilege and subjugation have been shown to function are also at play in inscribing normative notions of the student and producing educational inclusions and exclusions. Using this frame, then, all school-age children/young people are students, whether good or bad.

Yet while this understanding promises to be useful in thinking about good and bad students, I retain a sense that there may be some students who are constituted as so 'bad' in the terms of school discourse that this good/bad student binary might not account for them adequately. I wonder whether some students might even exceed the discursive terrain of the bad student. If this is the case, this subject will be outside student. If s/he is outside student in the school context, is s/he unimaginable as a subject? Is s/he a subject at all?

Being a good or bad student might not be the same as being a good or bad learner. In the discursive frame of the school, the learner is constituted through discourses of ability (or intelligence) and even educability and, in the context of marketisation and the benchmarking of high stakes tests, through discourses of attainment and predicted attainment. Just as the student might be good or bad, so the learner might be understood through an acceptable/unacceptable binary (Youdell 2004a).

Being a good student is not necessarily synonymous with being a good (or even ideal) learner, even though these may be tied together in school discourse. Similarly being a bad student is not necessarily the same as being a bad (or impossible) learner. Rather, while these may frequently intersect to constitute good student-ideal learner/bad student-impossible learner, these correspondences are loose and non-necessary. The ideal client of schooling, then, is an ideal that is constituted in and sustains a normative matrix of popular and educational discourse that frames what sort of student an individual might be and who can be a learner and who cannot.

In exploring the constitution of acceptable and unacceptable learners (and good and bad students) I also borrow from Becker (1970) to consider the possibility of the ideal learner. As in Becker's model, no student actually *is* the ideal learner (even the 'gifted' or 'talented' student, with her/his need for additional intervention, chapel is not 'ideal'). Rather, students approximate this ideal to greater or lesser degree and, after Derrida (1978), the ideal is defined through the proliferation of discourses of what it is not. That is, through those discourses that constitute the impossible learner. As I demonstrate in subsequent chapters, these discourses call up contemporary discourses of the struggling, the lazy, the disabled, the impaired, and the disordered. And these discourse continue to implicitly echo older but now formally discredited discourses of deficit, retardation and, indeed, ineducability. Despite the demise of these latter discourses in professional educational discourses, the notion of the inherent intellectual capacity or, lack thereof, that underpins these has not gone away. And while classificatory systems no longer feature the slow learner, the dunce, and the retard, these haunt contemporary classifications of special educational need and are silently invoked as the impossible learner is inscribed.

Technical measurements of intelligence quota, or IQ, and a vaguer, and less 'scientific' quality of 'natural ability' have long been invoked along with notions of gifts and talents in constituted differentiated learners. While for a period IQ was almost wholly discredited within the education community, both IQ and 'ability' have recently enjoyed a renewed ascendancy in academic (Herrnstein and Murray 1994) and policy discourse (Blair 2002). Furthermore, recent theories of multiple intelligences (Gardener 1983) and learning styles (Sternberg 2001) have attempted to add nuances to professional and academic understandings of the learner and have offered promises of enhanced educational outcomes. They remain, however, tied to the notion that these intelligences or styles are relatively constant and reside within the individual learner. These notions of innate intelligence, and the capacity of psychometric tests to identify this, is evident in the new IQism (Gillborn & Youdell 2000) and the practices of educational triage that this underpins which were discussed in chapter 1.

This is not to suggest, however, that formal theorizations of learning or the wider enduring discourses that are constitutive of learners have not been asked to engage with the individual learner in her/his social and biographical context. Such an engagement does not necessarily call into question either the interior nature of the learner's capacities (or lack thereof) or the given-ness of the biographical axes (such as race, social class and gender) or social factors (such as poverty, social exclusion, limited social capital, poor housing) that are taken to be mediators of learning. As such it incorporates the risk of remake old models of community deficits and their impacts on learning rather than undermining deficit notions of non-learners. Work concerned with learners and learning in increasingly making efforts to understand the learner as a subject in context and avoid slipping into such implicit deficit accounts. For instance the work of Pollard and Filer (1999 and 2004) offer important examples of such work that explores biographical, social, and cultural dimensions of learners and learning.

These markers of subjectivities are indeed crucial to understanding the intersections, correspondences, discontinuities and incommensurabilities between good student-ideal learner and bad student-impossible learner. *They are crucial because, as I will show, discourses that constitute students and learners intersect with, indeed are infused with, multiple discourses of sex, gender, sexuality, race, ethnicity and social class.* Indeed, the recent discourses of learning style that I touched on above might be argued to act to naturalise and formalise these links at the same time as they offer technologies for monitoring these links.

These good and bad students, acceptable and unacceptable learners must, in order to be intelligible as subjects, be intelligible within the terms of those discourses through which particular axes of identity are constituted. For instance all students must be intelligible in terms of prevailing gender discourses in order to make sense as subjects. But these multiple identity axes, and the discourses though which they are constituted, cannot be assumed to be discrete. Subjects must also make sense in terms of the *intersections across* those discourses through which axes of identity are constituted in order to be intelligible. So constellations of identity categories, and the discourses through which these are constituted, only render an apparently 'whole' person if these intersections are intelligible.

However, discursive matrices and circuits render some identity constellations meaningful and other unintelligible. For instance, I have argued elsewhere that in the discursive matrices that frame these study schools, alternative queer sexuality might be incommensurable with working-class masculinity such that a working-class-alternative-queer self would be unintelligible in these school contexts (Youdell 2004b, 2004c). I have also suggested that the school discourses of the good student and youth-cultural discourses of Black masculinity might be incommensurable (Youdell 2003). Rather than envisaging these identity markers in a single constitutive network or circuit, they might be better conceived of as discursive planes, with the discursive network of youth-culture and Black masculinity sheering against the discursive network of the good student, even as Black masculinity is constituted by the school institution as potentially constitutive of what the good student is not.

The learner might be constituted as desirable/undesirable or acceptable/ unacceptable; in the terms of the discursive networks that frame schooling. But the undesirable of unacceptable learner is still intelligible – s/he still makes sense as a person. But as well as subordinate intelligibility (here the unacceptable learner), there might also be unintelligibility (here the impossible learner). This impossible learner would be, in the terms of school discourses, not a subject (although my speaking of her/him might be constitutive – is not-subject some form of subjectivity?). Judith Butler (2004) has considered the subject who exceeds meaningful discourse and so is not a 'who' or a 'human' at all. Worse than being 'special' or 'bad', this threat of this not-subject, the impossible learner, would mean not being recognisable as human at all. Butler (2004) suggests that it is this threat that leads the subject to accept a constitution as the Other – this other is still intelligible and, therefore, human.

In this part of the book, then, I offer a series of four interlinked chapters, each of which explores an episode of data generated through my ethnographies in Taylor Comp and Plains High. Through these explorations I examine the parameters of good and bad students and acceptable and unacceptable learners; the ways that these are entangled with biographical and sub-cultural categories of identity; and the possibilities that some subjectivities might be so incompatible with school discourses of students and learners that they may be rendered *impossible*. These explorations allow a better understanding of the subjects of schooling and offer important fresh insights into processes of educational inclusion and exclusion.

CHAPTER 5

EXCLUDED WHITE-WORKING-CLASS-HETERO-ADULT- MASCULINITY

My readings of boys' bodily practices in Chapter 4 began to show how masculinities are constituted through discursive chains that deploy oppositions of male/female; masculine/feminine; masculine/(un-)masculine; heterosexual/homosexual. The chapter also began to consider how gender might be classed, illustrating class and gender discourses entangled in ways that produce particular, and hierarchical, possibilities for classed masculinities in school settings. The chapter also illustrated the constitutive effects of the race, ethnic and national discourses that circulate in particular contexts and began to identify how these intersect with sub-cultural, gendered and classed discourses. These readings began to suggest that particular social and biographical identities might, due to the incommensurability of discursive frames, sit uncomfortably with student and learner identities.

My readings of the episodes offered in this chapter interrogate the processes through which one student, Steve, comes to be excluded from the educational process through the simultaneous constitution of him as (hyper-)adult-masculine, a bad student, and an unacceptable, or even impossible learner. I suggest that it is the very success of his particular constitution as adult-masculine that excludes him from the possibility of being a good student and an acceptable learner. This is because in school discourse the student-learner is intrinsically child, passive, and, perhaps, feminine. Constituted as an adult, sexually desirable man, Steve is rendered an impossible student and learner. These constitutions are neither straightforward nor complete. Rather, they sediment and shift as they are struggled over through the day-to-day and moment-to-moment practices of Steve, his teachers, and his peers. The episodes that follow are moments in these constitutive struggles.

Episode 5: Bad bodies
Taylor Comprehensive, London, UK. Maths lesson. A mid-ranked teaching group. STEVE (boy, aged 15-16, White) walks into the room. The teacher (male, White, late 40s) asks "Are you on referral?" [sent out of his usual class]. STEVE replies: "Yes Sir." The teacher holds out his hand to Steve and says: "Your report card". Steve replies: "I haven't got it Sir." The teacher appears relatively unconcerned and continues with the lesson. Steve sits down near a group of boys who nod to him. Later in the lesson, another teacher (Male, White, early 40s) opens the classroom door and looks in. The teacher sees Steve, points at him and beckons with his finger. Steve gives an exclamation: "Ahhg". Steve pushes his chair back from the table through the combined force of feet pushing back against the floor and hands pushing back against the table. A space is opened up as the chair scrapes back along the floor and the table moves slightly forwards. Steve stands. Holding the chair back in his hand behind him, he lifts the chair

and moves it back creating further space. He strides casually through the aisle with his
hands hanging at his side. Other boys grin and make eye contact with Steve and/or call
out a mimicking "Ahhg!". Steve grins at them. Steve smiles at me as he passes. As he
walks out of the classroom and into the corridor he pulls the door behind him by the
handle but does not shut it fully.

(Fieldnotes)

In chapter 4 Steve was seen questioning the absence of a White British race
category in a questionnaire being administered by the school. While exploring how
the episode might be able to shed light on how race categories constitute raced
selves, I considered briefly how Steve's question might contribute to his constitution
as a particular sort of learner. In episode 5 (above) the way that learner identities
might be constituted through mundane teacher, student, and school practices
becomes more clear. The episode shows a series of confrontations between the
dispositions, attitudes, and conducts required of the male body by the school
institution and those valued within the student sub-culture and wider popular culture.

At the beginning of episode 5 Steve enters a Maths classroom 'on referral' – he
has been ejected from his own Maths class for conduct deemed unacceptable by his
teacher and, in accordance with practice in the department, he has been sent to
another class for the duration of the lesson. The teacher's assumption that Steve is
on referral, and Steve's acknowledgement of this immediately constitute Steve as a
bad student, a constitution that is clearly not new. This is underscored by the
teacher's second assumption – that Steve is already being monitored by the schools
higher-level disciplinary procedures by being required to keep a report card on
which classroom teachers record his conduct in lessons, reports that are then
inspected daily by a senior teacher. In not producing a report card Steve does not
deny being on report but instead suggests he does not have it, itself a serious breach
of the school's disciplinary processes. This apparent refusal to acquiesce to the
technologies of surveillance and correction deployed by the school again constitutes
Steve as a bad student.

In the second part of the episode another male teacher, presumably Steve's actual
Maths teacher, summons Steve out of the classroom. The teacher's authority is such
that no verbal request is necessary and Steve complies without any overt refusal,
argument, or challenge. Yet his exacerbation with and contempt for the school's
unquestionable authority is expressed bodily. Steve's movement of furniture as he
stands; slow, striding exit from the room; pulling the door to without shutting it, are
all bodily practices which technically obey the teacher without deferring to him.
These bodily activities simultaneously cite the bodily dispositions of entitled,
confident, anti-authoritarian, adult, masculinity – man – and are citations and
inscriptions of Steve's sub-cultural status within the student milieu. As such, these
bodily practices present a tacit challenge to the authoritative, adult masculinity of
the teacher. These are not the bodies of a student and a teacher, then, they are the
bodies of men.

In offering this reading I am not suggesting that Steve thinks "I'll get up like
this". I am suggesting is that he has a tacit, practical sense of the relative values of
his bodily performatives across the multiple, intersecting discursive frames (such as
school, sub-culture, sexuality) in which he is bodily located. By rising from a desk
and leaving a classroom in a particular way, Steve cites and constitutes himself

simultaneously as bad student *and* confident, anti-authoritarian, adult masculine man. This analysis demonstrates the different relative values of practices, and the selves they constitute, across school, popular- and sub-cultural contexts and the discourses that inform these. That is, the masculinity that is valued and sought after outside the classroom may well be the same masculinity that renders males students so constituted unacceptable inside the classroom.

It seems likely that such a scene is not new, Steve has experienced this many times, a tacit ritual is being enacted through which Steve's learner and sub-cultural identities are repeatedly cited and inscribed. Steve's subjectivity has congealed over a multitude of such mundane constituting incidents. This understanding begins to shed light on how particular groups of students repeatedly come to be excluded from the educational process across moments and contexts.

The incommensurability of adult masculinity and the good student is demonstrated further in my analysis of episode 6 which shows the masculinity constituted through Steve's bodily practices in episode 5 constituted and struggled over through the practices of Steve's teacher and fellow students as well as Steve's own practices. And while in the terms of high status or "known" sections of the student sub-culture this sexually accomplished and (proto-) adult masculinity is highly desirable, in other sections of the student community this mode of masculinity is at once denied to Steve and constituted as undesirable. And it is refuted and punished by at least one teacher for whom this masculinity appears such a threat to teacher/student (and man/boy) hierarchies that it leads to Steve's constitution as beyond the bounds of acceptability in the school context. Indeed, it seems that such masculinity is so far removed from official discourses of the good student that to be constituted as a man in school – that is, as not a school*boy*, is to be rendered an impossible student.

Episode 6: Wanker, Scene 1
Taylor Comp, London, UK. Discussion/Interview with STEVE, MARTIN *and* MARCUS *(all aged 15-16, boys, White)*

DY: Are there any teachers you don't like?
MARTIN: Mr Mills, he picks on people.
DY: Who does he pick on?
MARTIN: Steve, and other people.
STEVE: *(interrupting)* And he talks about your sexuality, your sex life, like the other week, he saw me out with my girlfriend and then brought it up in class.
MARTIN: Yeah.
STEVE: He goes "What were you doing with her, it wasn't looking too good" and I just had to sit and take it. After the lesson I went and said to him, really politely, "Please don't speak about my girlfriend in class" and I got shouted at again. You can't win.

The teacher's comments[xi] reported to me in Scene 1 of episode 6 can be seen as a challenge and threat to Steve's masculinity as well as his girlfriend's desirable femininity. Such comments are more than slurs, they have the potentially to performatively constitute Steve and/or his girlfriend in particular ways. The teacher's question suggests that there is something wrong with the girl and/or Steve's bodily practices of masculinity[xii]. That is, the question potentially constitutes the girl as undesirable and Steve as sexually inept and, therefore, boy. In the teacher's subsequent statement the "it" is significant. The "it" might refer to the girlfriend, potentially constituting her as lacking the desirable femininity to merit the designation 'she' (and so not human, and so animal? "dog" perhaps?). If the "it" is taken to refer to Steve and his girlfriend's practices more generally then it is, once again, a challenge to Steve's masculine sexuality and potentially constitutive of 'boy'. The obliqueness of the teacher's "it" might expose his wariness of mounting a more direct challenge to Steve. Yet the "it" also broadens the potential reach of the teacher's constituting linguistic practices. Furthermore, that the teacher's comments are made in front of the whole class renders this a public humiliation and potentially constituting moment. The potentially performative force of the teacher's comments is felt by Steve and recognised by Martin.

Steve's immediate response (sitting and taking it) and his later private, polite request provisionally recuperate the teacher's constitution. At the level of conscious awareness and intent it is likely that Steve felt injured/humiliated; knew (given the teacher/student hierarchy that frames the context) that an immediate, aggressive response would only lead him to be disciplined; and hoped that a polite, private request might make him feel better (recuperate the teacher's constitution of him/his girlfriend) and possibly guard against similar comments in the future. Steve's response did both more and less than this. His response did not save him from being disciplined – he was "shouted at again". It did not make him feel better – he felt "you can't win". But it may have had substantial, if only provisional, performative force.

Steve's private polite request cites and inscribes the quiet word, the man-to-man talk – it is a particularly adult, masculine response. Through these practices Steve recuperates the teacher's implicit 'boy' and constitutes himself as man. In turn, this constitution destabilises the teacher-adult-man/student-child-boy hierarchy that framed the teacher's comments. Indeed, Steve's man-to-man talk with the teacher might even momentarily transpose their locations within this hierarchy – it is the teacher who has behaved inappropriately, or even childishly, and Steve who offers a gentle but clear correction. Steve's tacit performative practices of man have not only effected his own masculinity, they have exceeded and even threatened the teacher's own. Steve has acted out of his place in discourse and in doing so he has risked the teacher's place.

While Steve's tacit performatives have some force, they do not enhance his standing in the teacher's eyes. Rather, it is the provisional force of these performatives (tacitly deployed in a multitude of Steve's apparently mundane practices) that make it imperative for the teacher (-adult-man) to recuperate these. One such recuperating moment is illustrated in Scene 2.

Episode 6: Wanker, Scene 2
Taylor Comp, London, UK. In the staffroom during a teaching period. MR MILLS (teacher, man, White, mid forties), who I see regularly around the school and exchange friendly "hellos" with, approaches me. We talk and it transpires that some content of my discussions with students has got back to him through a student in his tutor group. Mr Mills believes that he has been "slagged off" and, while I try to assure him that this is not the case, he conjectures on who it might be. He says: "I bet it was Steve. I hate that kid, he's a little wanker, one of those really arrogant kids who thinks he doesn't have to do any work. I bet it was him whose been slagging me off". I deny this (of course), reiterating that he has not been "slagged off".

(Fieldnotes)

It is the very force of Steve's ongoing performatives that provokes the teacher's potentially constituting tirade. If Steve has acted out of his place in discourse (again) and in doing so risked the teacher's place in discourse, then he must be constituted (again) in his proper place and thereby restore the teacher to his. The teacher's comments to me are not simply vilifications of Steve. They implicitly recuperate Steve's constitution of himself as man and the threat that this poses to the teacher-adult-man/student-child-boy hierarchy. While the particular language and vehemence of this commentary is unusual, teachers do regularly make comment about individual students to me, and they often engage in uncensored staffroom discussions with each other about individual students. While the teacher's particular comments here are unusual and inappropriate, and their staffroom setting might make them 'backstage', they are not off the ethnographic record.

By calling Steve "little wanker" and "arrogant" and suggesting that he "thinks he doesn't have to do any work" the teacher provisionally constitutes Steve in particular ways. As an injurious name that is both gendered and sexualised, "little wanker" might constitute Steve as a child-boy (feminine), as sexually incompetent and, by extension, as not-man. "Little" potentially constitutes Steve as small, diminutive and therefore child and not man. "Wanker" is more complex. Wanker cites and inscribes a discourse of masculinity in which the social and the sexual are closely entwined and constitutive of each other. While wanking is literally the act of masturbation, to call a man wanker can be seen as a tacit contestation of his masculinity; an indication of his incapacity to gain sex with (intrinsically available) desirably feminine women; an assertion of his unacceptability within a community of speakers; as well as a suggestion of an (in this context vilified) masturbatory act. Sexual experience and activity is, within prevailing discourse, crucial to the constitution of adult heterosexual masculinity – man. And while coitus and masturbation are clearly not mutually exclusive, when wanker is deployed as an injurious name they may well be. The potentially performative name wanker, then, simultaneously contests masculinity and man. The wanker lacks desirable masculinity; indeed, he may not be man at all.

Mr Mill's "arrogant" is also potentially constitutive of Steve. It suggests Steve is mistaken in his gender, sexual, and educational sense of himself – it acts to further underscore Mr Mill's contestation of Steve as man at the same time as it asserts him authority as the adult teacher (man) in a position to assess professionally Steve's merit as a student and learner. This account of Steve, then, is not simply suggestive of Mr Mill's apparent anger and frustration. More significantly, it is potentially constitutive of Steve as neither an acceptable learner nor a desirable man.

Mr Mills' "wanker" is echoed by a group of boys who are in the same tutor group as Steve.

Episode 6: Wanker, Scene 3
Taylor Comp, London, UK. Discussion/interview with RICHARD, ROB, JAMES, SIMON, CHRISTOPHER, DECLAN *(all aged 15-16, boys, White)*

CHRISTOPHER: Steve tries to act bigger than he is.
ALL: Laugh.
DY: What?
RICHARD: (*laughing*) If you were, if Steve saw that!
    (*simultaneously*) JAMES: (*earnest*) I won't tell.

(*simultaneously*) SIMON: (*laughing*) Git!
DY: He's What?
ROB: He's a bit of a (*hand-mimes the act of masturbation -- hand encircled to meet fingers and thumb with hand moved back and forth*).
    (*simultaneously*) ALL: (*Laugh*)
DY: I've put in my notes 'wank sign', OK?
RICHARD:(*laughing*) Put Declan next to it!

ALL: Laugh.
SIMON: We didn't say that either so!
DY: I saw somebody else do it, do you disagree?
SIMON: (*laughing*) I don't want my name right next to it.
    (*simultaneously*) JAMES: (*laughing*) Don't worry about it.
    (*simultaneously*) ROB: It won't get out.
CHRISTOPHER: He won't touch us.
DY: This is strange cos, I don't know what I thought, but you don't get on with him, you don't like him?
CHRISTOPHER: Often he appears without invitation and we just sort of ignore him or we don't really mind but, he gets angry without any reason, or start being mean to us.
SIMON: He's got a bad attitude.
CHRISTOPHER: Yeah, he's got a big temper as well.
RICHARD: He cries a lot.
ROB: Yeah.
DY: Does he? Does he cry when people wind him up?
RICHARD: (*laughing*) No, not like crying with tears, he whines, kicks things.

These boys' practices are also potentially constitutive of Steve and themselves. These practices draw on both a masculine/feminine hierarchical binary and a nuanced distinction between *forms* of masculinities. These boys are neither strongly positively nor negatively educationally orientated. Rather, in Christopher's words, they endeavour to "stay out of trouble" with both teachers and peers. They are not notable for either high or low attainment. Their mundane bodily practices (postures, gestures) cite and inscribe discourses of masculine physical ableness and entitlement but do not reflect the aggressiveness of the hyper-masculinities discussed earlier. Their group identity seems to reflect traditional working class/lower middle class notions of masculine paternalism, group consensus, and loyalty. These are ordinary boy-students. Girls in their tutor group describe them as "unknown" boys, the quickly dismissed counter to the desirable, interesting and popular "known" boys of whom Steve is one.

The boys do not call Steve wanker verbally, rather they interpellate him wanker through a familiar hand-mime. That they do not *say* the word does not leave the naming ambiguous, nor does it negate its potentially performative force. The bodily rather than linguistic naming might itself be seen as a practice of masculinity. To call names, to "bitch" or "gossip", has been denigrated by these boys as a girls' pass-time. To hand-mime wanker, itself a masculine doing (not saying), protects against the risk of (feminine) bitching/gossiping[xiii].

A number of the boys express concern over this naming of Steve being attributed to them – in the context of an audio-recorded interview the hand-mine pretends to stay off this recording. They assure one another of confidentiality *and* jokingly suggest that the comment should be attributed to a particular member of the group – this is a group interpellation and all the boys concur through repetitions of the hand mime, nods, laughter and assurances of safety. Nevertheless, the explicitness of this concurrence seems to vary according, perhaps, to each boy's degree of confidence in me and the rest of the group – that they do not want this to get back to Steve is a real, but minor, concern.

The boys also challenge Steve's masculinity by suggesting that he cries. An accusation of crying is intrinsically feminising within a discursive frame in which women/girls cry and men/boys do not. Yet this feminisation is retracted when I query their meaning – while my momentary belief in Steve's crying provides some pleasure to the boys (seen in their amusement), the boys' clarification of this (whining and kicking things) might act to reinforce Steve's hyper-masculinity, a masculinity whose sub-cultural status there boys privately contest.

The Scene is punctuated by moments of hilarity during which it is difficult to make out the boys' verbal contributions to the discussion. This underlines the excitement that suffuses the scene. The boys have taken a risk. As ordinary boys they have transgressed the boundaries and order of the hierarchical student sub-culture by calling Steve wanker – they have acted outside their place in discourse. Popular wisdom within the student sub-culture has it that Steve is a high status man who demands and deserves respect. This group of boys has taken the risk, which in their (constituting) understanding of Steve's hyper-masculinity might include a real physical risk, of contesting this position and potentially constituting Steve as wanker.

Steve's adult heterosexual masculinity is, in part, constituted through his refusal to defer to the authority of the school and his contestation of the givenness of the teacher/student hierarchy that school authority is constitutive of and constituted by. These boys have witnessed Steve's constituting practices a multitude of times. Unlike Steve, the boys in this group do defer to school authority, including the teacher/student hierarchy. This deference seems to be motivated by a practical desire for an easy life rather than an active approval of and belief in the school's authority. Steve's refusal exposes the boys' own acquiescence and the lack of adult masculinity that this implies. The boys' naming of Steve might expose a tacit recognition of the inferior status of their own masculinity within the student sub-culture and even a concomitant envy of Steve's masculinity and the status it cites and inscribes. In calling Steve wanker these boys differentiate between their own and Steve's mode of masculinity. This is a differentiation that implicitly suggests that, contra to the discourse of the mainstream student sub-culture, their own masculinity is not that of the ordinary boy but that of the mature, rational man. That is, it is more desirable than Steve's.

Steve's particular bodily masculinity is successful in student sub-cultural and youth cultural discourses of desirable heterosexuality (man). Furthermore, this masculinity may well also prove to be an asset as Steve moves out of compulsory schooling and into educational, training, or work contexts in which adult masculinity is not only valued but demanded. It appears possible, however, for such a masculinity to be too successful within the school context. It appears that both the teacher's and the boys' potentially performative interpellations of Steve are provoked by his *excess* of adult masculinity in the terms of the school's institutional discourses, particularly the teacher-adult-man/student-child-boy hierarchical opposition. In the context of official school values Steve's masculinity is a threat or challenge that must be recuperated – Steve is entrapped by the very success of his adult, heterosexual masculinity such that it renders him a bad student and an unacceptable, or even impossible, learner.

In school discourses the good male body is the instrument of the mind of the rational, Cartesian man who has subdued the body through its displacement onto woman and its taming through education and/or godliness. The bad male body, then, is the untamed and sexualised force that compels the ungodly, irrational, and uneducated man. Constitutions of these bodies deploy the historicity of colonial, eugenicist, and industrialist discourses that demand the management and correction of mass urban populations, the colonised, and the enslaved. As Foucault (1990) has suggested and Hunter (1996) has explored, the cultivation of the good body and the correction of the bad body have become key task of schooling.

Yet beyond the school this good male body is contested. Indeed on the urban street, in the city centre pub, on the football terraces and in (some) places of work, this binary is reversed – it is the hyper-masculine, sexually desiring and powerful body that is demanded. This male body is also classed and raced. Parkin in D.H. Laurence's *Lady Chatterly's Lover*; Heathcliffe in Emily Bronte's *Wuthering Heights*; and Scudder, the Under-gamekeeper, in E.M. Forster's *Maurice* each embodied a working class masculinity so desirable and desiring that it threatened the ruin of women and, in the latter case men, of the ruling classes. Steve, then, is the inheritor of this (White) working class bodily masculinity that is at once so desirable and so threatening. If this analysis is correct, it shows the long threads between contemporary common sense and social and political histories and the complexities and challenges of shifting this common sense.

This chapter suggests the plurality of masculinities that might be available for men and boys to take up as practices of self and in whose terms men and boys might be constituted through prevailing discourses. In this chapter perhaps just three of these are evident: the hyper-masculinity of Steve with its high sub-cultural status but low degree of school acceptability; the sensible, low-profile masculinity of the other boys with its low sub-cultural status but high degree of school acceptability; and the (contested and even fragile) adult masculinity of Mr Mills. Might there be moments in which sensible, low profile masculinity might bring with it low levels of school acceptability? Could Mr Mills still be adult-man if he allowed Steve to be adult-man? Could Steve be sub-cultural cool and a good student?

CHAPTER 6

EXCLUDED WHITE-WORKING-CLASS-HETERO-(UN) FEMININITY

In Chapter 4 I considered the constitution of femininity within school contexts and suggested that school requirements of good student conduct and popular expectations of femininity might be commensurate. I also suggested that discourses of the ideal learner might be implicitly gendered male, and so femininity might be schooled at some distance from the ideal learner. This might allow, or even require, constitutions of desirable femininity to be of greater value than those of desirable learners. Here I am arguing both an intersection *and* a lack of connection between discourses that have the potential to constitute the girl student in particular ways. This is not, however, to suggest a singularity of femininity. Nor is it to suggest either a degree of fit that guarantees girls school success, or a degree of separation that makes school success unimportant for girls. Rather it suggests that matrices of school and popular discourses create discursive frames that make being a girl and being a good student easy, at the same time as school and popular discourses create discursive planes that separate being a girl and being an ideal learner.

It is the particularities of these discursive frames and planes that I turn to in this chapter. Through my analysis of episode 7 I explore how particular modalities of femininity foreclose the possibility of being either an acceptable learner or a good student. In demonstrating these processes, I also show the inseparability of femininity from sexuality, social class, and race as well as from the student-learner subject.

Episode 7: Bitch, scene 1
Plains High, Sydney, Australia. History Lesson (students aged 14-15), The lesson takes place in a first story classroom that looks out over a concrete quadrangle, without air conditioning or fans the glass-sided room is extremely hot and sticky in the heat of the afternoon sun. There is a lot of noise and many students are chatting and joking together. The Teacher, MISS STARKEY (White, woman, mid thirties), is guiding the boy and girl sitting next to JULIE (girl, age 14-15, White) through the questions on the worksheet. Julie is working on her own worksheet, and looks up at the teacher to request help:

JULIE: Miss?
MISS STARKEY is standing close enough to hear her, but makes no response.
JULIE (shouting): MISS!
Again, the teacher does not respond.
JULIE: Don't ignore me, BITCH!
MISS STARKEY looks up at Julie.
Student seated nearby: Did she just say 'bitch'?!
JULIE: Yeah, well you ARE a bitch, aren't you bitch?

111

Miss Starkey gives Julie a disapproving glance, but goes on with what she is doing. Ten minutes later, Julie is still working on her worksheet.

JULIE: Miss? I can't figure out the answer to that one!

Miss Starkey goes to Julie and helps her with the answer. Once Miss Starkey moves on to someone else, Julie chats with some girls sitting nearby. After that line of conversation finishes, Julie says aloud, to no one in particular "I've finished my work for the day!". She commences playing with her hair and chewing her nails.

(fieldnotes)

Exchanges of this sort are regular occurrences between Miss Starkey and Julie, and, as is suggested by my consideration of Phil and Trent's wrestling in episode 4, such scenes are relatively common within Plains High. It is not my intention here to explore in detail the set of circumstances that might lead to such practices becoming everyday in a school. It is noteworthy, however, that in a context in which notions of marketisation and consumer choice are hegemonic and school reputation is all, Plains High struggles to attract and retain the highest attaining students from its locale and cannot hope to attract such students from further outside the area (Youdell 2004a). Those students who do attend the school do not report efforts to go elsewhere, but they are disdainful when speaking of the school, which they regularly describe as a "shit hole".

In order to understand the constitutive potential of this episode and how these practices might act to render Julie beyond the bounds of acceptability as a school learner and unsettle the constitution of Miss Starkey as teacher it is important keep in view the terms of enduring discourses of femininity, such as those illustrated by Nicola's brushing of her hair and her exchange with Miss Baxter in episode 3. These contemporary discourses of femininity, themselves bearing the historicity of Victorian/protestant discourses of the pure and pious woman, cite and inscribe, in multiple combinations: passivity; submissiveness; politeness; refinement; caring; empathy; nurturance; diligence; hard work; and sexual continence as key markers of a feminine ideal.

The practices of both Julie and Miss Starkey in the episode sit in a problematic relationship with such a feminine ideal. The version of the female (and perhaps feminine) constituted here is, I suggest, one that is framed by a discourse of girl-woman that continues to require passivity and service in relation to men (especially male partners and family member); nurturance in relation to children; but self-reliance, including the capacity for verbal and even physical combat in relation to outsiders, in particular other women. Put simply, Julie and Miss Starkey are engaged in a series of (ongoing?) cat fights, fights that are incommensurate with the femininity required by official school discourse but which do not undermine this particular (un-)femininity. In such a frame Julie and Miss Starkey's practices are marked by, and constitutive of sub-culture, gender, sexuality and, perhaps, social class. This version of girl-woman is recognisable in youth and popular culture, but it is incommensurate with school values and is contested in out-of-school youth and popular cultural contexts. This begins to suggest that femininities that are compatible with the acceptable (girl) student of schooling are intrinsically marked by sub-culture and class. And these constraints to the femininities that are commensurate with acceptable girl-students begin to shed light on how, despite media headlines proclaiming all girls' school success; it is in fact particular groups of girls who are the main beneficiaries of this school success.

At the beginning of the scene Julie asks Miss Starkey for assistance. While her first request "Miss?" reflects usual expectations of such an exchange between student and teacher, when this help is not immediately forthcoming Julie rapidly shifts her request to a demand: "MISS!". While Julie's request meets expectations for appropriate student conduct, her demand does not. In this shift from request to demand, then, it seems that Julie's practices shift her from being potentially constituted as an acceptable learner to being potentially constituted as an unacceptable learner.

That the teacher does not respond to the first request might simply indicate that she is busy with another student and, in the silence of this non-response, requires Julie, acting her place in discourse as an acceptable student, to wait her turn. But Julie does not wait. Rather when her demand is also ignored she commands "don't ignore me BITCH!". While there is a degree of possibility that Julie's demand 'MISS!" remains compatible with the conduct of the acceptable learner, her "BITCH!" certainly is not. A student who uses such an injurious expletive to and against a teacher is, in using the expletive, constituted an unacceptable learner. Indeed, such a practice may well be so far beyond the bounds of what is recognisable as a learner that it may render the student an impossible learner.

Formally, bitch refers to a female dog and, in so doing, it has no injurious effects. When applied to a girl or woman, however, the potential for injury, including the potential to constitute and denigrate simultaneously is ever present. As an injurious name bitch is gender specific – it is girls and women who are bitches. To call a woman a bitch is to call her a dog – to render her less than human. It is also to speak of the *sort* of woman she is – the bitch is unpleasant, unkind, vindictive, untrustworthy, scheming, malicious, spiteful, and coarse. The 'bitch' is the bad woman, what woman can be if she is released from the restraining paternalism of church, state, and family. Eve's culpability for the fall echoes in the contemporary injury 'bitch'. The bitch, then, is constituted through a web of enduring discourses that set the refined, prudent, and sexual continent (White) middle class wife in opposition to the coarse, careless, promiscuous low class whore. In silent or explicit citation of the virgin and the whore, the godly and the fallen, bitch constitutes the fish-wife, guttersnipe, slag, slapper, tart (see also Youdell 2005b).

While bitch is implicitly classed by the commensurateness of refinement, kindness, and sexual continence on the one hand, and coarseness, cruelty, and promiscuity on the other, embedded in discourses of femininity, this is not a final constitution. The upper and middle class girl/woman can also be bitch. She, however, may be constituted as retaining her refinement, and perhaps even her sexual continence, while being wily, cruel and spiteful (think, for instance, of the Marquise de Merteuil in Choderlos de Laclos' *Les Liaisons Dangereuses*, or Kathryn Merteuil in *Cruel Intensions*, the film based in contemporary New York but inspired by Laclos' book). And in continuing to be constituted as refined (if not, in either the Marquis' or Kathryn's case, chaste) bitch may even become a desirable quality (think the Vicomte de Valmont's and Sebastian's respective admiration of the Marquise's and Kathryn's spite).

Similarly, while I have suggested that bitch is intrinsically (un-)feminine, this does not mean that men or boys cannot be interpellated bitch. While in many contexts the performative force of bitch is likely to be diminished if it is directed at a man/boy, in other contexts such a name is likely to have effects. For instance, in popular gay discourse bitch contributes to a successful camp parody of femininity and, as such, compliments as it identifies the injury inflicted not by the name bitch, but by the bitch 'her-'self. In this discursive frame the gender, and injury, of bitch is shifted. Indeed, being called bitch may often be at once an injury *and* a moment of admiration – to be a bitch is an accomplishment as well as a flaw.

While the meaning and injury of 'bitch', then, is not determined, in the context of this history classroom the injurious intent of Julie's "Bitch" is indisputable. And yet, as I have indicated, for a student to call her teacher 'bitch' is to act well beyond the bounds of the hierarchical teacher/student relationship. In calling Miss Starkey bitch, Julie introduces a discourse into the classroom interaction of the student and teacher that has not belonged there – and which is barely intelligible there. It is unintelligible for a student to call a teacher bitch, and yet Julie has done so. Furthermore, it is arguable that bitch is all but unintelligible in this moment because, in personifying the authority of the school, the (woman) teacher is constituted as ungendered or even as an honorary (if impossibly and sub-standard) man. But the teacher is a woman, and in calling her bitch Julie drags the teacher out of her institutional subject position and constitutes her not just as an ordinary woman devoid of institutional authority, but as low class, denigrated woman. The teacher is, even if only momentary, not teacher. This challenge is not restricted to Miss Starkey, by introducing this disallowed discourse in the school context, the school's authority and its right to require particular conduct of students is refused, and in refusing Julie also constitutes herself outside the discourse of the school. The degree to which Julie's practices have exceeded the bounds of those school discourses that define the student, the learner, and the teacher is highlighted by her classmate's shocked request for confirmation of what she has said.

Miss Starkey initially ignores what Julie has called her – in doing so she acts her place as teacher (not entertaining bad behaviour, insisting through her silence that students conform to school conduct requirements) and so potentially recoups Julie's constitution of her. And yet, to assist students who are in need of help with their work is integral to being teacher – and so Miss Starkey at once is and is not 'teacher' in her mode of response to Julie. That the teacher ignores Julies "BITCH" might be read as a refusal (tacit or intentional) to accept this naming, that is, as a refusal to concede this subjectivation. Yet, as a discursive effect, this subjectivation exceeds Miss Starkey's–Julie's naming, while non-ordinary in this context, is recognisable and so the constitution has performative effects. Irrespective of the teacher's refusal to acknowledge the name, she is at least provisionally constituted 'bitch'. As such, Julie at least partially unseats Miss Starkey's teacherly authority and constitutes her as a denigrated woman in terms of student and popular discourse instead of a respected woman in terms of school discourse. Ultimately Miss Starkey does help Julie – perhaps she has a tacit sense of the way she has been constituted through Julie's practices and, despite herself, helps Julie in order to reinscribe her identity as teacher and her concomitant teacher authority.

These performative practices have significant implications for Julie. As I have noted, and as the other student's response indicates, to call the teacher 'bitch' is well beyond the bounds of the good student and acceptable learner. And so Julie's practices constitute her as an unacceptable learner, even as she asks for help with her schoolwork. And this unacceptability is underscored by the teacher's failure to respond to her request. The teacher's non-response, then, itself has performative potential: by ignoring Julie, Miss Starkey constitutes her as an unacceptable, even impossible learner – the student who calls the teacher 'bitch' while asking for help cannot be a learner. Further, by constituting Julie as an impossible learner, the teacher is acting her place in institutional and professional discourses of the teacher, and in so doing constitutes herself teacher.

Ultimately Miss Starkey does give Julie the help she has sought, they are teacher and learner in teacher/student discourse (if only just). Julie, it seems, actively seeks out this dangerous space between acceptability and unacceptability: once she has been helped and finished this piece of work her practices once more promise to constitutes her as bad student and unacceptable learner – she plays with her hair and fingernails. These bodily practices, however, are not at odds with the acceptable girl-student – like Nicola's hair-brushing in episode 3, these are acceptable off-learning task practices that are constitutive of proper femininity. So, when Julie plays with her hair and nails she is not working but she is (just?) an acceptable learner, when Julie calls the teacher bitch she is not just unacceptable as a learner, she is unintelligible as a learner.

The fragility of these teacher and learner subjectivities are shown again in scene 2 which illustrates further the way that Julie and the teacher's practices destabilise the teacher/student hierarchy, and constitute Julie as an unacceptable learner even as they challenge the teacher's status as teacher and constitute her instead as a denigrated, low class woman.

Episode 7: Bitch, scene 2.
Plains High, Sydney, Australia. History Lesson (students aged 14-15), the following week. Books and worksheets are distributed. Six students in the class are doing the worksheets, and MISS STARKEY is talking them through it. Everyone else is left to their own devices. There is a good deal of talking and laughing. One boy sitting in the far corner of the room is listening to a portable cd-player with earphones on. The music is loud enough to be heard clearly across the room. JULIE is drinking water from a water bottle, when she spills a bit on her shorts. Miss Starkey looks over at her:

MISS STARKEY (yells): Julie! Wo-ork!
JULIE: No-o!
MISS STARKEY: C'mon, work!
JULIE: I don't have to work now. I'm not on a conduct card.

Miss Starkey returns to helping another female student on whom she has focused her attention. A few minutes pass.

JULIE: Miss, do you have the time?
MISS STARKEY: Yes, I've got the time.
Miss Starkey returns to helping the girl, and does not tell Julie what the time is. Once the girl finishes her work, Miss Starkey tells the class that their reports will be marks over the whole year, and that in this class the average has been 67 out of 100.

JULIE: I better be around the 160.

MISS STARKEY: Yeah, from the top maybe.
JULIE: Shut up, you bitch.
MISS STARKEY: Put it this way, you won't be anywhere *near* where you could be if you *tried*.
JULIE: I try.
MISS STARKEY (dropping her mouth open in mock astonishment): The initials B.S. are coming immediately to mind.

(fieldnotes)

As is often the case in this classroom, lots of students are not engaged in any work and, instead are listening to music, socialising and so on. These are the practices of unacceptable learners. In terms of educational triage, these are hopeless cases and, therefore, there is no point or need to enforce (if this were possible) usual classroom requirements. It is in this setting that Julie spills her bottle of water and the teacher identifies her for a low-level disciplinary intervention and entreaty to work. It is important to note that drinking in class is not a breach of conduct requirements – Australian summer temperatures mean that school students are often allowed to drink water in class. It is also noteworthy that during observed lessons the teacher regularly makes such low-level disciplinary interventions regarding Julie's conduct. And that Julie regularly highlights this to the teacher. She also points out the extreme behaviour of other students – for instance, Phil and Trent's wresting match seen in chapter 4 – which Julie judges to receive less frequent and less robust disciplinary interventions that those directed at her own behaviour. When Julie raises these apparently uneven disciplinary approaches Miss Starkey responds by suggesting that Julie is "whingeing".

Julie, it appears, does not take Miss Starkey's instruction to "Wo-rk!" seriously, mimicking the teacher's enunciation she replies "No-o!". While Miss Starkey's instruction has the potential to constitute her and Julie as teacher and student, Julie's response unsettles both of these constitutions. It seems that, in recurring moments, the relationship between Miss Starkey and Julie is not bounded by institutional and popular discourses of teacher and student. Instead, it appears as a relationship framed by the combative terms of gendered and classed sub-cultural discourse that does not normally belong (or exist) between teachers and students in classrooms. In the terms of this discourse the relative status of Julie and Miss Starkey is less clear. It might be anticipated that Miss Starkey greater age (perhaps distinct from 'adult') might enhance her status in this alternative discourse, as may her capacity (high, on the basis of these scenes) to be bitch.

Yet Julie is not cowed and she refuses to work. Within the terms of the teacher/student hierarchy Julie 'should' defer. And in the terms of this alternative discourses Julie may also be of lesser status that Miss Starkey. But, despite practices that unsettle her constitution as a teacher, Miss Starkey *is* a teacher, and so cannot act fully, or claim status, in terms of this alternative discourse. Yet by deploying a discourse that is disallowed by the school and by which she can only be partially constituted, Miss Starkey also ensures that she cannot act fully in terms of school discourse. This simultaneous occupation of teacher and sub-cultural subject positions, constituted through two incommensurable discourses as these are, renders Miss Starkey's practices harmless, she is constrained by both discourses but without the full authority of either.

By refusing to work, and by offering the absence of monitoring by a conduct card as her explanation for this, Julie infers that her motivation to work bears no relationship to learning but is instead influenced by her desire to fulfil minimum requirements of the school's disciplinary procedures. As such, she constitutes herself once again as an unacceptable learner. And this constitution is inscribed once again when she asks Miss Starkey the time and Miss Starkey ignores her. Miss Starkey's silence construes the query as being concerned only with how far away the end of the lesson is – the concern of an unacceptable learner. And by ignoring, and so constituting, the unacceptable learner, Miss Starkey once again cites and inscribes discourse of the proper teacher and so, constitutes herself once again in these terms. In this moment Julie is not an acceptable learner, but Miss Starkey might be an acceptable teacher.

As the teacher announces likely marks, and Julie engages her on this, further constitutions of Julie as an unacceptable learner are seen. The score that Julie announces she is seeking is meaningless on the scale that Miss Starkey has indicated. Perhaps Julie has misheard, or perhaps this is hyperbole, a feigned caring about results that suggests that she does not care at all – a hyperbole that would contribute once again to Julie's constitution as an unacceptable learner. And once again, Miss Starkey's response "160 from the bottom" is not that of a teacher. The teacher has, it seems, discarded the requirements placed upon her by professional and bureaucratic discourses to fulfil a duty of care (including emotional and psychic well being as well as educational progress) towards the student. Rather, acting outside her place in school discourse, Miss Starkey deploys the spite and cruelty that is valuable in the alternative discourse through which she and Julie compete with each other. Here she is the older neighbourhood girl who, in her greater years, is able to be sharper, crueller, more cutting: she is the 'bitch' that Julie said she was. And Julie responds in kind. These interlocutors are not teacher/student – they are woman/girl and they are both trash. And constituted as these sorts of bad women, neither can be reconciled with those forms of femininity required of the good teacher or the good student and acceptable learner.

But ultimately Miss Starkey reinstates a teacherly discourse of effort – "if you tried" – into this scene But it is half-hearted, and too late. And Julie's retort that "I do try!" (and maybe she does, perhaps she is working that space between acceptability and unacceptability?) is enough to once again constitute in this moment Miss Starkey as not-teacher but, instead, as a low class, coarse and spiteful woman engaging in a slanging match or handing down cruelty to a girl-child. And Miss Starkey acts her place in this discourse – she suggests obliquely (she has not given teacher up entirely, she too is working a space between two discourses) that Julie is talking bullshit. Not only is Julie and impossible learner, but Miss Starkey might be an impossible teacher.

The exchanges between Miss Starkey and Julie represented in this chapter sit far beyond what might ordinarily be expected of the interactions between a teacher and her student. Indeed, it may seem almost shocking that a student and teacher – in particular a female teacher and female student – would engage in such a dialogue, or that some exceptional circumstances must have prompted them to act in this way towards each other. That is, in institutional, policy, and popular discourses of appropriate student and teacher conduct, conduct of this sort is unacceptable. And in prevailing popular (but not all) discourses of appropriate female, that is, feminine behaviour, such conduct is disallowed.

Nevertheless, this conduct is intelligible. In a discourse of good/bad student and acceptable/unacceptable learner, Julie's conduct is that of the bad student and unacceptable learner. Indeed, the constellation of discourses and identity markers circulating in this episode acts to constitute Julie an impossible learner. Similarly, in a discourse of the good/bad teacher, the good (female) teacher – charged with the moral and social as well as academic education (in Foucauldian terms, disciplining) of the student – is self-reflective, controlled, and, above all rational, even if she is no longer kindly and nurturing. Miss Starkey conduct, however, does not meet these requirements of the good teacher, she is unreflective and uncontrolled – she is a bad teacher. Furthermore, the adult-teacher/child-student hierarchy, and the institutional and popular discourses that cite and inscribe this, appears to be discarded during moments in this episode. In their place, it seems, Miss Starkey and Julie's practices deploy an alternative discourse that is at odds with the discourses of the school. Indeed, this pop-cultural-style verbal battle is far beyond acceptable teacher or student behaviour – could Julie be a bitch and a good student and acceptable learner? Could Miss Starkey be a bitch and a good teacher?

Students and teachers are more than simply this inside school context. Gender, sexuality, class, race, sub-culture all press on who students and teachers are and can be, or whether they are students and teachers at all. I will continue to tease out these intersections and exclusions are I go on to consider the subjectivation and practices of self of a group of Black girls in a London school.

CHAPTER 7

EXCLUDED BLACK FEMININITY

In previous chapters I have demonstrated how the understandings of race and ethnicity that circulate amongst students in both Taylor Comp and Plains High are underpinned by discourses that fuse biological race with cultural expression to produce an essentially based certainty about race and ethnic identifications. I also borrowed from my earlier exploration of the 'hierarchy within the Other' (Youdell, 2003), a discursive hierarchy that steps past White hegemony and constitutes Black students as particularly high status and desirable amongst minority ethnic students and within the terms of student and street sub-cultures. In my reading of episode 2 in chapter 4 here, I suggested that the discussion of the Australian students in Plains High concerning ethnically based groups in the school was constitutive of a similar hierarchy within the Other, albeit it one that constitutes hierarchically a different set of race/ethnic/national identities to those that exist in the London school. I also drew a parallel between the institutional constitution of a 'Black challenge to White hegemony' (Youdell 2003) in Taylor Comprehensive and an institutional const-itution of Islander student culture as a similar challenge in Plains High (see also Youdell 2004a).

These analyses suggest that young people's practices of self that constitute particular race/ethnic subjectivities and institutional practices that constituted these as sub-cultures and as a challenge to a school authority are entangled. Specifically, the sub-cultural identities that imbue these minority ethnic students with particular status and prestige within the student milieu are the very identities that are deployed within institutional discourse as 'evidence' of their challenge to authority. Yet these institutional practices are constituted as neutral, so eliding the way that the institution is invested and implication in White hegemony.

The *specific* minority raced/ethnicised sub-cultural forms that are taken within institutional (and wider) discourse as a challenge *shifts* across setting. These shifts evidence the reach of White hegemony and the continuities of empire and colony in the prevailing discourses of post-colonial and post-empire settings. Furthermore, the contextual specificity shows how these discourses constitute particular race/ethnic groups as a threat even as they claim to simply recognise this threat. Finally, and perhaps most importantly, the shifting nature of the race/ethnicity taken as threat within institutional/popular discourse demonstrates the *constituted* nature of the very threat these discourses claim to narrate and, by extension, the constituted nature of race/ethnicity itself.

This does not mean, however, that in a south London context all Black students are inevitably banished to an educational wasteland, or that in a Western Sydney context all Islander (or other minority ethnic) students are on such a trajectory. Nor does it mean that in each setting such destinations are reserved exclusively for these minority race/ethnic students. As I have stressed throughout my analysis, discursive constitutions always risk failure and misfire, as well as recuperation or reinscription. There is always space for subjects to be constituted differently.

My analysis of episode 8 below examines these possibilities. Drawing on the notion of resistance within accommodation (Mac an Ghaill 1988) I suggest that through their practices within the 'Leaving Day Show' – a show performed by and for the year group and their teachers on their last compulsory day of school at Taylor Comprehensive – a group of Black girls can be seen to assert the legitimacy of a Black sub-culture, an assertion that at once exposes and resists the institutional constitution of Blackness as synonymous with a challenge to White hegemony.

On the morning of Leaving Day students are expected to attend lessons as usual. During the period that would usually cover the lunch break and part of the afternoon teaching session, students and their teachers gather for a series of activities. First, there is a show in the Drama Studio where a number of students and staff entertain the assembled group with songs, dances, poems, and skits. The group then moves to a sports field. A photograph of the year group is taken and then the tutor or roll groups have a mini inter-tutor group sports contest. The mood is informal and celebratory, students gather in groups hugging, crying, joking, taking photos, and writing on school t-shirts and sweatshirts. There is a sense of this being the students' time, of the event being captured by/surrendered to the students. It also seems that the teacher/student hierarchy is blurred – while not equalised, the distance between the status' of teacher and (almost) ex-student seems to be narrowed.

Episode 8: Cool Black girls
Taylor Comp, London, UK. Drama Studio, Leaving Day Show
Performers: MARCELLA (*aged 15-16, girl, Black*)
JASMINE (*aged 15-16, girl, Mixed-race*)
NAOMI (*aged 15-16, girl, Black*)
MARCIA (*aged 15-16, girl, Black*)
NATASHA (aged 15-16, *girl, Mixed-race*)
Audience: Students, form (roll) tutors, School senior managers, DY.

The auditorium has tiered seating on three sides arranged around a large empty floor space. The forth side of this floor space is flanked by a low-level stage. The seating capacity of the Drama Studio is barely adequate to accommodate the entire year group. FORM TUTORS, members of the SENIOR MANAGEMENT TEAM and STUDENTS are squashed together in their seats, with an over-spill of STUDENTS seated on the floor at the edges of the central floor space. The HEAD OF YEAR, who is hosting the event, is on the stage. He also provides some musical interludes along with the school MUSIC TEACHER and a FORM TUTOR. The room is illuminated only by stage lighting on the stage and, when in use for performances, the central floor space.

The Head of Year announces that the next entertainment will be a dance performed by MARCELLA, JASMINE, NAOMI, MARCIA, and NATASHA. The girls enter the auditorium and assemble in the large performance space in the centre of the room.

The girls are wearing tight fitting micro or circular cheerleader skirts or cycling shorts. These are paired with cropped vests and bra-tops; some sports style, others beach style with fabric ends dangling from where they have been knotted between uplifted breasts. Skirts and shorts are in shinning, lycra-mix synthetics, tops are in cotton-lycra mix. These outfits combine black and white with bright blues, reds and greens. All the girls have bare legs and wear trainers with well known brand labels. Hair is perfect. The Mixed-race girls have long hair worn slicked back from the face into a tall bun. This bun is worn high on the top of the head and given added elevation by fabric accessories

bound up from the base. The Black girls have shorter hair worn in straightened jaw
length graduated bobs, with slicked side-parted fringes and kiss-curls. The outfits are
not matching but their shared sub-cultural source is evident.

The performers receive an uproarious welcome as they enter the room. There is
loud applause; cheering; wolf whistling; bent elbows circling clenched fists above heads
and in front of bodies accompanied by "boo boo boo"; some boys call out to the girls by
name and make sexual propositions. The girls are smiling to one another and to friends
they see or hear in the audience, including some of the propositioning boys. They look
to one another: "ready?" "ready". They stand in two staggered lines of 3 and 2, feet
apart, arms held out diagonally, heads turned to one side. Naomi, on the front row,
bends, hits the play button on a tape recorder and gets back into position. A moment of
silence then the music starts.

The watching students repeat their welcoming noises and gestures when the music
starts -- a well known song that has recently been successful in the mainstream music
charts. While it's hip-hop roots are clear, it has a R and B feel which undoubtedly
contributes to its mainstream success. The lyrics are overtly sexual but the extremely
explicit lyrics of some hip-hop are absent. The girls begin to dance. They perform a
synchronised dance routine of the sort commonly seen in promotional videos for music
of this genre. Its execution is proficient but is not outstanding. Included in the dance
routine are moves where the girls bend over forwards, rocking their upper torsos from
side to side accentuating the display of plunging cleavages. It also includes moves that
involve the girls thrusting their hips back and forth while standing with feet apart and
knees bent. At times they do this while straddling one another's thighs. These moves are
greeted by more appreciative noises and gestures from students in the audience.

When the music ends the student audience gives a similar display to that which
welcomed the girls. The girls laugh and smile and take repeated bows before leaving the
auditorium. Once they have gone, it takes the head of year some time to quiet the
student audience ready for the next act.

(Fieldnotes)

The group whose practices are represented in the episode includes girls who identify
themselves as both Black and Mixed-race. The three Black girls – Marcella, Naomi
and Marcia – have had conflicts with the school institution throughout their school
careers. Marcella was originally in the same tutor group as Naomi but was moved
part way through her time in the school. Marcella suggests that the school perceived
her and Naomi as "trouble makers" and removed her from this tutor group in an
effort to "separate" them. Inside her new tutor group Marcella had ongoing conflicts,
of varying degrees of severity, with the Tutor. Marcella returned to school from her
sixth fixed-term exclusion only days before Leaving Day. Naomi and Marcia both
reported having received multiple "threats" of exclusion and being warned that they
were on their "last chance". These girls, then, are constituted as bad students. Unlike
Marcella, Naomi and Marcia, Jasmine (Mixed-race)[xiv] does not have a history of
disciplinary conflict with the school. Indeed, she appears to be immensely popular
with teachers despite her close alliance with Marcella, Naomi and Marcia. On a day-
to-day basis it seems that Jasmine sustains good student and acceptable learner *and*
(moderately) status sub-cultural cool[xv].

This group of girls is highly critical of the school and at varying moments in my
research with them they struggled to articulate and evidence the sorts of subtle
racism that might be understood as institutional. However, all of these girls
recognise the qualifications market place that now frames even compulsory
schooling (Gillborn & Youdell 2000) and seek to attain the benchmark in high-
stakes end of compulsory schooling exams that act as a gatekeeper to further
education, training and, increasingly often, employment. The girls' co-existing

criticism of the school institution and regard for educational qualifications suggests that they are anti-school and pro-education, a relationship to schooling detailed by Fuller (1984), Mac an Ghaill (1988) Mirza (1992)[xvi].

In classes that are set by ability and / or tiered examinations and syllabuses the girls are positioned towards the middle of the set/tier hierarchy. Such placements are not always satisfactory to the girls. The girls, most notably Marcella and Naomi, suggest that within certain subjects their set / tier placement is too low and see this as a result of having an unjustified "bad reputation" amongst staff. This suggests that their constitution as bad students – a constitution that I will argue is inseparable from their subject positions as Black girls – clashes with a normative notion of the good student-ideal learner to render them on the margins of acceptability as learners.

My analysis suggests, then, that the girls' relationships with education, the school, and individual teachers are entwined with and underscored by their identities as Black girls. A provisional identification of the girls as pro-education and anti-school suggests that their practices of self might involve intentional and/or tacit resistance within accommodation. At the same time, however, the school institution disavows Black subjectivities (real or imagined) and simultaneously deploys these in the constitution of a Black challenge to White hegemony – discursive manoeuvres which render Black sub-cultural identities and acceptable learner identities incommensurable (Youdell 2003). These institutional practices are likely to interact with the girls' resistances and constrain the success of their accommodations. In this context it is interesting to examine both the fact and mode of the girls' participation in the Leaving Day Show.

The episode is a moment in the citation, inscription and potential *re*inscription of the girls' sub-cultural, student and learner identities. While the girls' participation in the show may appear on the surface to be an acquiescence to school values, it is also a moment of resistance to school values and particular schooled subjectivities – a moment of resistance that cites a multitude of minor skirmishes throughout the girls' educational histories. The girls' Leaving Day Show performance might be also seen as a moment that contributes to the constitution of the day as captured by/-surrendered to the students.

In the discursive frame of the mainstream student milieu, it is the girls who are constituted within the terms of a coveted Black sub-cultural identity who are the key figures in this group. While Jasmine and Natasha's race identity is less prestigious (but still substantial) in these terms, they have both studied drama and are (relatively) experienced performers. It is possible to conjecture, therefore, that Marcella, Naomi and Marcia might not put on such a public performance without the performance skills of Jasmine and Natasha. Conversely, it is possible to conjecture that Jasmine and Natasha's sub-cultural status might not be high enough to put on such a performance without the other girls. Furthermore, given the specificities of the race identities cited and inscribed through the Hierarchy within the Other it seems unlikely that these *Mixed-race* girls would put on *this* performance without the sanctioning participation of the *Black* girls. That is, the dance is racialised – it cites and inscribes gendered Black sub-cultural identities. In the discursive frame of discreet and authentic races that frames the mainstream student milieu, such a performance by Mixed-race girls alone might be received as an expropriation of Blackness and, therefore, open to considerable censure.

The Black girls' sub-cultural identities seem to assure a positive reception from peers. Yet this very identity is constituted, in part, through its oppositional relationship with the school institution. This suggests that these girls might be unlikely to (ask or be allowed to) participate in such an event and that to do so would undermine the very identity that secures peer support. That is, participation could be construed as pro-school. However, these girls' long-standing sub-cultural status and anti-school positions; the nature of the performance; and the capture of the event guard against this. At the same time, Jasmine's apparent (almost/partial/sometimes) pro-school identity may deflect the risk posed to the Black girls' sub-cultural identity by their participation. The performance itself is made possible, therefore, through a particular constellation of multiple biographical, sub-cultural, and student subject positions.

The girls have discursive agency – their citational bodily practices have the potential to performatively constitute, whether intentionally or otherwise, themselves and others in particular ways. The dance can be understood as being performed for two overarching audiences – teachers and students. The student audience is by no means homogeneous. Rather, it is self-consciously categorised along biographical and sub-cultural lines. Likewise, the teacher audience will also be differentiated, for instance, along biographical, cultural and professional axes. These multiple audiences also have discursive agency – the meanings made and subjectivities potentially and provisionally constituted through the girls' dance are mediated through the discourses that frame the (multiple) audiences' reception of it. Understanding these audiences as discursive markets suggests that the cultural capitals citationally displayed and inscribed through the girls' bodily practices are likely be imbued with values that vary across these markets. The meanings cited and inscribed through the girls' dance, therefore, are multiple, multi-directional and always at risk.

In terms of the (multiple) student audiences the girls' discursive practices – their dress, bodily movements, and the music to which they dance – cite and inscribe a highly sexualised heterosexual femininity that is raced by a sub-cultural discourse of Black hetero-femininity (think Destiny's Child) and, in tension (and inadvertently), by colonial discourses of Black hyper-sexuality and the exotic Other. This femininity contrasts with (is Other to) the feminine Ideal that I discussed in relation to Julie and Miss Starkey in chapter 6. Simultaneously, these practices lay claim to, demonstrate and constitute the girls' location at the pinnacle of the Hierarchy within the Other. As such, the dance is a dramatic flaunting and inscription of the (almost indisputably) high value of the girls' cultural capital within the discursive market of the mainstream student sub-culture. It also alludes to the existing (or potential) value of this within youth cultural markets that exceed the bounds of the school. The value of this cultural capital has been accrued and constituted over time through the ongoing citation of the status of Black heterosexual femininities within the Hierarchy within the Other and youth culture more broadly. The dance (silently and provisionally) 'says' to the student audience 'this is how cool, high-status, and desirable we are, and how cool, high-status and desirable you (through multiple, varied but intersecting identities) are also/nearly/not'.

In terms of the teacher audience(s) the girls' practices might constitute a Black sub-culture marked particular genres of music, dance, bodily gestures and adornments as well as particular urban experiences, lifestyles and relationships to the State. In the person of Black R 'n' B and hip-hop artists within the music industry, these subjects have had notable professional and financial success. They have also had a significant influence on mainstream youth cultures globally. By citing these Black subjectivities the dance 'says' to the school 'this is what you have refused to allow me to be and punished me for being. This is what you have forced me to deny/compensate for/retain at high cost. Now we are leaving school and you can no longer make any intervention. *And* there are places where this/I am sought after and valued – you know that just from listening to the radio, watching TV, and looking around at what everyone wears (including your own trainers)'.

However, as Connell (1995) has noted in relation to Black sports men, these R 'n' B and hip-hop artists are *exemplars* – their success in the entertainment industry does not elevate Blackness generally, nor does it improve the material conditions of the majority of Black people. These exemplary Black subjects are restricted to this sub-cultural milieu without being generalised to other discursive markets. That is, just because some Black artists are professionally successful, have massive global record sales, and are emulated by young people from across diverse social, biographical, and national backgrounds, this does not mean that these girls (Black young people in general) become more desirable as students, potential employees, citizens. Indeed, the success of the girls' emulation of these exemplary figures may well contribute to their undesirability beyond this specific sub-cultural milieu. The teachers undoubtedly recognise this citation *and* the exemplary status of successful Black R 'n' B and hip-hop artists. Furthermore, the sub-culturally status-laden and exemplary Black identities the girls are flaunting, citing, and constituting are the very identities that the school has simultaneously disavowed as being intrinsically beyond the bounds of the good student and acceptable learner and deployed in constituting these identities as anti-school and a challenge to White hegemony.

The citations and inscriptions of the girls' dance, then, can be understood as a moment in which the Black sub-cultural identity that is *institutionally* disavowed is provisionally reinscribed through the citation of *popular* sub-cultural discourses as the most desirable and prestigious identity. In this sense it might be understood as a moment of a politics of performative reinscription. Yet in doing this, the dance also confirms (cites) the school's discourse of the Black challenge to White hegemony and this confirmation (citation) means that any reinscription is highly tenuous and open to rapid recuperation, a recuperation that constitutes the girls once again as bad students and unacceptable learners. Beyond the Leaving day Show (where institutional discourse might have been partially and temporarily suspended) could these girls be Black sub-cultural cool *and* good students and desirable learners?

So far in this part of the book my discussion has focused on the commensurability, or otherwise, of student and learner identities on the one hand, and biographical and sub-cultural identities on the other. In the next and final chapter of this section, I focus in on the notions of the student and the learner to consider particular institutional constitutions of these. Specifically, I ask what sort of student a boy classified as having special education needs can be, and whether this classification can allow him to be a learner. In asking these questions, I interrogate the boy's practices of self and ask whether in a different discursive frame these practices might be constitutive of biography or sub-culture and not of 'specialness'.

CHAPTER 8

EXCLUDED 'SPECIALNESS' (WHITE-WORKING CLASS-HETERO-(HYPER-) MASCULINITY)

As my discussion in chapter 1 indicated, there is significant debate over the understandings and terminologies as well as the diagnostic, organizational and pedagogic tools and approaches (if any) that are most useful for educators and most appropriate/least damaging for students deemed to have disabilities or special educational needs. Some scholars and activists argue that the proliferation of diagnoses of special educational needs tells us more about the neo-liberal context in which contemporary education takes place than it tells about the students diagnosed, even as these classifications become both mechanisms for surveillance and correction and constitutive of the students that classify (see for instance Slee 1995). Others suggest that such specificities remain helpful in understanding the development and needs of these children (see, for instance, Layton *et al* 2003). And while the last decade has certainly seen a proliferation of diagnosed learning, emotional and behavioural disorders (Slee 1995), a tendency seems to remain in mainstream education to work with general markers of special need, disability, difficultly and disorder. Indeed, this is reflected and sanctioned by recent moves in the UK government's Department of Education and Skills to replace an emphasis on the diagnosis of the student to the identification of their specific educational needs in their specific learning context. Nevertheless, the argument remains that the language of special educational needs cannot escape its deficit connotations and so remains intrinsically detrimental to the students to whom it refers (See Corbett 1996).

In the UK it is common to speak of students with 'special educational needs' (SEN) or emotional or behavioural difficulties (EBD). Yet in the Australian educational context it remains the student who is special and who has 'emotional difficulties or behavioural disorder' (EDBD). While the language used in the UK and Australia is not exact, there are clearly close links across these settings. In Australian popular culture a charity discourse identifies the special child and special person through their intellectual (learning difficulties), physical (disabled), emotional (organic or environmental), behavioural (again organic or environmental) and economic (the child in poverty) deficit or deficits. These identifications are also mirrored in UK popular discourse.

Reflecting the argument I have made in previous chapters, these various designations are not descriptions of objective facts about the way that students *are*, rather they are constitutive of the student in these terms. This assertion clearly resonates with the 'social model' of disability that I discussed in chapter 1. Indeed, in my discussion of the shift from thinking about the disabled person to thinking about how the impaired person is disabled by social structures and practices,

I argued that the notion of impairment was itself problematic in that, despite the best efforts of scholars of disability studies, it remained locked into the subordinate side of a normal/abnormal binary within normative discourses of both the mind and the body.

This chapter takes up these arguments to examine the way that teacher and student practices are constitutive of a 'special' (bad) student and unacceptable (impossible?) learner identity for one boy in Plains High, Sydney, Australia. It examines how the discourse of special-ness, or perhaps more accurately disordered-ness, is deployed in ways that subsume and incorporate other discourses and render all of this student's discursive practices constitutive of his EBDB status and his location outside the normative centre of student, learner and subject-hood.

> *Episode 9: Mad, bad, special, scene 1.*
> *Plains High, Sydney, Australia. English Lesson (students aged 14-15).* On route to my first observation the teacher, MISS ELLIS, who is Head of Department, describes the group as "delightful", including "problems from other classes" and using "a lot of language". They have, she says, a "working arrangement".
>
> *Ten minutes into the lesson.* MISS ELLIS is reading aloud from the textbook, *Rock and Rap*, about styles of popular music. The section is discussing Jimmy Hendrix. There is low-level activity and discussion while the teacher is reading. As Miss Ellis continues to read the room goes quiet. PAUL is sitting upright in his chair with his hands on his head. As he sits he makes popping noises. The two boys sharing the six-seater table with Paul do not appear to pay any attention to him. Miss Ellis says "Paul, I really do object!". Paul replies "Sorry Miss" and removes his hands from his head. As Miss Ellis continues to read Paul becomes restless, fidgeting in his seat, tapping his fingers on his desk. Several boys at an over-crowded six-seater table of boys are tapping and drumming in time together while the teacher reads. Miss Ellis does not acknowledge the drumming and tapping coming from this table of boys. Occasionally she looks over at Paul. Paul stands up from his seat and leans against the window that is directly behind his chair. Miss Ellis stops reading and asks Paul to move to another seat. Paul objects and the teacher asserts there will be "No argument" and instructs him to stand in the quad outside the classroom door. Paul leaves the room but instead of standing outside the door as instructed, he appears to walk off across the quad. A student calls out laughing: "where's he going?" and another replies "to spend the period with Miss" as others call "Miss he's going!" and "You're losing him Miss!". Miss Ellis does not acknowledge these comments and continues to read. A few minutes later Paul returns to the door of classroom, he stands at the window of the closed door, looking in and grinning and making faces at students in the classroom.
>
> (Fieldnotes)

Miss Ellis's account of the whole English group at the scene offered unbidden on route to my first observation of the class deploys a discourse of a classroom, and by extension a school, of deficit behaviour – before I enter the classroom for the first time, the teacher has deployed a citational chain which potentially constitutes the as yet unobserved group as naughty children, bad students and, potentially, impossible learners.

While Miss Ellis does not make any distinction between Paul and the rest of the class in her brief account offered to me, a significant distinction does appear to be played out in her practices in the classroom represented in scene 1. On the basis of ongoing discreet talking while Miss Ellis is reading aloud to the class, and more obtrusive drumming on the table top by one group boys, it seems that the behaviour of a number of members of the class might be understood as outside the normative bounds of the good student and acceptable learner. Yet Miss Ellis makes no intervention into these behaviours – these students remain intelligible as learners, even if they are far from ideal. In contrast, Miss Ellis's interventions in Paul's classroom practices and his ejection from the room appear to constitute Paul as so far outside the bounds of acceptability that his is not a learner at all, he is an impossible student. This apparent constitution – as it is played out through what appears likely to be Paul's regular censure and ejection from the classroom – demands to know what it is about Paul's bodily practices that render them so different from the practice of other students (for instance, the boys tapping and drumming in the table).

It is difficult, if not impossible, to pin down precisely what it is that is different about Paul. It seems that what he wants to be is a cool-naughty-boy, like the boys drumming on the table. And yet here, and again elsewhere, he doesn't quite get it right. It may be his audience, or more precisely apparent lack of encouraging audience, that is significant. It may be his failure to be the Larrikin (Australian Joker) or, indeed, his *failure to attempt to be* the Larrikin here (he does attempt it elsewhere). Or it may be his failure to amass counter-school cool (he does amass it sometimes, in some (limited) ways elsewhere). Or his *failure to attempt to* amass counter-school cool while engaging in the practices of the Larrikin or the counter-school-cool boy that render him so Other. It seems that his practices constitute him as impossible because they are unintelligible in the terms of the Larrikin or the counter-school cool boy that are *legitimate* 'unacceptable' positions in this setting. The boys drumming on the next desk drum with at least the tacit intent of constituting themselves counter-school-cool. And there is extra opportunity here because the 'contemporary' popular music subject matter possibly renders drumming 'legitimate', and if it does not, then for the teacher to intervene in the students' drumming exposes her 'inauthentic' engagement with what is believed to be (but probably is not) contemporary youth culture. The boys are almost daring Miss Ellis to tell them to stop drumming rhythmically on the table while she is reading about Jimmy Hendrix.

What Paul is doing is different. This difference is subtle and nuanced, relying on questions of intent, bodily execution as well as reception by the multiple audiences in the classroom. But it is different. At the crux of this difference seems to be questions of intent; awareness of self and audience; bodily mastery; and at least tacit understanding of the discursive networks that frame this setting.

When Paul sits with his hands on his head and makes a repetitive popping sound with his mouth his behaviour is not notably more intrusive that the low-level talk that has continued at a number of the desks in the classroom after Miss Ellis has begun to read. And it is notably less intrusive than the drumming from the boys' desk that followed it. Similarly, standing silently against the window is arguably less disturbing than the restless fidgeting that preceded it, and which Paul may well have stood up to relieve. And yet, despite the minimal disturbance that his behaviours actually cause, and the fact that none of the students in the room appear to pay any attention to it, Miss Ellis quickly moves to censure and ejects Paul from the classroom[xvii].

This can be understood by considering Paul's behaviour within the discursive frame of normative student and normative student behaviour. While Paul's bodily practices sit outside the bounds of normative student body, in doing so it exposes the arbitrariness of the body that the school requires (Moore 2004). In addition, Paul is undoubtedly constituted here in the context of multiple prior constitutions as 'special' – Paul is 'already' 'special and so his bodily practices are immediately defined in the terms of an EBDB discourse, despite the similarity of some of these practices to those of his classmates (for example, the drumming boys), and the relatively limited nature of the disturbance he causes (for example, standing in silence).

And yet Paul's bodily practices in this classroom are disturbing. That is, while they do not disturb the classroom in a literal sense, they may well disturb because of their non-normative nature. While Paul is ignored, the teacher, the students and I do notice what he is doing – we are disturbed from our work, from the comfort of the normative student-subject, from the comfort of ourselves. Perhaps it is this social and psychic disturbance that is censured.

Paul then, breaks the sedimented and well-known tacit norms and explicit rules of student classroom deportment. And yet so do many other students – students who slouch, students who drum the table, students who lean in and put their heads close together to whisper while the teacher reads. It is the *way* that Paul breaches these requirements that renders him 'special', EBDB, and which demand he is ejected from the classroom. Miss Ellis, the students and me all have a nuanced, practical sense (Bourdieu 1991) of what constitutes, and is constitutive of, normal and non-normal practices and so normal and non-normal students. And so Paul is constituted not only an impossible student and learner, but also an impossible subject.

When Paul leaves the classroom, instead of standing outside the classroom door but remaining in view as school convention expects, he walks off and students call out to Miss Ellis that this what he is doing. The students are clearly unconcerned that Paul has walked off, they are not really entreating Miss Ellis to intervene (although it may be good sport if she did). While this walking away is yet another breach of school conventions of normative behaviour – even normative bad behaviour – it seems clear that Miss Ellis and the other students have seen all of this before. This is a ritualised set of practices that constitute Paul, his classmates, and Miss Ellis (and me) in particular ways again and again. When Paul walks off, then, he continues to act his place in the discourse that constitutes him as beyond the bounds of the normal student, that constitutes him emotionally disturbed and behaviourally disordered, as 'special'.

In calling out to the teacher their jovial 'warnings' of Paul's departure, the students inscribe the invisible, but irresistible divide between the 'naughty' student (what they are constituting themselves as by calling out and disturbing the lesson, although, of course, part of the pleasure of this is that it is disguised as helpfulness and so the practice of the 'good' student) and the 'special' student. And in this classroom it seems that for a student to put his hands on his head or to stand at the side of the room without being instructed to do so as a corrective by a teacher is enough to be constituted as such. This demonstrates the incredible reach of conventions of normative bodily practice.

Paul's practices, then, while not disruptive, or even particularly remarkable in themselves, sit so far outside the bounds of normative behaviour that they must be disciplined. And while his classmates at once delight in his breach and contribute to his constitution as 'special', Miss Ellis's responses join a citational chain that constitutes Paul not just an unacceptable learner, but beyond learner altogether. He is constituted here an impossible learner. Yet this constitution is on one day, in once classroom. Is it possible that elsewhere in the school Paul might be constituted differently and/or might practice differently? Scene 2 tries to address this question as it considers events in Computer Studies lessons with Miss Carter, a teacher who has taken a particular pastoral interest in Paul and where Paul might be constituted differently.

> *Episode 9: Mad, bad, special, scene 2*
> *Plains High, Sydney, Australia. Computer studies Lesson (students aged 14-15). The students are doing an open book examination in silence.*
>
> PAUL is sitting across from OHAN and is openly looking at his work. The teacher, MISS CARTER, says to him "busy eyes" and he responds "I've got an eye problem, I have to look at other people's work". Paul calls to Miss Carter and she comes over and he asks her a question, she asks him what topic the exam question is about and if he remembers doing that in class. I wonder whether my presence is impacting on the exam. Paul looks across at me and at my notepad, he nods and smiles – it seems he is pleased by his deduction that I am making notes about him. Paul calls to Miss Carter for help again and quietly, but across the classroom she tells him which lesson in his exercise book he needs to refer to answer the exam question:
>
> PAUL: Arrg, Miss, I wasn't here, I was as Mitcham House [the special school]!
> MISS CARTER: use a textbook then.
> PAUL drops his jaw open as he looks at her in mock shock or outrage.
> MISS CARTER: I'll come and help you
> Boy (sitting nearby) passes Paul a textbook: page 15-16
> MISS CARTER: It's chapter 4 I think
> PAUL: Its page 15 to 16
>
> (Fieldnotes)

In the scene the Computer Studies class is undertaking an open-book examination and Paul is taking part in this. His inclusion in the exam might be taken to suggest that he is constituted here, through this inclusion, as an acceptable learner. And yet his exemption from the formal and informal rules that govern even the open-book exam constitute him otherwise – he is not a learner and so there is no need for Paul's exam to be invigilated. That Paul's exemption from these requirements of examination conduct is understood, at least tacitly, not only by Miss Carter and Paul, but also by the other members of the class is indicative of the repetitious citation of these discourses of the 'special' (and so impossible) student and Paul's constitution in these terms. And Paul underscores this constitution when he asserts that he has missed work because of his attendance at the special school. Nevertheless, Paul does do the test. As such, his impossibility is perhaps not absolute, perhaps the possibility for him to be an learner of some kind, even if this is an unacceptable learner who calls for, expects, and receives assistance from both teacher and students during an exam, remains?

Episode 9: Mad, bad, special, scene 3
Plains High, Sydney, Australia. Computer Studies Lesson, 2-3 weeks later.
Students are sitting at computers while the teacher, MISS CARTER, explains the idea
of morphing and that they will be learning to use a software programme that will allow
them to morph the image of one student in the class into another. As the teacher is
explaining morphing, PAUL calls out "leaching?", the teacher, echoed by 2 or 3
members of the class, says "No!" and, continuing her input, suggests that they might
morph PAUL into IAN.

PAUL: Ah no, no way, Ian's a fag!
MISS CARTER: No Paul
PAUL: He is! Ian's gay!
MISS CARTER: Paul, enough
PAUL (louder, to the whole class): Hands up, hands up who agrees Ian's a puff!
PAUL turns around in his chair and looks at OHAN: he is, he's queer!
MISS CARTER: Paul, NO!
PAUL: Everybody listen, hands up who agrees
OHAN puts his hand up
MISS CARTER: Everybody, you can't hear Paul, you can't hear him. (To Ohan): Ohan,
you need to carry on with what you are doing
Through all of this Ian says nothing, his cheeks flush deep pink as he continues to look
at his computer screen.
PAUL: Hey miss, you think we could turn KEVIN (a high status 'Smoker') into IVAN
(a low status 'Special' student)?'.
IAN is the first in the class to laugh "Yeah, Kevin!" and others join in.

(Fieldnotes)

After the lesson in which I observed this scene, Miss Carter approached me and
spoke about Paul. She describing him as a "special student" and told me of his
"behavioural problems" and "learning difficulties". This represents a peculiarly
Australian version of the now well-worn international professional discourse of
special educational needs. This professional discourse of problems and difficulties
that bring with them special educational needs is one which has, in common
professional parlance, replaced an older, outmoded discourse, now acknowledged as
discriminatory, of retardation and educability (or not) that locates a deficit, be this
genetic or environmental, firmly in the student. Special educational needs and
'specialness', in contrast, is widely accepted has having shifted the approach away
from identifying the student's deficit and towards identifying their special needs.

The apparent promise of this move proves limited on closer inspection. The
removal of a gateway to education based on educability is clearly essential. Further,
a move away from nomenclature that is almost inevitably injurious and, in line with
the theoretical frame I am pursuing here, constitutive even as it injures is welcome.
Yet, the notion of 'specialness' and the 'special student' circulating in this
Australian context appear to disguise, rather than intercept the constitutive injury.
'Specialness' is undoubtedly meant within the educational profession to present a
'different' without being 'less', and indeed the 'special' might in its more romantic
deployments be considered to bestow extra value upon the student so named. In
contexts framed by matrices of normative discourses in which the Same is being
constantly constituted through the proliferation of discourses of the Other (the 'less
than', the lacking), however, this 'equal-but-different' never materialises, and a shift

to 'specialness' merely disguises the continued inscription of the normal and the not-normal child.

The special student, then, is constituted as beyond the bounds of normative discourse of behaviour and learning (if not intelligence) and, outside these bounds of normativity, the special student is abnormal, s/he is Other. And s/he is an impossible learner.

When Miss Carter offers me an account of Paul's special-ness, including his part-time attendance at Mitcham House, a state special school for students diagnosed as having EDBDs, he deploys this professional discourse of special needs. She goes on to describe the causal relationship between his "work" at Mitcham House on "social skills" and the subsequent positive impact of this on both his behaviour and learning. This is significant for several reasons. First, while Paul is discussed in general EDBD terms, the distinction and relationship between his behavioural and learning difficulties are specified: his behavioural problems are primary and are causative of his learning difficulties. On the surface at least, this seems to function in beneficial ways for Paul: the primacy of his behavioural problems, and their susceptibility to professional intervention protect his educability – his learning difficulties stem not from an interior intellectual deficit, but from his behaviour and so, if his behaviour can be corrected, which by Miss Carter's account it can, then Paul can learn. The possibility of being an acceptable student remains open to him. Likewise, by framing Paul's behaviour as an indicator of 'special-ness', this professional discourse protects Paul from being constituted as simply a bad student, or, indeed, an impossible student. Instead it draws him back into student-hood, albeit a restricted one. That Miss Carter offers this account unbidden at the end of a lesson in which Paul's behaviour has been particularly 'disruptive' suggests her insight into these constitutive processes: by explaining Paul's behaviour to me, the researcher, she potentially intercepts my interpretation (constitution) of him as a bad student and her as a bad teacher.

In the final scene, then, Paul objects to Miss Carter's lesson illustration that sees him being 'morphed' with Ian, a boy regularly injuriously alleged to be "gay" by other boys in the class, by calling out that Ian is gay. In the discursive frame of the school, this might be understood as the practices of a very bad student or as the bad behaviour of a student so disruptive that these practices are constitutive of him as 'special. Or these practices might be understood as reflecting Paul's practical sense that such an imagined morphing has the potential to threaten his own hetero-masculinity and constitute him as the denigrated homosexual, or even that the suggestion itself might effect such a constitution. In the hetero-normative terms that dominate this discursive terrain, then, Paul's objection to the teacher's suggested morphing might be taken as a reasonable and predictable response to a threat of 'gay' rather than as the outside-meaning act of an EBDB student. Indeed, we might wonder what the teacher was intending – for both Paul and for Ian[xviii] (whose injury in this scene is evident in his flushed cheeks and eyes fixed on his computer screen) when she drew on this particular example.

And Paul's practices are once again inappropriate, as a student and learner. Good students do not engage in defamatory name-calling, nor do they call out, and they certainly do not call out repeatedly while being instructed to be quiet. These practices are so far beyond the good student that Paul might not just be a bad student, he may be an impossible student. And if his behaviour is so far beyond that of the good student, given the extent of his breach, he may well also be an impossible learner.

Paul's practices in scene 3 are also inappropriate as a subject of student sub-culture. As I have noted above, being the Larrikin in class and disrupting the lesson through joking is a valorised practice within sections of the student sub-culture, But like his practices in the English lesson of scene 1, Paul's practices here do not fit and so constitute him outside the student sub-culture. As well as being aware of the inappropriate timing, content and style of Paul's calls, it seems the other student's in the class also anticipate in advance Miss Carter's intervention. That is, they already know that they 'cannot hear' Paul. Paul is not only outside the student and school sub-culture, he is outside subject-hood. Like the boy seen sitting crying on the floor outside the staffroom whom passing students are instructed 'is not to be spoken to' in Laws and Davies' paper (2000), Paul is no longer "special", instead – his practices of hetero-masculinity so exceed the bounds of acceptable student conduct and acceptable subject-hood that he is rendered inaudible – he is an impossible learner and an impossible subject.

However, this is not a final, once and for all constitution. Paul's subject-hood is inscribed, if only momentarily, when he suggests an alternative morph: Kevin the high status Smoker into Ivan the low status special student with the mole and the un-cut hair. Paul gets a collaborative laugh from the class (from a relieved Ian first of all) and in getting that laugh Paul is constituted Larrikin and perhaps even a little counter-school cool.

While Miss Carter spoke to me of Paul's specialness at the end of this lesson, that is, *after* I had observed all of the scenes explored in this chapter, I already 'knew' this when I was told. This is not because my professional artillery enabled me to recognise diagnostic features of EDBD. Rather, it is because I – like the teachers and students here – share the practical sense and am implicated in the ongoing constitution of normal/abnormal. This is not just a 'recognition' of Paul's 'aberrant' behaviours, but also of the 'normal' behaviours of the teachers and students with, by and in comparison to whom Paul is schooled as 'special'.

While Miss Carter's account of Paul locates and constitutes Paul openly in a professional and popular discourse of 'specialness', he is already located there by Miss Ellis' quick ejection of him from her classroom and the other students' participation in this and by Miss Carter's lifting of the examination regulation and removal of his voice (the other students cannot not hear, *they cannot hear Paul*). While Miss Carter's professional discourse of specialness maintains the possibility of something like 'normalness' for Paul (if his behaviour correction works), it is unlikely that even this champion of Paul could shake off the discourse of specialness entirely. Nevertheless, Miss Carter does believe that Paul could 'do normal' (after Laws and Davies 2000) in a way that Miss Ellis seems unlikely to contemplate.

The student constituted as 'special' then, is not tied irrevocably into this subjectivity, but it is a deeply sedimented location that is not easily shifted. In the discursive frame that bounds this school, 'specialness' subsumes other constitutions of other subjectivities, from class and masculinity and sexuality to naughtiness and limited ability. Might being a bad student and an undesirable learner offer this student more room for movement? Might it be 'better' for Paul to be naughty and low ability than confined in/by subjectivity singularised as 'special'? And might any other intelligible subjectivities be available to him here?

PART 4: NAVIGATING EDUCATIONAL INCLUSIONS AND EXCLUSIONS

INTRODUCTION

In the chapters that make up part 3 I showed how school practices, framed by institutional and enduring popular discourses, exclude some students from the educational process, from being a good student and/or an acceptable learner. Indeed, in some moments the subjects constituted appeared unintelligible in the terms of schooling – these were impossible students and learners. Through this analysis I demonstrated how the student and learner identities constituted in schools are entangled tightly with constellations of biographical and sub-cultural identities. Gender, class, race, ability, disability, sexuality, culture, sub-culture, themselves apparently inseparable in the constitutive moment, were shown to be entwined with the sorts of students and learners it is possible to be.

Yet the young people who populate schools are not passive surfaces on which student and learner identities are mapped; my analysis showed students actively engaged in linguistic, bodily, textual, and representational discursive practices. While these active students are not necessarily fully cognizant of the discourses they deploy or their effects, it remains evident that students, as well as teachers, act with discursive agency.

The entanglement of biographical, sub-cultural, student and learner identities stresses that student-learner is not 'all' the subject of schooling is. Hammersley and Turner (1984) noted that studies of schooling that imagine that the school, its norms, values and project, is the central concern of students may well proceed from a flawed position. Students, they suggest, may well foreground alternative sets of norms and values – sub-cultural norms and values, for instance – and that this prioritization *may or may not be* the result of prior institutional positionings; in today's terminology, it may be entangled with, but is not necessarily a direct result of, educational exclusion. The school student, then, may not be centrally concerned with schooling. Instead, s/he may be engaged in alternative project(s) of self, community, sub-culture; projects that may be more or less consciously recognised as such and which may be more or less compatible with schooling.

In this part of the book, then, the student milieu, or milieus, are fore-grounded. Extending my examination of the intersections of biographical and sub-cultural identity categories with educational exclusions, I turn to the intersections of subjectivities marked by biographical categories and educational *and* sub-cultural inclusions. That is, I begin to ask 'who' the student needs to be in order to be included in the project of schooling and 'who' s/he needs to be in order to be included in student sub-culture(s). In responding to these questions my analysis suggests that just as educational exclusions appear to be tightly entwined with students' sub-cultural locations, so educational inclusions appear to be tied to sub-cultural exclusions.

The analyses that are offered in the following chapters insist that inclusion/exclusion in/from either the project of schooling or student sub-cultures is not a once and for all act. It does not necessarily remain fixed over time. Nor does the inclusion/exclusion of a person in one moment or setting necessarily translate across all moments or settings. And while at times there appears to be an inverse relationship between educational exclusion and sub-cultural inclusion, and vice versa, the nuances of contexts and discursive frames mean this is far from straightforward. This is not to suggest, however, an illimitable capacity for free play of subjectivities and exclusions/inclusions – constellations of identity categories and their implications can and do become enduring, as suggested by my analyses in part 3 and by the ongoing commitment to Cartesian man in Western discourse. Nevertheless, as the subsequent analyses show, students do have the potential to deploy discourses differently, challenge exclusions (and inclusions), and reconstitute themselves again but differently from before.

In the chapters that follow, then, the capacity for discursive agency and the potential mobility of subjectivities will be focused on as I explore students' navigations of sub-cultural and institutional inclusions and exclusion. In doing this I turn away from Plains High and focus on students from Taylor Comprehensive. This allows a cluster of students' navigations and shifting constitutions to be revisited across moments and settings. By doing this, the analysis is able to show practices of discursive agency, the effects of such agency, and the extent to which particular instance of such agency change 'who' a young person can be in particular discursive moments.

CHAPTER 9

INCLUDED AND EXCLUDED?
MIDDLE CLASS-WHITE-QUEER-HIGH ABILITY-ALTERNATIVE YOUTH-CULTURE/WORKING CLASS-WHITE-BLACK-HETERO-LOW ABILITY-MAINSTREAM YOUTH-CULTURE

This chapter turns to consider how students come to be inside or outside the educational process *and* inside or outside the student sub-culture as well as how these are linked. I explore how a group of White, high attaining students from professional, middle class backgrounds constitute themselves and other students. I examine how a discourse of sub-cultural difference is deployed by this group of students in a way that deflects pro-school, White, middle class identifications and constitutes sub-cultural cool *at the same time* as it masks and constitutes class, race and learner privilege.

This group of students constitutes itself as marginal, as Other, in the student milieu. And yet, as the group extrapolates *what they are not*, they inadvertently expose the institutional and social privilege – a privilege that rests upon middle class Whiteness – that their practices eschew. These practices join the citational chain that constitutes these students as the learner (social?) ideal, and the student mainstream as less than good students, less than ideal learners, and less than desirable citizens.

In offering this reading the chapter shows how discourses that constitute difference as both *sub-cultural* (nothing more than youthful tastes) and *neutral* (different but equal) obscure the constellations of categorical identities that underpin these sub-cultures and mask these insider/outsider, Same/Other locations. It also shows how this masking conceals the privilege of particular identity constellations and their correspondence with particular good and bad student and acceptable (even ideal) and unacceptable learner identities. Finally, it shows how the inclusion of some students and the exclusion of others are inseparable because it is the constant invocation of the 'Other' that constitutes, and renders invisible, the (privileged) 'Same'.

> *Episode 10: Dir'y 'ippies / Shazas and Bazas Part 1*
> *Taylor Comprehensive, London, UK.* Sitting in a group around a table in the Year Base, an infrequently used classroom that is designated as the social space of the year group. DY is with VICI (girl, White), PIPA (girl, White), SUZI (girl, White) and TOM (boy, White) all students aged 15-16. The rest of the tutor group are in a PSE lesson. The group begin to talk about how they believe they are perceived in the school.
>
> VICI: We are seen as very very un-cool because we are seen as (laughing and imitating a south east London accent) dirty hippies.

[...]
DY: Dirty hippies, who thinks you're dirty hippies?
    (simultaneously)TOM: Everyone.
    (simultaneously) PIPA: It's actually (changing pronunciation to imitate a south east
London accent) dirty hippies.
SUZI: (imitating east London accent) Dirty hippies.
ALL: (laugh)
DY: (trying to repeat and write as pronounced) Dirty hippies?
VICI: Spelt: D, I, R, apostrophe, Y...
PIPA: Apostrophe, I, double P, I, E, S.
ALL: (laugh)
DY: (pronouncing as instructed) Dir'y 'ippies.
[...]
VICI: The opposite end of the scale to (repeating imitated accent) dir'y 'ippies are
Shazas and Bazas.
SUZI: Have you heard of them?
DY: No, I don't think they self-identify in the way that you do.
VICI: No they don't, cos they just sit here and go (whining) 'Ner ner'. No, they don't
know that they're referred to as Shazas and Bazas but we know that we're refereed to as
Dir'y 'ippies cos we are, (with slight laugh in voice) on the ball.

The group engages in an extended discussion of the different styles of clothing, hair,
jewellery, shoes, bags that distinguish between Dir'y 'ippies and Shazas and Bazas.
Hair wax or hair gel, and in what quantity; record bag or sports bag; silver or gold
jewellery. When I offer Mridula, an Indian girl in the tutor group, for classification she
doesn't fit: she is not a Dir'y 'ippie but, says Vici, "she's not a true Shaza, (laughing)
her hair is not solid and she doesn't wear quite enough gold jewellery either!". Music is
also crucial. While Dir'y 'ippies listen to alternative rock and brit-pop, Shaza's are
imagined nursing broken hearts to R&B love songs. And while homophobic Baza's use
"gay" as a catch-all insult and term of derision, Dir'y 'ippies celebrate queer. Vici
summarises: "You could almost write out a set of definitive rules for Shazas and Bazas
and Dir'y 'ippies" and Tom elaborates: "The point is, Shazas and Bazas keep to those
rules".

At a superficial level this might simply be seen as a group of students who, having
been called a name (Dir'y 'ippie), retaliate by first, insisting that the name is not,
after all, an injury and second, by retorting with another name (Shazas and Bazas).
Further, it is not clear that a Shaza or a Baza has actually ever addressed one of these
pupils as Dir'y 'ippie. These students are most notable in the talk of Shazas and
Bazas by their *absence*. Where they do appear, (usually at my instigation), they are
named as "Bods" or "Boffins" and quickly disregarded. (At Plains High in Sydney a
student minority noted for its relative high attainment and social class background
calls itself "the performing arts crowd" while their peers in the mainstream student
sub-culture refer to them, on rare occasion, as "the goodie goodies"). In the context
of the (absent) relations between the two groups of students; the names (Bod,
Boffin) that these students *are* called; and the recognisable quality of the names
under discussion[xix], it is plausible and even likely that such an address did not take
place. Rather, it seems that these students are citing names that circulate in
discourses reaching far beyond the specific context of this school, and whose
historicity lends them their performative force. The names at stake here have the
potential to constitute the student population in very particular ways.

In chapter 2 I explored Helene Cixous' (1986) question *'Where is she?'* as she
offered a series of pairs whose privilege/subordinate and masculine/feminine
relation were clear. Taking the categorical identities through which the young people

in this episode are made as recognisable subjects, and recognisable subjects of schooling, it can similarly be asked, *Where is the ideal learner?*

Middle class/working class
White/Black
Hetero/homo (queer?)
Mainstream/alternative
High ability/low ability

When these hierarchical pairs are taken individually, enduring discourses suggest that it is the leading term that will be synonymous with the ideal learner. And yet when these are drawn into constellations, and when the question is applied to the pair 'Dir'y 'ippie/Shaza Baza', as they are in the students' discursive practices here, 'who' might approximate the 'ideal' becomes more equivocal.

As the Dir'y 'ippies extrapolate the minutiae of the differences between these two sub-cultural styles, it is almost possible to imagine that this is all it is. On the surface these names might appear to reference nothing more than a nebulous array of 'teenage' 'choices' concerning clothing, hair styles, musical genres, effort in school work, But Bourdieu's (1987) analysis of distinction presses: these apparent 'tastes' have differential values in differentiated markets and it is the relative values of the wearer/user/listener's capitals in varying markets that is at stake. And the class and race privilege that is cited and inscribed through these students' discursive practices, while implicit, is unavoidable. This is because these apparent choices at once mask and cite an array of discourses that constitute subjects along intersecting lines of social class, gender, race, sexuality, and intelligence/ability. Indeed, these 'choices' are the very discursive practices that cite and inscribe these discourses and the identities that are constituted through them. As Mike Apple (2003) has argued in relation to race; the insistent absent presence of professional middle-classness and Whiteness are inescapable here.

Dir'y 'ippie/Shaza and Baza is also constituted through, and inscribes, particular modes of intelligible masculinity, femininity and sexuality. Of immediate note is that Dir'y 'ippie incorporates both female and male students, whereas, the female and male parts of Shaza and Baza are distinct. The group's discussion of Shazas' and Bazas' cites discourses of compulsory heterosexuality and traditional modes of passive femininity and active masculinity, whereas their account of themselves cites liberal discourses of gender and sexuality equality/alternaeity. Indeed, a key feature of Dir'y 'ippie is its embracing of non-heterosexual identities and the additional value of these identities within the Dir'y 'ippie discourse and milieu. The ideal learner is asexual (Epstein and Johnson 1998) and hetero-normativity suggests that the good student is proto-(but not actively) heterosexual within institutional discourse. Yet the desirability of middle class professional home backgrounds, Whiteness, and supposed high ability, mediates this queer self-identification and it is rendered acceptable. Indeed, in a discursive frame of liberal-progressive education, the sub-cultural alternaeity of the Dir'y 'ippies and the claim to queerness that intersects this may even become evidence of their social, cultural and so intellectual creativity. That is, it is possible that they are ideal learners not in spite of identifying as queer, but because they are constituted through a constellation of discourses and identity categories that at once compensate for and valorise queerness (of course, it may be that this not-so-queer reading is one that would not be meaningful to the school institution).

Dir'y 'ippie/Shaza and Baza is also marked by, and in turn inscribes, race. The group does not explicitly state any race affiliations but this does not mean that race discourses are not present in the student' practices, or that their practices do not have raced effects. Perhaps most straightforwardly, that the opposition is synonymous with middle class/working class infers that it is already raced: the disproportionate poverty of the non-White population in Britain implies that the middle class Dir'y 'ippies are predominantly, but not exclusively, White. The racialised nature of the opposition becomes more explicit when the group discusses named individuals: named Dir'y 'ippies are all White students, named Shazas are White and Mixed-race, named Bazas are White, Mixed-race and Black. The most notable absences are Black girls and Asian students. When I name Mridula, an Indian girl, the binary momentarily becomes a "spectrum". Nevertheless, in discussing (constituting) this spectrum, the opposition persists: Mridula is more of a Shaza than a Dir'y 'ippie. As such, the apparently Same/Other binary of Dir'y 'ippie/Shaza and Baza also functions as a totality of intelligibility in which there is no place for students from certain minority ethnic backgrounds. Those students who fit neither category, it seems, become the other-Other who are impossible subjects in the terms of this the student milieu.

The silence around race, combined with the normative status of Whiteness, might suggest that both sides of the binary are implicitly marked by Whiteness. This does not mean, however, that the fashion and musical preferences that the group enlist to Dir'y ippie and allocate to Shaza and Baza are either race-neutral or simply 'White'. Instead, the group identifies a Dir'y 'ippie eclecticism that is on the surface racially-inclusive (a pop-sub-cultural multicultural pluralism?). Yet this also appears the sort of expropriation of minority ethnic cultural forms that has been and remains constitutive and indicative of the operations of Whiteness. Simultaneously, the group rejects for themselves and allocates to Shazas and Bazas a particular, narrow set of 'mainstreamed' 'Black' fashion and musical styles. While this allows Shaza and Baza a degree of racial diversity, it is precisely one that is allowed and one that denies counter-cultural forms that have not been incorporated into the mainstream. it is once again a practice of Whiteness.

At the end of Part 1 of the episode the Dir'y 'ippies suggest that that "know" how they are referred to, while the Shazas and Bazas' 'failure' to know is indicated by their (imagined) "ner ner". As the group moves to this distinction between the two 'sub-cultures', a discourse of differential intelligence is deployed. That this intelligence is constituted as classed – through silently cited discourses of predetermination, eugenics and meritocracy – remains implicit. As the group turns to discuss modes of speech, however, the discourse of classed intelligence that runs through these subjectivating discourses becomes clear.

> Episode 10: Dir'y 'ippies / Shazas and Bazas Part 2
> [...]
> SUZI: Another thing is speech. You see, we all speak quite clearly so you can understand what we're saying.
> PIPA: (squeals)

DY: Is there a social class thing about being a Dir'y 'ippie or a Shaza or Baza?
PIPA: Erm...
VICI: If we're honest, sort of, not strictly but it does tend to be.
    (simultaneously) SUZI: A trend.
VICI: It's not a definite decision but, a trend. Probably anyway.
PIPA: Sort of.
    (simultaneously) SUZI: If you take a case study in Taylor, that is.
TOM: And the people who are more inclined to work in school. The people that are more inclined to work and come from slightly more middle class backgrounds tend to be, don't you think?
SUZI: Erm, not exactly. I'm not sure that I'd quite agree with that. I wouldn't say Dir'y 'ippies tend to work.

The specific pronunciation of Dir'y 'ippie is central to both Dir'y 'ippie and Shaza and Baza. Dir'y 'ippie as an injurious name is pronounced with an (imagined) 'real' east London accent. As a recuperated and *re*inscribed self-identity it is pronounced with a self-conscious parody of this 'real' east London accent. Distinct modes of speech are also positioned as crucial markers of difference – Dir'y 'ippies "speak quite clearly so you can understand" and implicitly, the reverse is true for Shazas and Bazas. These assertions of differential modes of speech expose how the categorisations are infused by, and inscribe, a discourse of distinct and hierarchically organised social classes. The assertion of distinct educational orientations, albeit one that is internally disputed, also draws on and inscribes discourses of social class. Indeed, the group hesitantly confirms the social class distinctions between the categories when asked explicitly. That the opposition Dir'y 'ippie/Shaza and Baza is synonymous with the opposition middle class/working class becomes inescapable.

Vici, Suzi, Ben and company believe that they are (and constitute themselves as) excluded ("outcast") from the mainstream of the pupil population on the basis that they are "uncool" Dir'y 'ippies. In this sub-cultural discursive frame it is the Dir'y 'ippies who are constituted (constitute themselves) as Other. They 'respond' to this Othering by constituting this marginalisation as a radical alternative and thereby recuperate it through an ironic/parodic/radical *re*inscription of the injurious name through which their marginality has been (fictively) constituted. As such, the marginal Other is constituted as a radical and, therefore, desirable identity – indeed, it is constituted as über cool, but only to the marginalised (elite) that is "in the know".

This identity contrasts with the alternative identity apparently available to these pupils: Bod or Boffin. Acknowledging a positive educational orientation (which might also be pro-school) and confirming middle class status threatens to undermine this radical Other identity and recast it as the sub-cultural minority *and* the privileged Same (middle class, white, high attaining). That is, it might be exposed as being Bod or Boffin. If this discursive shift occurs, then the conservative Same (sub-cultural majority) appears as the marginalised (working class) Other, particularly within those discursive frames that exceed the limits of the school's pupil sub-cultures.

This turn to sub-culture(s) cannot erase either the classed nature of these constituting names or their oblique but enduring intersection with school cultures. By extension, this turn to sub-culture cannot overwrite the respective privilege and disadvantage embedded in them: in the classroom, the GCSE examination, the further and higher education market places and, ultimately, in the employment market, it is the Dir'y 'ippies – the White, middle class, high attaining, and positively educationally orientated pupils – who score highly for Bourdieu's social, cultural, symbolic and linguistic capital (Bourdieu 1990 & 1991). It is students' identities within these broader, official contexts that are likely to have the most bearing on educational experiences, outcomes, and futures.

And so these students are themselves implicated in the discursive production of privileged middle class-ness and Whiteness through their apparently benign practices of youth sub-culture. And these practices are implicated even as they are produces as a site of injury, of being called a name – Dir'y 'ippie – by a Shaza or Baza.

The intertwining of the discourses that are deployed explicitly and implicitly by the Dir'y 'ippies is such that particular discursive markers of difference come to appear synonymous. 'White-middle class-intelligent-liberal (radical?)-positive educational orientation (but not pro-school)-good student-ideal learner (Dir'y 'ippies) becomes opposed to '(White or Black but not necessarily other minority ethnicities)working class-unintelligent-conservative (reactionary/traditional?)-negative educational orientation (and possibly anti-school)-bad student-undesirable learner (Shazas and Bazas).

At a superficial level Dir'y 'ippies and Shazas and Bazas are readily recognisable, and the distinctions between the two groups draw upon established social 'truths'. Yet while the Dir'y 'ippies report and offer a commentary on these 'truths', they also participate in a citational chain of classed and raced practices that constitutes these. These students constitute themselves and others as particular subjects. In so doing, they inscribe those discourses of embedded, distinct, hierarchically organised, and *classed* and *raced* identities that are both necessary for the success of these performatives and entwined with educational inclusions and exclusions.

This analysis shows how middle class Whiteness (but not just White) might come to be synonymous with the good student and the ideal learner and how working class (White, Black and some minority ethnic but not Whiteness) might come to be synonymous with the bad student and the unacceptable (and sometimes even impossible) learner. In the following chapter I continue to examine these entanglements and the ways that sub-cultural and educational exclusions and inclusions are tied together.

CHAPTER 10

INCLUDED LEARNERS, IMPOSSIBLE GIRLS: THE INCOMMENSURABILITY OF INDIAN-NESS AND DESIRABLE FEMININITY

This chapter picks up the preceding chapter's concerns with the sub-cultural and institutional locations of students. This chapter traces the threads of the Dir'y 'ippies inability to locate Mridula on either side of their sub-cultural binary or my suggestion that this might leave her nowhere and nobody. It examines how Mridula and her friend Avtar are variously constituted by their own, their peers' and their teachers' discursive practices. The chapter shows how, in the terms of the discourses that prevail in the mainstream student sub-culture, Indian-ness is incommensurable with a femininity that is recognizably desirable, and given the centrality of this to girls, so Mridula and Avtar are constituted on the margins of the student sub-culture. Yet further discourses press upon the scene and an apparent need for the exclusion of Mridula and Avtar from desirable femininity to be constantly policed emerges, exposing the tenuousness of this incommensurability. This exclusion from the femininity valued in the student sub-culture is entangled with (but does not necessarily require) the girls' constitution of themselves and their teachers' constitution of them as good students and acceptable (that is hard working and attaining but not intrinsically gifted) learners. This constitution might itself be raced through Orientalist discourses of Asian submission and work ethic. While this constitution as good students and acceptable learners is implicitly raced, it also masks the raced underpinnings of the girls' location on the periphery of the student sub-culture and contributes to their constitution as (un-)feminine.

> *Episode 11: Samosa, munchers, and white princesses*
> *Taylor Comp, London UK. Food Technology Lesson.* MRIDULA *and* AVTAR *(both aged 15-16, Indian, girls) are making samosa and have invited* DY *to observe. This practical session contributes to their examined coursework that they have opted to work on together. This work is set in the context of a fictional 'Multicultural Wedding'. A boy at a similar stage in his coursework is also cooking during this lesson. The rest of the group is expected to work independently on ongoing written work.*
>
> Mridula and Avtar are making pastry. Avtar holds up the bag of flour for me to look at. It has several lumps of pastry stuck to it. Avtar pulls her mouth down and says "Urrrg!". The pastry is sticky and the girls grimace as they knead it. While kneading, they pause regularly to pick lumps of pastry off their hands. Once the pastry is rolled, it is stuffed with a filling which Mridula has made at home with the help of her mother.
> [...]
> Avtar is taking photographs for their coursework folders. She asks me to hold the food and utensils for the photographs. I point out that my finger nails are a bit chewed. She counters that her own are much worse. Mridula and Avtar laugh as I roll up my

sleeves and remove my watch and ring. Lucy, who has come to watch, reminds Avtar: "make sure you can't see she's not in uniform!". Avtar takes photographs of my hands holding cooking utensils and pinching together the pastry seams of an uncooked samosa.

[...]

Intermittently various students come to the cooking area. The (White) girls look to see what Avtar and Mridula are doing and ask: "Are you cooking those thingies again?" and "You're making what's it called?". They do not wait for an answer before moving away. Only Lucy and Bridget (White), who stop to chat and contribute cooking advice, refer to the samosa by name. The (Black, Mixed-race and White) boys demand: "When will it be ready?", "What am I getting to munch?", "Isn't it ready yet?", "I better get a munch". Mridula ignores the boys. Avtar becomes annoyed, her face is unsmiling and set. On one occasion Avtar shouts: "Miss!" and the teacher calls the boys back to their seats. Mridula asks Avtar: "Why are you getting stressed?", Avtar replies: "I'm not, I dunno...". After a moments pause she looks at me and says: "All they want is a munch." Turning to Mridula she says: "'Mrid, I'm going to save 2 each for us and Debbie and they can have the rest. We'll cut them up". She looks back to me and tells me: "Last time we let them have them all. The boys won't do the survey, they just want a munch".

[...]

Mridula crosses the path of Stuart (Black boy), one of the boys who has been hassling for a munch, as she walks into the kitchen area. As Mridula passes, Stuart throws his weight into a head-butt and shouts "Uurrgh". He pulls the head-butt a few centimetres before it makes contact with Mridula's face. Mridula ignores him. When she reaches Avtar and me she says: "That boy's a nutcase".

[...]

A girl approaches the kitchen area. Avtar nods towards the girl and says to me: "Watch this". The girl is White and noticeably overweight. The girl stands close by and watches. Avtar and Mridula ignore her. She walks away. I ask: "What was I watching?". Avtar chuckles as she replies: "Her coming to see if it was ready yet".

[...]

Avtar and Mridula fry the samosa they have made along with a packet bought from a shop. We try the samosa as they are cooked. Mridula finds the samosa "too hot" and says that she cannot eat a whole one. She laughs as she tells us that she is known within her family for being unable to eat hot foods. Avtar and me laugh as we eat a number of samosa during the cooking process and agree that shop-bought variety are far inferior to the ones that she and Mridula have made.

[...]

When all the samosa are cooked, Avtar and Mridula put the shop-bought samosa on a plate together. Six of their own samosa are set to one side for us to eat and the rest are cut into smaller pieces and put on a plate with a survey sheet next to it. The boys who have been demanding a munch throughout the lesson come over saying: "Where's mine?". Avtar indicates the plate of cut up samosa. One boy responds: "I don't want that, I want a whole one". Avtar says: "No, those are the ones for tasting". The boys hassle Avtar for a whole samosa. Avtar says: "They're for us". The boys indicate the shop-bought samosa and say: "What about those?". Initially Avtar refuses but, with persistent hassling, she tells the boys that they can each have a whole shop-bought samosa. The boys walk away grumbling about the quality and quantity of what they have been given. They do not offer any thanks. Once the boys have left the area, a number of girls come to taste the samosa for the survey. These girls do not complain about the size of the portions. As they eat, several girls say that the samosa are "Hot!". One girl takes a bite, puts her hand over her mouth, reels, and says "I've got to get a drink of water!". The girls' responses on the survey sheet are uniform: the colour is "golden"; the appearance "nice"; the smell "spicy"; and the flavour "HOT!".

Avtar and Mridula are engaged in a tacit, if not intentional, affirmation of Indian-ness and themselves as Indian. At the same time, but Mridula in particular, they (try to?) constitute themselves within sub-cultural (and popular) terms of desirable femininity. That it, they appear to constitute Indian-ness as valuable, valued and legitimate *and* commensurate with desirable heterosexual femininity. As these potential constitutions are made through a serious engagement with examined coursework, these practices are simultaneously constitutive of Avtar and Mridula as good students and acceptable (or even ideal?) learners.

The girls' decision to make samosa is significant. It seems that making samosa acts as an assertion and affirmation of their race identity; the specificities of this race identity; its cultural difference from the White majority; and *also* its legitimacy within the school context. It is notable that 'Indian' food is common-place within UK popular culture – while the reasonably priced Indian restaurant and post-pub curry remain staples of any UK town, Indian food has also made it into the supermarket in the form of ready meals and cooking sauces. It is almost certain, then, that every student in the school lives within a walk of an Indian restaurant and that most will have eaten this food. In this context, making samosa neither introduces an unfamiliar cultural artefact into the school nor acts as an assertion of race that is likely to disrupt hegemonic notions of Asian-ness or good Asian students. At the same time, the linguistic and bodily performatives deployed by Mridula and Avtar as they make pastry cite and inscribe a desirable heterosexual (and middle-class) femininity that is clean, sensitive and unused to domestic and/or menial tasks, for instance, their distaste for the pastry sticking to their hands cites and inscribes femininity of and for beauty and ornamentation, not domestic work. At the same time, however, they are competent cooks, citing and inscribing the 'natural' capacities of the feminine service provider and the good student and acceptable learner of Food Technology.

While Mridula and Avtar may have a tacit intent to constitute themselves as simultaneously Indian, desirably feminine, and good student-learners, my analysis of the episode suggests that such a constitution is likely to fail on several counts. First, despite the likely familiarity of samosa to the other students in the class, Mridula's and Avtar's assertion and affirmation of Indian-ness is strongly resisted. Second, their practices of desirable femininity seem to be subsumed by the other students' constitutions of them as Asian, that is, as Other, and, therefore, beyond the bounds of desirable femininity. Finally, the girls' own tacit knowledge of the income-mensurability of Indian-ness and desirable femininity appears a various moments within the episode. What their practices seem to constitute, then, is an Indian (servicing) femininity and a good student-learner.

It is not Indian-ness itself that is contested by other students in the group. Rather, it is the simultaneous *affirmation* of this and the attempt to constitute it as *commensurable* with desirable femininity that is resisted. The refusal of the majority of the other students to *name* the samosa acts to recuperate Mridula's and Avtar's assertion of it as a legitimate food. By not 'knowing' the name of the food they reassert its Otherness – the food (and by extension the girls making it) are provisionally constituted as the exotic/racial Other.

The White girls' practices concerning the spiciness and hotness (flavour not temperature) of the food are constitutive of themselves, Avtar and Mridula, and English/Asian. These practices cite and inscribe their own desirable White (English) femininity (which is too sensitive and delicate to eat Asian food) and, therefore, the Otherness of Asian girls who lack this desirable femininity. The boys' practices also constitute Mridula and Avtar as Other to desirable femininity. The boys' desire to eat the girls' food inscribes the (English) (Colonial?) masculine consumer (who is not too delicate to eat spicy food) in opposition to the (Asian) (colonised?) feminine service provider. Yet this is not an *exchange* of constitutions of desirable masculinity and femininity. The boys do not *request* feminine services, thereby citing and inscribing this femininity. Rather, they *demand* and their demands do not allow for any legitimate refusal. These practices are potentially constitutive of the boys' aggressive masculinity (bad students?) and of the girls' racial Otherness. Within the discursive frame mobilised by the boys, Mridula's and Avtar's services are citations and inscriptions not of their femininity but of their subordinate Asianness and lack of desirable femininity. Beneath these contemporary constitutions, the echoes of colonial relations between the English colonised and the colonised (feminised but not feminine) 'Oriental' resound.

This constitution of Otherness and lack of desirable femininity is also apparent in the head-butt sequence. Stuart does not attempt to engage Mridula, to extract her (feminine) submission. Rather, his shout and head-butt appear as particularly aggressive and intimidatory performative practices. These practices are potentially constitutive of Stuart's aggressive hyper-masculinity, bad-studenthood and impossibility as a learner, a subjectivity that is itself raced as it cites racist discourses of a Black challenge to White hegemony. They are also potentially constitutive of Mridula. Stuart's practices do not simply overlook Mridula's femininity, they deny it, that is, they cite and inscribe the subordination of Asianness and its intrinsic lack of desirable femininity. Yet Stuart's constituting practices do offer Mridula a position as speaking subject from which she can resist this constitution. To me and Avtar she calls Stuart a "nutcase" (impossible subject?) and this naming is at least provisionally successful within the restricted context of our corner of the kitchen.

The boys and girls who engage with Mridula and Avtar recuperate the girls' affirmation of Indian-ness and neutralise, if not subjugate, this race identity. This recuperation may be effected intentional or through a tacit knowledge of the potentially performative force of these practices. That is, the other students cite and inscribe the place of Indian-ness discourse and this is a place of subjugation in the discourses that underpin both White hegemony and the Hierarchy within the Other that permeate this student sub-culture. At the same time, the students' practices deny any possibility of desirable femininity. They cite and inscribe the incommensurability of Asian-ness and desirable femininity[xx].

Mridula's and Avtar's awareness of the Otherness of Asian in and the incommensurability of Asian-ness and desirable femininity within White hegemonic discourse can be seen within the photographing sequence. While asking me to hold the utensils and samosa in my (White) hands could simply be indicative of Mridula's and Avtar's like for me and desire to include me in their activities, it might also be understood as an attempt to ratify samosa as a genuine and legitimate food within White hegemonic culture. That is, *White* hands making samosa might suggest that samosa are more than the exotic food of an exotic/racial Other – if a White woman makes them they are staples of contemporary British cuisine. At the same time, this might indicate Mridula's and Avtar's acquiescence to the intrinsic Whiteness of desirable femininity. They are captured by discourses of hegemonic femininity in which the hands of a White woman (irrespective of how chewed the fingernails) are intrinsically more desirably feminine than the hands of an Asian woman. In such an analysis it appears that Mridula and Avtar are at least tacitly aware of the likely failure of their attempted simultaneous constitution of Indian-ness and desirable femininity. Their constitution of affirmed Indian-ness traps them within a discursive chain that excludes the possibility of desirable femininity.

This can also be seen in Mridula's assertion that the samosa is too spicy and hot for her to eat. This is despite having chosen to cook samosa (and thereby affirm her Indian-ness) and the filling having been made by her and her mother (suggesting she may well have eaten it in the past). Furthermore, Mridula attempts to give this potential constitution some endurance and broader legitimacy (performative force) by asserting that she is known for her inability to eat hot and spicy food (feminine delicacy and sensitivity) within her family. These practices cite those of the White girls. In doing so, they cite and inscribe the Whiteness of desirable femininity and its incommensurability with Asian-ness. In this discursive frame it appears that Mridula acquiesces to, cites and inscribes the incommensurability of Indian-ness and desirable femininity and is prepared to jettison the former in favour of the latter. Such a trade, however, seems unlikely to be effective. In earlier chapters I have demonstrated the endurance, significance and force of phenotypes and/or physiognomy in constitutions of natural, authentic and distinct races. In addition, the performative practices of the students within this episode demonstrate the force of constitutions of Indian/Asian Otherness and its incommensurability with desirable femininity. Mridula is trapped by and through these discursive constraints. She cannot simply jettison her Indian-ness in favour of desirable femininity. Her inability to eat the samosa might risk the *affirmation* of her Indian-ness, but in this moment it cannot undo either her Indian-ness or her lack of desirable femininity.

Avtar seems to navigate the constraints of this discursive frame in different ways. Avtar's "Watch this" constitutes the watching White girl as fat and greedy[xxi]. Avtar's 'fat-ing' and 'greedy-ing' of this White girl can be seen as an attempt to claim a degree of desirable femininity – she is *more* desirably feminine than this girl because she is neither fat nor greedy. This might also be understood as a momentary retaliation against the White girls' recuperation and inscription as Other of Avtar's attempted constitution of affirmed Indian-ness. If these girls recuperate her Indian-ness in order to inscribe it as Other, then she will cite and inscribe another Otherness – (un)feminine fatness and greediness. Through these practices, Avtar appears to claim a degree of desirable femininity in this moment within our corner of the kitchen without this being at the expense of her affirmed Indian-ness. Such unkindness or, indeed, breach of the school's prohibition against bullying/name calling, might, however, risk the constitution of Avtar as a good student. If it does, it seems this is a risk she is unaware of or willing to take.

Avtar's controlling of the munching boys seems to suggest that she may have given up (at least momentarily) on desirable femininity within the terms of the mainstream student sub-culture. Having given up on this (impossible) desirable femininity, it cannot be risked by refusing to provide services to the boys or by calling for the intervention of the teacher. In this sense, she contributes to the constitution of her absent femininity and good student-hood but at the same time offers herself possibilities for practice. Put simply, if she is debarred from desirable femininity anyway then she will withdraw the feminine submission and services that this femininity cites and requires. While Avtar is trapped by her own and others' discursive constitutions of Indian-ness/Asian-ness and desirable femininity, she is constituted as a good student and an acceptable learner. Furthermore, her practices offer momentary resistances to the prevailing constitution of Asian-ness, albeit resistances that might ultimately contribute to these discursive traps.

This chapter shows how, within the constraints of particular discursive contexts, race, gender, sexuality, and student and learner identities are constituted in constellations that make certain subjectivities possible – being a good-Indian-girl-student – and other subjectivities impossible – being a good-Indian-desirable-feminine-student – and further subjectivities likely – being a bad-Black-masculine-student. That these possibilities and limits are the effects of the discourses that frame contexts and make practices meaningful (or not) *should* mean that while these constitutions might be likely across contexts like this one, they are not absolute or necessary. But in what discursive context might Avtar be a good-Indian-assertive-student *and* desirably feminine? And in what discursive context might Stuart be Black-masculine *and* a good student?

CHAPTER 11

INCLUDED STUDENTS, IMPOSSIBLE BOYS: THE 'RACING' AND 'SPECIALING' OF (UN-) MASCULINITY

In this chapter I continue to pursue the theme of raced exclusions from gendered subjectivities by exploring the processes through which a Vietnamese boy, Quoc Trinh, is constituted as outside recognisable masculinity – as (un-)masculine or feminine. While Quoc Trinh's own practices (playing with a miniature toy doll) are clearly implicated in this exclusion from masculinity, these practices might be understood as the hyperbolic citation of prior exclusions that are underpinned by discourses of Asianness or, to use Said's (2003) term, Orientalism. Such a hyperbolic citation of Orientalism might have the potential to trouble Orientalism and the normative (White) masculinity against which Oriental (un-) masculinity is compared.

Just as Avtar and Mridula's exclusion from desirable femininity was easily reconciled with (or part of) their constitution as good students, so Quoc Trinh's exclusion from masculinity does not exclude him from being a student. Indeed, while Quoc Trinh's classroom ministrations to his doll, as opposed to his work, might be expected to constitute him as a bad student and unacceptable learner, the nature of these practices – quiet, seated, unobtrusive (their femininity?) – mean that they are not taken by the teacher to be either disruptive or challenging. Quoc Trinh is not recognisable as a masculine subject in prevailing discourse, and his apparent wilful floating of practices of masculinity might be taken to be so strange as to suggest an absence of free will, but he is not a bad student. The chapter goes on to extend this analysis of the commensurability of (un-)masculinity with acceptable student-hood by considering the practices of Manny, a White boy described by teachers as having "special needs". Like Quoc Tran, Manny's (un-) masculine/-feminine classroom practices (here singing a song about being a Barbie doll) exclude him from recognisable masculinity and, in combination with his "specialness", might threaten to exclude him from subjecthood.

Episode 12. Quoc Trinh's Doll
Taylor Comp, London, UK. Science lesson. Mixed ability. VICI (age 15-16, girl, White), SUZI (age 15-16, girl, White) and DY are sitting together at a table that seats four.
Vici points to the other side of the room QUOC TRINH (aged 15-15, boy, Vietnamese) is sitting on a stool next to a radiator. A small doll, approximately 6 centimetres tall, is lying on top of the radiator. Quoc Trinh appears to be drying the doll's hair. While the doll lies on the radiator, Quoc Trinh brushes its hair with a miniature, pink plastic hairbrush. Vici calls to Quoc Trinh. Quoc Trinh looks over, smiles, picks up the doll and comes over to our table. Vici introduces me to Quoc Trinh

saying "This is our friend Deb, she wanted to see your doll". Quoc Trinh smiles and hands the doll to me. The doll is made of moulded plastic and is the standard orange-pink of Caucasian dolls. The doll has silver-white hair that is longer than the doll is tall. Pink and purple streaks have been drawn on the dolls hair with felt-tip pen. The doll has large blue eyes and a plump but narrow pink mouth formed in a pouting smile. The doll is wearing a short pink dress with a cheerleader style skirt. I hold the doll and inspect it saying: "she's gorgeous". Quoc Trinh smiles and nods. Suzi laughingly suggests to Quoc Trinh: "you should give her plaits!". Again, Quoc Trinh smiles and nods and, puts the miniature hair brush down on the table, goes back to his seat on the other side of the room. Vici, Suzi and I laugh as we experiment with the doll's hair. We plait it and then coil the plait into a cone around the doll's head. Vici laughs and shakes her head as she points out that glitter make-up has been put on the doll's face. We stand the doll on the desk.
[...]
    The teacher comes over to our table to check on progress and offer assistance. She notices the doll and says: "Can you put her away?" before moving on to the next table.
[...]
    HIEU (boy, Vietnamese), who has been sitting with Quoc Trinh comes over to our table. As he approaches he announces: "I've come for a visit!". He asks me: "What year are you in?". Vici and Suzi laugh and, before I can respond, Vici introduces me. Quoc Trinh and GREGG (boy, White) follow Hieu over to our table. Quoc Trinh picks up the doll and admires the hairstyle we have given her. He smiles and tells me: "her name is Chelsea Page". The teacher approaches and the boys go back to their desk leaving Chelsea Page behind. Vici takes Chelsea Page and her hairbrush over to Quoc Trinh and speaks briefly with him. Vici returns and, in mock earnestness, assures Suzi and I that Quoc Trinh is very pleased with the hairstyle we have given to Chelsea Page.
[...]
Quoc Trinh picks up Chelsea page. Holding her horizontally above his head he moves her around in a flying motion and makes a "Chhhh" rocket/aeroplane sound. Vici and Suzi observe this and exchange glances, chuckling and shaking their heads.

                                                                                                                    (Fieldnotes)

This episode represents the moment in which I was introduced to Quoc Trinh's constant companion – the miniature doll Chelsea Page. In prevailing discourses of masculinity, it is inappropriate, if not unintelligible, for a 16 year old boy to own a doll, keep it constantly with him, and regularly display and even celebrate this inside school. Yet this is exactly what Quoc Trinh does. In this discursive frame, the 'abnormalness', the 'madness', of Quoc Trinh's practices is striking. Yet Quoc Trinh is not simply 'abnormal' or 'mad', rather, his practices have the potential trouble the gendered and raced discourses that frame the student milieu without placing his acceptability as a learner or his good-ness as a student at serious risk.

Within the discourse of discrete and natural races that frames the context, a Vietnamese race identity potentially constitutes, and is constituted through, Quoc Trinh's lack of status within wide-reaching discourses of the Orient (Said 2003) and the specific Hierarchy within the Other that frames this student sub-culture. Similarly, the implicit exclusion of Asian students from both sides of the Dir'y 'ippie/Shaza and Baza binary suggests that Quoc Trinh might be constituted as other-Other within this minority student discourse of alternative marginality. Yet Quoc Trinh's discursive practices appear to effect some degree of recuperation of these multiple marginalisations. Indeed, it seems that his practices may effect at least a partial and provisional *re*inscription of these marginalisations and, therefore, *re*constitute him *again differently* as a subject who is at once intelligible and beyond intelligibility.

Quoc Trinh's practices seem to parody discursive constitutions both of the feminine and the feminised Asian man. His practices simultaneously transgress the bounds of appropriate and intelligible masculinity, itself constituted through the discursive opposition of masculine/feminine. Such parody and transgression might appear to pose significant risk to Quoc Trinh – he might be rendered unintelligible as a subject and/or he might be punished by his peers for his transgression. Yet, if the masculinity of hegemonic discourse is understood to be denied Quoc Trinh through an Orientalist discourse of the feminised Asian man, then transgressing the bounds of this does not risk Quoc Trinh's masculinity because it is a masculinity from which he is already debarred. Furthermore, his parody of the feminised Asian man can be seen to expose the constituted nature of this raced (un-)masculinity and, therefore, masculinities more broadly. Understood in this way, it seems that through his practices in relation to Chelsea Page, Quoc Trinh revels (at least tacitly) in breaching the limits of both this raced (un-) masculinity and hegemonic masculinity and exposing the constitutedness of these. In this sense, Quoc Trinh might be understood to mimic the marginalised raced and gendered subjectivity ascribed to him by and through hegemonic discourses and simultaneously redeploy these in order to *re*inscibe himself otherwise.

I was with Suzi and Vici, two of the Dir'y 'ippies encountered in chapter 9, when I met Chelsea Page. Quoc Trinh gave Chelsea Page to Suzi and Vici to play with and they were clearly already well acquainted. While my presence may have informed Quoc Trinh's choice of who to give Chelsea Page to on that particular occasion, these practices were a moment of repetition of ongoing practices. Quoc Trinh is one of the few non-White students in the year group who appears to be aligned (to some degree) with the Dir'y 'ippies. While Chapter 9 showed that a Dir'y 'ippie identity was synonymous with and masked middle class Whiteness, it seems that the emphasis placed on alternaeity by these students, particularly in respect to gender/sexuality, makes Quoc Trinh's practices potentially constitutive of a Dir'y 'ippie identity irrespective of his social class and race locations. Indeed, his Vietnamese-ness might, in its marginality, itself be potentially constitutive of D'iry ippie, despite the Orientalism implicit in this constitution. Yet Quoc Trinh also has alliances with many popular girls. On subsequent occasions I saw a number of these girls ask to play with Chelsea Page and, while Quoc Trinh did not always consent, the doll was frequently passed between groups of girls during lessons. In this way Quoc Trinh's practices might offer him a degree of movement between Dir'y 'ippie and mainstream student sub-cultures as well as social access to popular girls that might not usually be open to him.

This does not mean, however, that his practices somehow create a fissure within the Hierarchy within the Other and the 'schema of raced hetero-sex' (Youdell 2003) that this underpins. The schema of raced hetero-sex extrapolated (but not necessarily practiced) by students in the school appears to take up and invert a discourse of prohibited miscegenation that excludes the possibility of certain, but not all, inter-race couplings. This schema renders Black boys' ultra desirable and makes legitimates their relationships with Black, White and mixed race girls; it insists that Black girls are desired by all races but should restrict their relationships to Black boys, thereby protecting the location of both at the pinnacle of the Hierarchy within the Other; and denies South Asian and South East Asian girls and boys desirability to anyone other than a corresponding intra-race heterosexual partner. As might be expected from the schema, then, while Quoc Trinh's practices seem to facilitate his friendships with girls, they do not appear to constitute him as a legitimate sexual subject. Indeed, it is possible to suggest that while his parody of the feminised Asian (not-) man is troubling, it is also open to a recuperation that insists that Quoc Trinh (and Chelsea Page) is confirmation of the femininity with which Asian (un-) masculinity is inscribed within discourses of Orientalism. That is, in this discursive frame Quoc Trinh practices – playing with a doll – are explained by and constitutive of his lack of masculinity. This lack is constituted as a prior and natural fact of Asian-ness, and in opposition to (valorised) White hegemonic masculinity and (feared and desired) Black hyper-masculinity, and so positions Quoc Trinh as a legitimate friend but an impossible sexual subject.

While Quoc Trinh's practices transgress gender, sexual and racial boundaries and clearly trouble heterosexual masculinity and femininity, he does not appear to be explicitly censured for this. In exploring possible reasons for this apparent absence of censure it is useful to consider the ways in which Quoc Trinh's practices might be recuperated through the discourses of the mainstream student sub-culture.

Quoc Trinh is not (could not be) a popular 'known' boy. Nor is he like the White ordinary 'unknown' boys who called Steve 'wanker' in chapter 5 and, in doing so, asserted the superior value of their own masculinity. While Quoc Trinh appears to be almost universally popular amongst girls, this is not the case with boys. It seems that a small number of boys – Vietnamese and Dir'y 'ippie – are friends with Quoc Trinh and, as seen in the episode, ride on the wave of his access to girls. These boys' practices in the episode seem to deploy a strategy of proximity to, approval of and *difference from* Quoc Trinh. As such, these boys benefit from Quoc Trinh's practices without risking their own masculinities (such as they are).

Given the destabilising potential of Quoc Trinh's practices, it might be reasonable to expect those boys with the greatest investment in masculinity – the known boys – to explicitly censure Quoc Trinh. Yet known boys simply ignore Quoc Trinh. While such silence can, as argued in earlier chapters, act to performatively interpellate the subject in particular ways, the question of why Quoc Trinh is not explicitly censured for this behaviour seems to press on this analysis.

Within popular discourse, dolls are for children and, therefore, playing with dolls is childish. As such, Quoc Trinh potentially and inadvertently constitutes himself as infantile and so simultaneously his troubling of race and gender might easily be recuperated through an adult-masculine/child-feminine binary. If Quoc Trinh's practices can be recuperated through discourses that cite the feminine child, the intrinsic adult-ness of man and, therefore, the man/boy binary, it may be possible that his practices are not explicitly challenged, censured or punished because he is constituted within this discursive frame as *so* feminine as to pose no threat to masculinity. It may be possible that by being 'proof' that Quoc Trinh is a child (boy), his practices are simultaneously 'proof' that the known boys are adult (man). Such an infantilising and feminising recuperation may also insist that the known boys' masculinities would be risked if they were to censure, through verbal or physical violence, Quoc Trinh's practices. That is, the recuperation of Quoc Trinh's practices involves an implicit citation and inscription of a discourse of paternal masculinity in which the 'real' man is risked if he hits the woman, child or 'sissy'.

This would suggest that the known boys do not explicitly censure Quoc Trinh's practices in a tacit effort to protect against the potential threat to masculinity. Furthermore, it may be that Quoc Trinh's practices are *so* unintelligible within the discursive frames that bound identity constitutions within this context that Quoc Trinh is inaccessible to the known boys. That is, Quoc Trinh may constitute his place in *this* discourse as no place. He may refuse to respond to/be subjected by the constituting hail of masculinity and, in so doing, sacrifice his subjecthood within *this* discursive frame.

And yet, as his practices potentially sacrifice subjecthood within the discursive frame of the student sub-culture, his subjecthood as a student and learner appears to remain. Playing with a doll in class might be expected to also render Quoc Trinh beyond the bounds of the good student and the acceptable learner. And yet, as Quoc Trinh plays with Chelsea Page he is quiet and unobtrusive and, until Vici and Suzi call him over, he remains seated at his desk. That is, his 'feminine' mode of engagement with his 'girls'' toy does not breach the terms of good student beyond the fact that it is off-task. It might be imagined, then, that the teacher does not censure Quoc Trinh's practices because they are not taken as either disrupting the classroom or challenging the teacher's authority. Yet the teacher *does* censure Vici and Suzi for playing with Chelsea Page when the doll is simply lying discarded on the desk-top. This suggests that the teacher *does* take playing with the doll to be a breach of good student behaviour. That the teacher censures Vici and Suzi, and not Quoc Trinh, might simply reflect the moment at which she saw the doll. And yet it is also possible that Quoc Trinh's – a boy's – possession of and playing with a miniature doll is so far off-gender, so far beyond the bounds of intelligible gender discourse, that the teacher 'could not' intervene intelligibly until the doll was in the possession of the girls. To say that the teacher could not intervene does not mean that she was somehow prevented from intervening, but that for an intervention to be intelligible it had to be directed at girls – the 'proper' possessors of dolls. In this analysis, it is the unintelligibility of Quoc Trinh's practices of (un-)masculinity that protect him from censure from the teacher and so ensure his ongoing constitution as a good student and acceptable learner.

It is useful to compare Quoc Trinh's practices with those of Manny, another boy in the year group. While cooking alone during a Food Technology lesson that I observed, Manny, a White boy described by his teacher as having "special needs", accompanied his cooking by wandering/dancing around his kitchen area singing "I'm a Barbie girl, in a Barbie world..." – the chorus to the *Aqua* pop song which was in the charts during 1998. As he sang he imitated the accent, pitch and intonation of the woman singer in the group. Manny's practices, Like Quoc Trinh's, breach the boundaries of the masculine/feminine binary and might be expected to be met with ridicule and censure. Yet while "known" boys firmly ignored Quoc Trinh, they laughingly encouraged Manny's song and dance.

This reception might be explained through Manny's formal educational classification of special educational needs (SEN) (the precise diagnosis is unknown and it is unimportant here beyond what it might reveal about its likely constitutive effects). It seems that as the disciplinary technologies of the school formally categorise Manny as SEN and the students designate him the 'fool' or 'clown', the potentially disruptive performative force of his practices is minimised. If Manny is constituted as having no practical sense of appropriate bodily dispositions within the masculine/feminine binary then his practices can be disregarded – Manny 'doesn't know any better'. In this discursive frame Manny cites and inscribes his own SEN or 'fool' designation and his practices are rendered so unintelligible that they pose no threat and have no broader implications – he is beyond the bounds of gender discourse, he is an impossible subject.

Yet this constitution as an impossible subject is not absolute or final. Manny remains 'included' (in the version of inclusive education that is concerned with 'mainstreaming') in this comprehensive school, in its classrooms, and in (at least parts of) its curriculum – Manny is baking a cake as he sings. And students continue to engage with him, albeit in ways that are constitutive of his special-ness, of his location well beyond the normative centre. Manny may be unintelligible as a boy, but he remains a good student and, while his designation as SEN may threaten his viability as a learner, it does not seem to have rendered this impossible in this classroom.

Quoc Trinh and Manny are boys who play with or sing about dolls and who, in so doing, risk their constitution as boys and so their subjecthood. Nevertheless, Quoc Trinh and Manny remain intelligible subjects of sorts, despite their location beyond the bounds of the normative centre.

Despite the various possible recuperations of Quoc Trinh's practices, these retain the potential to trouble the normative centre and the prevailing discourses of race, gender and sexuality that underpin it, and Quoc Trinh may well have a practical sense of this trouble his practices cause. In troubling this normative centre, Quoc Trinh's practices have the potential to reconstitute his marginalised subjectivity differently, as something or someone else. But if Quoc Trinh is not a good-(un-)masculine-Vietnamese-student, what/who else might he be?

Manny may also have a practical sense of the potential impact of his practices, and he surely knows that these practices will be encouraged by his classmates. So while the song may be taken by its audience as a citation of and moment in Manny's SEN-ness, it remains an eruption within masculinity. Manny's SEN or 'fool' designation means that this masculinity is unavailable to him and constrains the performative reach of his practices, but this does not completely negate the effect of this performative eruption. Manny's student-hood and subjecthood remains and so does the gender trouble caused by his practices. Yet as a *special* student, can Manny also be boy or learner? And might a discursive context be imaginable in which he could be a boy-student-learner but *not* special?

CHAPTER 12

INTELLIGIBLE IMPOSSIBILITY:
THE (UN-)FEMININE SUBJECT-HOOD
OF A 'GEEZA-GIRL'

Chapter 11 explored the (un-)masculine subjectivities and student-hood of Manny and Quoc Trinh and asked whether these subjectivities might trouble hegemonic masculinities and/or whether Many or Quoc Trinh night be constituted in other ways, In this chapter the identity constellations that constitute viable subjecthood and viable student-hood in this school and sub-cultural context are again the focus as I explore the various constitutions of Molly, or "Geeza-Girl".

Molly's practices of (un-)femininity/masculinity might be expected to exclude her from the student sub-culture in ways similar to those seen for Quoc Trinh and Manny. Yet it seems that in an androcentric discursive frame 'girl doing boy' (tomboy not lesbian?) is acceptable in ways that 'boy doing girl' (the sissy, the homosexual, or the lady-boy) is not. As a White working class girl whose deviation from 'proper' gender orientates around footballing skill (as distinct from the 'strange' behaviours of Quoc Trinh and Manny) and who has the friendship (and so warrant) of Black girls (including Marcella from chapters 4 and 7) whose sub-cultural status is high, Molly is protected, perhaps unexpectedly given her practice, from being constituted as outside acceptable girl-hood.

Simultaneously, and again perhaps unexpectedly, Molly's friendship with Black girls who are constituted in school discourse as anti-school/a challenge to White hegemony does not constitute Molly a bad student or unacceptable learner. For Steve (chapter 5), Stuart (chapter 10), and Marcella, sub-cultural cool is inversely related to acceptability as a learner. This is not the case for Molly who unexpectedly constituted inside the student sub-culture, a good student and an acceptable learner, despite her practices of impossible masculinity and her proximity to blackness.

This is not a simple series of constitutions. The scenes analysed in this chapter represent three moments in the constitution of Molly's subjectivity. My analysis suggests that there is considerable ambiguity amongst students over the viability and legitimacy of Molly's (un-)femininity and this gendered subjectivity is contested and policed in ways that restrict Molly's access to both femininity and masculinity and maintain her on the margins of meaningful subjecthood. Yet Molly's constituting practices of self do trouble enduring constitutions of masculinity and femininity as well as their complementary opposition and natural discreteness. Through these practices Molly reinscribes the subjugated identity that is (tentatively and potentially) assigned to her and renders legitimate (at least partially and provisionally) a gender that is implicitly proscribed within hegemonic gender discourse.

Episode 13: Geeza-girl, scene 1
Taylor Comp, London, UK. During a discussion/interview with RICHARD, ROB,
JAMES, SIMON,CHRISTOPHER, DECLAN *(aged 15-16, boys, White).*

JAMES: Molly is like a ...
RICHARD: *(interrupting)* Geeza!
ALL: *(laugh).*
DY: Molly's what?
JAMES: *(laughing)* A geeza!
SIMON: *(laughing and curving his hands out over the front of his chest)* she's built like
a brick shit house!
ALL: *(laugh hysterically).*
RICHARD: *(laughing)* She's built like Sylvester Stallone!
ALL: *(laugh).*
DY: When you said "she's built like a brick shit house", the actions were like you were
talking about breasts.
ALL: *(laugh).*
JAMES: *(laughing)* She has got so much breast.
   (simultaneously) CHRISTOPHER: I would never argue with her, if she want
   something done I'd do it.
   (simultaneously) ALL: *(laughing uncontrollably).*
DY: Sorry, was I not suppose to point that out?
SIMON: *(laughing)* No, I mean she's like, big like *(juts elbows out to the side, clenches
fists in classic 'muscle-man' pose).*
ALL: *(interrupting, laugh hysterically).*
DY: You said she's built like a brick shit house and went...
SIMON: *(Interrupting and laughing so hard that he can barely speak)* No, I meant, I
meant to go like... *(repeats 'muscle-man' pose).*
ROB: She's a footballer, her legs are just like. .. *(laughing so hard that he can barely
speak)* ginormous, they make us look puny!
CHRISTOPHER: She plays football a lot, and when she takes a shot everyone just like
jumps out of the way, dives for cover!
DY: Does she play football with you lot?
JAMES: Used to.
RICHARD: She used to.
CHRISTOPHER: When she does, she was such a great player.
DY: Why doesn't she play football with you anymore?
CHRISTOPHER: She's hanging around with the girls more.
SIMON: She's realised she's not a boy.
RICHARD: She's turned more feminine.
[...]
CHRISTOPHER: As long as you're not in goal when she shoots.
ALL: *(laugh).*
CHRISTOPHER: *(laughing)* Feel sorry for whoever is.
RICHARD: She is a bit dangerous.
ROB: Yeah I know, I used to get...
RICHARD: *(interrupted)* Jump out the way.
CHRISTOPHER: Just kick the ball for your life.
ROB: Yeah Molly, oh dear, 'cos I got booted by the ball in the groin area once, it really
hurt.
DY: Off Molly's shot?
ROB: Molly's shot.

In scene 1 a group of boys (some of them the same boys who deployed the injury "wanker" in their constitution of masculinities in chapter 5) deploy a series of names that are potentially constitutive of Molly as a sexed and gendered subject. The boys name Molly "Geeza" (admired working class man) and "Sylvester Stallone" (actor turned generic for the macho hero), she is "built like a brick shit house" (literally outside toilet, colloquial for very well-built), her legs are "ginormous" and make these boys "look puny" (small and weak). These are not neutral namings. Within prevailing discourse, biological sex – male/female – is constituted as a natural opposition that exists in a linear and causal relationship with gender – masculinity/femininity. In the discursive frame of sex-gender[xxii], masculinity is active and physically powerful while femininity is passive and physically delicate. The boys' linguistic and bodily practices appear to constitute Molly's physical masculinity. Yet within the discursive frame of sex-gender Molly – a girl – *cannot* be masculine. These namings of Molly are impossible constitutions.

The boys also assert Molly's physical sex (her breasts) and her realisation that she "isn't a boy" – a sexing that forecloses her masculinity and demands her femininity. The boys' hilarity throughout the scene suggests that they have a practical sense of the impossibility of Molly's masculinity. Rather than being constitutive of Molly's masculinity, the boys' practices appear as injurious namings that potentially constitute Molly's lack of, unacceptable, or unintelligable femininity. Molly cannot be man or boy, but she is not appropriately girl or woman either and she is subject to censure for this.

Yet there is a degree of ambiguity within the boys' constituting censure of Molly. She is introduced into the discussion through being identified as a girl with whom the boys have a preferred friendship. Furthermore, and citing the discourse of the tomboy, the boys are respectful of Molly's footballing skills. Yet these concessions are not straightforward. Molly is identified as a friend but is accused of inconsistency within this friendship. While her football skills are praised, it seems that she is denigrated for being *too good* – a denigration which seems unlikely to be applied to a boy. Her football skills deserve respect but are simultaneously deployed in the ongoing constitution of her unacceptable femininity. Molly's masculinity is also a potential threat to the boys' own – on the football field and in thigh circumferences Molly's masculinity exceeds the boys own[xxiii]. This is a threat that appears to be protected against by simultaneously asserting Molly's masculinity, the impossibility of this and, therefore, transforming this into an unacceptable lack of femininity. In short, Molly has acted outside her place in discourse and implicitly threatened the boys' place. The boys' discursive practices tacitly attempt to recuperate this and return Molly to her 'proper' place.

However, the recuperating effect of the boys' discursive practices is by no means guaranteed. Indeed, it seems that the boys are in something of a quandary concerning Molly. Within the boys' discourse Molly is potentially constituted as at once masculine *and* feminine – an identity that hegemonic discourse suggests is an impossibility and which the boys' tacitly attempt to disavow. Is it possible that Molly's discursive practices effect an intelligible identity which is somewhere between, straddling or outside the man-masculine/woman-feminine binary?

Episode 13: Geeza-girl, scene 2
Taylor Comp, London, UK. During a discussion/interview with MOLLY *and* NICOLA
(age 15-16, girls, White), MOLLY *takes her school diary out of her bag and offers it to*
DY *to look at.* DY *flicks through to the 'Commendations' section at the back.*

DY: (*reading aloud from* Molly's *school diary*) Commendations: "For being very
masculine and for being a dedicated geeza, well done".
MOLLY: (*indicating* Nicola) That was her. She calls me that all the time, look:
(*indicating several other instances in her school diary and reading aloud*) "geeza".
    (*simultaneously*) Nicola: (*laughs*)
DY: How do you feel about that?
MOLLY: (*still reading*) "for being a school bod and for being the biggest and best
geeza-girl".
DY: How do you feel about being called that?
MOLLY: It doesn't really bother me, it doesn't really bother me.
DY: Do they think you should be more girlie?
MOLLY: But then I wouldn't be me would I? They do say stuff about wearing girls
clothes, I do out of school, but not in school.
NICOLA: (*shrieking*) I've seen her wearing her bridesmaid's dress!
MOLLY: See, it's a big thing.
    (*simultaneously*) NICOLA: (*laughs*)
NICOLA: It depends on if she likes the attention or not. Even what Molly wears, she
don't care what anyone else says.
MOLLY: Just cos I play football and, OK, I'm kinda big, but I don't get it, they've been
doing it for years now, 5 years now, all the boys used to do it really bad.
NICOLA: (*laughing*) But you shut em up!
MOLLY: No, but they just don't give a toss anymore. But I don't care. She still calls
me it.

In scene 2 the 'commendations' that students have written in Molly's school
diary – their textual performative practices – are repeated and discussed. Molly has
been called – "masculine", "geeza", "school bod", "geeza-girl". The boys' namings
in scene 1, then, are not isolated potential constitutions. Rather, Molly's (un-)
femininity-/masculinity is constituted through citational chains that suffuse the
student milieu and which are reported to have endured throughout her time in the
school. Within the scene it appears that these are names that have injured Molly in
the past and, despite her assertion that she is "not bothered", continue to at least
confuse her. Yet Molly is not named in these ways by students with whom she has
conflictual relationships. The boys identify Molly as a friend and Nicola, who is the
author of many of the 'commendations' being discussed in scene 2, has a very close
friendship with Molly.

In scene 1 the boys offer Molly's body – her stature, strength and physical skill –
as 'evidence' of her (un-)femininity-/masculinity. In scene 2 it appears that Molly is
well aware that playing football and being "kinda big"[xxiv] are deployed by other
students as 'evidence' of her (un-)femininity-/masculinity. Within popular discourse
football is constituted as a pursuit of boys and men, and this scene unfolds prior
to the global success of the girls' footballing film *Bend it like Beckham* and the
popular take-up in the UK of the notion of the 'ladette'. And despite these more
recent inclusions of girls in football, it remains the domain of men, a constitution
that cites and inscribes discourses of physical strength and mastery and is, in turn,
constitutive of masculinity. In this discursive frame physical size is also sexed and

gendered. Constituted by and constitutive of the man/woman binary, man is physically big (and strong) while woman is physically small (and delicate).

In scene 2 the way that Molly dresses is added to the bodily 'evidence' of her (un-)femininity-/masculinity. Molly suggests that other students think she should wear "girls' clothes", a suggestion that inscribes clothing as intrinsically differentiated by gender and infers that, in the context of this differentiation, Molly wears 'boys'' clothes[xxv]. Molly seems to be in a double bind here. Her usual clothes are deployed as (constituting) evidence of her (un-)femininity-/masculinity. Yet when these clothes are contrasted with that most feminine of garments—the bridesmaid dress – this is worthy of comment and a source of hilarity for Nicola. Molly's assertion that she "wouldn't be me" if she dressed otherwise infers that she and other students have a practical sense of the potential performative force of such bodily practices and that they subscribe tacitly to a Cartesian model of the essential, enduring and self-knowing subject. Even as Molly is pressured to wear "girls' clothes", then, the comment and hilarity when she does so highlights the endurance of Molly's bodily performatives and the unintelligibility of her doing/being otherwise. In turn, this suggests that girls' clothes might not be appropriate attire for Molly – femininity might not be her 'proper' place after all. Indeed, the contradiction and ambiguity around how Molly 'should' dress might suggest that her subjectivity is constituted through and constitutive of a possible fissure within the discourse of sex-gender.

Molly does not concede these potentially performative constitutions of her (un-)femininity-/masculinity, asserting "I don't get it". Molly might not adhere to these discursive imperatives of sedimented and enduring sex-gender discourse, but it is almost certain that she is well aware of these. Indeed, the discussion represented in scene 2 is itself illustrative of Molly's awareness. It is possible, however, that Molly does not "get" quite *how* she transgresses these imperatives. Her body and mode of dress is not markedly different from those of many other girls. Indeed, apart from her exceptional footballing skill, Molly's 'difference' seems almost intangible. Could it be subtle and almost inscrutable 'differences' in the dispositions of her discursively formed and formative bodily *habitus* that underpin this (un-)femininity-/masculinity? Are these made accessible and intelligible by being attributed to her footballing, her stature and her clothes?

When Nicola claims that Molly "don't care" what she is called by the boys and asserts that Molly has "shut them up" (inferring actual or threatened physical violence) she (gleefully) contributes to the ongoing constitution of Molly's (un-)femininity-/masculinity. Nicola implicitly cites and inscribes a hegemonic discourse of binary sex-gender in which the absence of emotional sensitivity to name calling and the capacity for physical violence are positioned as masculine. But as I discussed earlier, the discourse of sex-gender excludes the possibility of Molly being masculine. Nevertheless, Nicola is identified here as the author (but not the originator) of the name "Geeza-girl" – a name that appears to have some enduring performative force.

Geeza-girl is potentially constitutive of Molly's (un-)femininity-/masculinity. At the same time, however, geeza and girl are incommensurable within the prevailing discourse that positions geeza (man) on one side of the sex-gender binary and girl on the other side. Yet geeza does not supersede girl here. Rather Nicola hyphenates these terms and deploys this sutured geeza and girl to name a single subject (rather than dual, opposing subjects). This suggests that these terms might not be as mutually exclusive as they appear within prevailing discourse. Through the interpellation of Molly as "Geeza-girl" a fissure within the sex-gender binary becomes evident. If Molly can be (is) Geeza-girl, then could it be that the relationship between sex and gender is not quite as linear and causal as it appears? Could it be that female sex and masculine gender are not as incommensurable as prevailing discourse constitutes them? Furthermore, if Molly can be (is) Geeza-Girl then could other subjects can also transgress the sex-gender binary?

In scene 2, as in scene 1, Molly is performatively constituted (un-)feminine-/masculine and the potential for this to be an injury persists. But these performative names simultaneously problematise the givenness of the binary oppositions that Molly is constituted as having transgressed, exceeded or troubled. Geeza-girl is constituted through and constitutive of a fissure in the prevailing discourse of binary sex-gender.

Episode 13: Geeza-girl, scene 3
Taylor Comp, London, UK. Standing in a ragged line in the corridor outside the tutor room before a PHSE lesson. MOLLY walks up behind NICOLA and wraps her arms around her upper torso restraining her arms. Without looking around to see the face of her assailant, Nicola giggles and exclaims: "Molly!". Molly laughs and loosens her hold, allowing Nicola to almost wriggle free. Nicola turns so that she is sideways on to Molly and tries to take hold of Molly's wrists. Nicola giggles, squeals and exclaims: "Molly!" and Molly chuckles. They continue to grapple in this way until Molly again takes hold of Nicola from behind and laughs. Nicola lets her arms drop to her sides. They stand in this restraining embrace for a few moments. As Molly lets go they both smile and laugh.

(Fieldnotes)

Scene 3 represents a sequence of bodily practices that contribute to the constitution of Molly as Geeza-girl. These practices also trouble the sex-gender binary while simultaneously contributing to the constitution of masculinity and femininity as discreet, oppositional and complementary. Physical contact between girls is commonplace within the student sub-culture, yet the physical contact between Molly and Nicola represented in Scene 3 seems to diverge from the everyday bodily practices of girls that tends to cite and inscribe discourses of the cohesive and consensual nature of girls' friendships as well as feminine bodily practices of caring, comforting and nurturing.

It seems that Molly's bodily practices in Scene 3 cite and inscribe her physical strength and mastery – her masculinity. On the other hand, Nicola's bodily practices cite and inscribe her physical weakness and passivity as well as her (half-hearted/feigned) resistance to this masculine strength and mastery – her desirable femininity. As such, Molly and Nicola's bodily practices cite and inscribe heterosexual masculinity and femininity and the oppositional relationship between these *at the same time* as they trouble the givenness of masculinity and femininity and their correspondence to male and female[xxvi].

These analyses suggest that Molly is constituted in a way that hegemonic discourse suggests 'should' be unintelligible but which, nevertheless, appears viable within this context. Through censure and attempted recuperations, students attempt tacitly to return Molly to her 'proper' place in discourse – femininity. Yet, these practices often seem to misfire and *contribute to*, rather than disavow, the ongoing constitution of Molly as intelligibly (un-)feminine-/masculine. Indeed, in this specific context and in relation to this specific student, this (un-)femininity-/masculinity appears to have such enduring performative force that it appears to have become Molly's 'proper' place. Molly exceeds authorised femininity, so much so that it seems that it is within these terms that Molly might be rendered an unintelligible subject. The discursive practices represented within the episode appear to expropriate masculinity and constitute an intelligible *un*femininity. In doing this, the constitutedness of masculinity and femininity; binary sex; binary gender; and the linear and causal relationships between sex and gender are exposed. In the discursive frame of the student milieu Molly causes sex-gender trouble.

While these constitutions do not speak of Molly's relationships with teachers and schooling, she is friendly and cooperative, without being so compliant as to be constituted a "bod" and so is constituted a good (enough) student and an acceptable learner. Her close friendship with Marcella, one of the Black girls whose Black-street-sub-cultural status was shown to be incommensurable with the good student in chapter 7, might be expected to also constitute Molly as outside the bounds of the good student. However, this is not the case – Molly remains popular with school staff and students alike. Could it be that it is Molly's exceptionality, her status as an exemplar that allows her to sit between being a good and a bad student, just as she sits between masculinity and girl-hood?

CHAPTER 13

GOOD STUDENTS, ACCEPTABLE LEARNERS, INTELLIGIBLE GIRLS: CLASS, RACE, GENDER, SEXUALITY AND THE ADORNMENT OF FEMININE BODIES

Preceding chapters have demonstrated the inseparability of student and learner identities and subjectivities marked by race, class, gender, sexuality, disability and other categorical identities. In this chapter I explore how raced and classed femininities as well as students and learners identities are constituted through the bodily adornments, especially styles of dress, of the Taylor girls at an end of school awards ceremony ('NRA Day'),

The privilege of middle class Whiteness and its all but automatic equivalence with good student and ideal learner is again evident as "Dir'y 'ippies" engage in hyperbolic enactments of femininity or even female drag. The normative hetero-sexual femininities (whether virgin or whore) of White working class girls and their entanglement of these femininities with good(ish) student and acceptable (but unimpressive) learner identities is demonstrated. And the group of Black and mixed race girls whose sub-cultural cache was constituted through their dance in the Leaving Day Show (chapter 7), are seen engaging bodily and symbolic practices that have the potential to constitute them not as high-status Black girls and bad students, but as respectable Black girls and good students.

On 'National Record of Achievement Day' (NRA Day) parents and families are added to the multiple student and teacher audiences in the school. NRA Day is a formal occasion that cites the Speech Day of the prestigious grammar school. As such, it is an event dominated by the school organisation. Nevertheless, NRA Day does take on an unofficial, secondary function for many (if not all) girls. Through clothing and adornments (the subjects of much discussion in the preceding weeks and even months) the event becomes a fashion gala. The outfits represented in the episode that follows indicate both the differences between and continuities across girls' bodily practices of femininities.

When exploring clothing as potentially performative bodily practices, it is important to bear in mind a number of practicalities that are likely to have some influence on them. For instance, when shopping for an NRA Day outfit girls are likely to have been constrained (to varying degrees) by the cost, durability and transferability of a particular outfit or garment. Parental consent/permission for particular clothing to be bought and/or worn for the event may also have been an issue for some girls. In addition, girls' personal 'taste' and 'style', as well as that of their friends/family, is undoubtedly a key influence on these outfits. While this may seem a banal point, understanding such 'taste' and 'style' as *citational and constitutive of dispositions of a performative bodily habitus* suggests that these NRA Day outfits are potentially constitutive of particular sorts of subjects (see also Youdell 2005).

Clothes are not neutral items that are imbued with meaning only when they enclose the body of a wearer (Barthes 1967). The observer sees the cut and quality of the cloth, the style of the garment, the material and design of the jewellery. In a glance gender, class, race, sexuality is seen and constituted. This is the mundane, routine, everyday practice of the ongoing constitution of subjectivities. The subject who clothes his/her body has at least a tacit, practical sense of the potential performative force of the observer's mediations. The girls in the episode know that their clothes and bodily adornments are potentially constitutive of who they are. These constitutions are not simply imposed by an audience. The performative bodily *habitus* of the wearer also mediates and brings meaning to clothes. In addition, the wearer has intent, albeit discursively constrained, and can seek to constitute him/herself in particular ways through his/her bodily adornments. My representation and analysis here, then, attempts to access and convey a layer of bodily practice that is often taken to be so obvious that it goes unexamined, or so impolite that it goes un-commented.

My representations of girls' NRA Day outfits within the episode and the analysis that follows runs the risk of appearing judgmental; citing and deploying caricatures and stereotypes; and inscribing particular gendered subjectivities. Yet these are judgments, citations, deployments and inscriptions that are made, often unintentionally and tacitly, on an ongoing basis. Without them the subject is inaccessible (*not* a subject). These practices contribute to 'who' and 'what' the subject is and are an integral part of the discursive practices through which identities are constituted.

Episode 14: Adorning bodies
Taylor Comp, London, UK, The main hall, National Record of Achievement Day,
Participants: Students (age 15-16), form tutors, Head of Year, Headteacher.
Audience: Parents/carers, family members, guests (including DY)

A low level platform is against the centre of one wall. Above it hangs a painted banner which read "All the Best for the Future, Class of 98". The HEADTEACHER, who is the keynote speaker, is seated on the platform behind a cloth draped table. The MUSIC TEACHER is seated at a piano. The HEAD OF YEAR, who is hosting, sits on a stool in the middle of the platform. At his side are JASMINE and NATASHA who are assisting the HEAD OF YEAR in hosting the event. Flanking each side of the platform and facing in towards it, each TUTOR GROUP is seated together with their FORM TUTOR. The AUDIENCE of parents/carers, family members and other guests are seated facing the platform and rows of students.

The main event is the presentation of NRA folders. Each form (roll) tutor goes onto the platform in turn to present the folders to their tutor (roll) group members. The head of year calls out the name of each individual student. As their names are called, students rise from their seats and walk up onto the platform. They shake hands with their form tutor and are handed their NRA folders. Some students plant a hesitant kiss on the cheek of their tutor. Women teachers are kissed by both girls and boys. Men are kissed only by girls. Having been handed their NRA folders students return to their seats. In sum, students are required to sit, walk, shake, accept, walk, sit. This process is repeated for almost every member of the year group which includes more than 200 students. There is persistent polite applause throughout this process.

Outfits

1. Bridget, Pipa, Suzi, Vici (White, middle-class, high achievers, "Dir'y 'ippies")
Evening dresses. To the floor (occasionally mid-knee) contour skimming bit not skin tight. Bootlace shoulder straps and cleavage. Metallics, negligee synthetics and lace, velour. Black, inky blue, sliver. Tyre-soled or high heeled platform sandals. Chokers, leather corded pendants, and a feather boa. Expensive and high quality fabric and manufacture -- top end of the high street or small label designer/boutique.

2. Annie, Diane, Molly, Mridula, Lucy, Su Lin (White, Indian, Chinese, working-class, ordinary and high status)
Mix and match separates. Fitted jacket over skinny rib vest worn with bootleg pants or mid thigh straight, or kick pleat skirt. Variations on high heeled strappy sandals (except Molly in boots). Gold hoop earrings, fine or chunky twist/link gold chains, gold pendants especially initials and names in script, gold rings often sovereigns. White, grey and pastel blue, pink, lemon. Inexpensive and low quality fabric and manufacture -- bottom end of the high street or mass produced for the market.

3. Juliet, Nicola, Sarah (Mixed-race, White, working-class, high status, named 'Shazas" by the "Dir'y 'ippies")
Mix and match separates and one pieces. Tight fitting mini dresses or skirts. Stretch and/or see-through fabric. Skinny rib tops or uppers with cleavage. Black, white and brights. Variations on high heeled strappy sandals. Gold hoop earrings, fine or chunky twist/link gold chains, gold pendants especially initials and names in script, gold rings often sovereigns. Inexpensive and low quality fabric and manufacture -- bottom end of the high street or mass produced for the market.

4. Marcella, Naomi, Marcia (Black, working-class, high status)
Two and three piece tailored suits. Long line jackets with skirt to top of knee. Mid chest square or diagonal neckline. Ivory or cream. Alternatively, tailored separates long line jacket and trousers. Brights. Flat heeled black leather fashion court shoes. Quality heavy cotton/linen/silk. Department store, bridal, hand tailored.

(Fieldnotes and photos)

The outfits of the first group of girls can be understood as *costumes*; an ironic masquerade of the ultra-feminine prom queen. As such these costumes are a moment in the constitution of Dir'y 'ippie as an alternative, marginal and anti-school identity and exposure of the constitutedness of femininity[xxvii]. As in chapter 9, however, the relative privilege of the girls' race and social class is also evident. The cultural capital and practical sense of the discursive markets of NRA Day that enables this masquerade; the obvious high quality and cost of the outfits; and the confident and entitled sashay with which these girls mount the stage to collect their "best in subject" awards as well as their NRA folders, are made possible by, cite and inscribe these girls' middle class Whiteness and their concomitant constitution as good students and ideal learners *despite*, and perhaps even because of, this masquerade. While the masquerade constitutes Dir'y 'ippie and troubles the naturalness of femininity, it simultaneously exposes these girls as the "bods" and "boffins" that the Shazas and Bazas always said they were.

The outfits of the second and third group of girls cite and inscribe the heterosexual femininities constituted through the discourse of the virgin/whore binary (see Youdell 2005a). The attire of the second group cites the office job interview, the registry office wedding, the family function. These clothed bodies (potentially and provisionally) performatively constitute a conservative, passive, subdued, oblique heterosexual femininity – the virgin, and even the unknown girl. These are good girls and good students in transit to good young adult femininity, replacing childish a-sexuality with modesty and sexual restraint.

The outfits of the third group cite the pub, the nightclub and the party. These clothed bodies (potentially and provisionally) performatively constitute an overtly (hetero-)sexualised desirable femininity – the known girl, the slapper, and even the whore. These are adult and sexualised femininities that are incommensurable with the childish a-sexuality of the good student and the study-focused priorities of the ideal learner. It seems that the third groups of girls might want to constitute themselves as the prom queen that the Dir'y 'ippies masquerade so effortlessly. Yet if these girls were given the money that the middle class girls spent on their NRA Day costumes, it is unlikely that they would come up with the same outfits. These girls do not have the bodily dispositions and discursive capitals to choose them. If they were handed Bridget, Pipa, Suzi and Vici's dresses to wear it is unlikely that they would wear them in the same way. These girls do not have the bodily dispositions and discursive capitals to sashay onto the stage in this formal, school dominated and public context. The evident (relatively) low quality and cost of the clothes worn by the girls in the second and third groups exposes their working class status, or even poverty. This contrasts with the ample and often copious amounts of gold jewellery that these girls have worn to school every day – a persistent assertion of their (relative) affluence within this working class milieu. While these outfits potentially constitute these girls as women, they also expose them as the Shazas that the Dir'y 'ippies said they were.

The outfits of the fourth group of girls – Marcella, Naomi and Marcia – might be expected to explicitly reflect their practices self seen on Leaving Day in chapter 7. That this is not the case underlines the contextual specificity of such constitutive practices of bodily adornment. It also underlines the ongoing constitution of subjectivities; the multiplicity of the subject's bodily dispositions; and the subject's deployment of his/her practical sense of multiple markets and the relative values of capitals within them. On NRA Day the girls are not the high status cool Black girls (and bad students) they were on Leaving Day, and this being otherwise exposes the constitutedness of these subjectivities and of subjectivities in general.

This is also a moment in the citation, inscription and *re*inscription of students and learners. Like their participation in the Leaving Day show, the dress of Marcella, Naomi and Marcia for the National Record of Achievement Day ceremony might suggest that they have finally acquiesced to the school's values and are attempting to constitute themselves, at this last moment, as the ideal student. While this might be the case, it is also a moment of resistance to the constitution of the Black challenge to White hegemony in general and the girls' unacceptability as learners in particular. As such, it is moment in which good and bad students and ideal, acceptable and unacceptable learners might be *re*inscribed *again differently*.

In contrast with the Leaving Day Show of chapter 7, these girls' bodily practices here assert their overt respect for the event (a respect perhaps not shown by the first and third groups of girls) and their willingness to go to considerable expense and effort for it. The styling and obvious high quality and cost of their attire cites and inscribes respectability, and the conservatism and affluence that are constituent parts of this in mainstream discourse. In this way it cites the well-dressed Black woman migrant alighting at the docks during the post-war wave of immigration from the Caribbean. Or, indeed, the same women gathered for Protestant worship, inscribing in turn Black Christianity and concomitant respectability. In this way the girls' clothing seems to be imbued with the historicity of colonialism and slavery, the sedimented meanings of Blackness that cite colonial discourses of Blackness, and Black communities' responses to and resistances of these. The girls' attire, then, is potentially performative of Black respectability, affluence, conservatism, religiosity *and* resistance. That is, it might be understood as a final attempt (whether tacit or conscious) to simultaneously resist the school's constitution of the Black challenge to White hegemony (to convince the school that it has misjudged them) and to potentially *reconstitute themselves *again differently* as Black *and* good students and ideal learners. At the same time, the girls bodily practice here might be understood as a display of the group's solidarity and a celebration of their collective and individual literal survival of the school institution and its embedded, business-as-usual, everyday racism.

The prevailing institutional discourses that frame this context mean that the success of such performative reinscriptions cannot be guaranteed and is may well be fleeting or not work at all. The need for the girls to jettison the Black sub-cultural cool of Leaving Day in order to enhance the likely performative force of their good-student-desirable learners of NRA Day indicates the potential costs of this *re*inscription. As well as the sedimented meanings of the discourses that frame the school context – what would need to happen for these girls to be Black-sub-cultural-cool *and* good students and desirable learners?

CHAPTER 14

BETWEEN GOOD AND BAD STUDENT, BETWEEN ACCEPTABLE AND UNACCEPTABLE LEARNER

Preceding chapters have been concerned with the way that discursive and bodily practices constitute young people in terms of sex, gender, sexuality, race, ability and social class categories that are more or less commensurable with institutional discourses of the good student and ideal learner. One key set of assertions that I have made is that constitutions of (certain White but perhaps all Black) heterosexual masculinity may be fundamentally at odds with school constitutions of the ideal student. Conversely, even when prevailing constitutions of (White) femininity are privileged over institutional requirements of student conduct, this does not appear to preclude girls from being constituted as acceptable students within school discourse. That is, my analyses have suggested that particular discourses of femininity and masculinity respectively may be intrinsically within and beyond the bounds of the good student and the acceptable learner. In the light of this suggestion, it becomes crucial to understand further how sex-gender constitutions interact with school discourses of the acceptable and unacceptable student. This is crucial, first, because it enables better understanding of the processes through which particular groups of students come to be excluded from the project of schooling and, second, because it facilitates consideration of how these exclusions might be interrupted.

This final chapter of part 4, then, explores how desirable hetero- femininities and masculinities that are high-status in the student sub-culture come to be constituted in a Science classroom as commensurate with the good student and acceptable learner. Such a constitution might be unexpected or unlikely if the relationship between ideal student/learner and sub-cultural status is imagined as simply inverse. The chapter shows, however, how these discursive domains are navigated in the everyday in ways that allow desirable hetero- femininities and masculinities to be constituted through practices that simultaneously constitute good(ish) students and acceptable (but not ideal) learners. These navigations show that educational and sub-cultural inclusions are not mutually exclusive, even if the possibilities for simultaneous inclusion are constrained.

Episode 15, Flirting and working
Taylor Comp, London, UK. Science Lesson, 'mixed ability' students aged 15-16.

MATT (boy, south east Asian) walks over to the table where JULIET (girl, Mixed-race), JOLENE (girl, White), MRIDULA (girl, Indian) and DY (woman, White) are sitting. Matt holds out a splint and says: "Can I get a light?" and nods towards the Bunsen burner. In unison, Juliet and Mridula say: "No!". Matt lights the splint saying: "Too late!". Juliet and Mridula simultaneously blow out the splint, look at each other, then look at Matt and laugh. Matt smiles and shakes his head as he walks away. Juliet

chuckles and says: "Mrid!". Mridula laughs and protests: "It was you!". Later in the
lesson Juliet is copying the results of the lesson's experiment out of Mridula's book
when Nat (boy, White) calls to her asking to borrow a rubber. Juliet doesn't look up at
him, with her eyes still on her work she picks up Jolene's (who has gone to see the
school counselor) rubber and throws it to Nat. Nat uses it. A few moments later the
rubber lands back on the table by Juliet's arm. She looks at the rubber and glances
disdainfully at Nat. Around five minutes later, without any verbal or non-verbal prompt
apparent and again without looking up from her work, Juliet pick's up the rubber and
throws it to Nat. Nat uses it. The rubber lands back on the table. Mridula watches this
silent exchange and lets out a small laugh. Juliet does not acknowledge Mridula's laugh.

(Fieldnotes)

Matt and Nat's practices cite and constitute a particular sub-cultural masculinity
that is irreverent to school norms while participating in educational processes and
that prioritises (implicitly sexual) engagement with (particular) girls. Juliet's
practices cite and constitute a desirable heterosexual femininity whose marginally
positive educational orientation facilitates its effortless fulfilment of the needs of
boys (men?) whose heterosexual masculinity is renders them worthy of such
services. These heterosexual masculinities and femininities are mutually constitutive
– by seeking Juliet's services the boys cite and inscribe her desirable heterosexual
femininity, and by refusing and/or consenting to fulfil these requests, Juliet cites and
inscribes the relative success of these boys' heterosexual masculinities. Mridula
(who was barred from desirable hetero-femininity in chapter 10) practices in ways
that augment Juliet's desirable femininity and suggest Mridula has access (at least in
some moments) to a legitimate femininity in the student sub-culture through her
friendship with Juliet.

Juliet and Mridula tell Matt he cannot light his wooden splint and blow it out
when he does light it – they are engaged in a playful battle over whether or not Matt
can use the girls' bunsen burner. It seems unlikely that the girls expect or intend
their "NO!" to be heeded, or that their blowing out of the splint is a display of
indignation at their refusal being ignored. When the girls playfully chastise and
blame each other, this is for refusing to service Matt *and* for flirting with him, and
this refusing to service, flirting, and chastising are all constituted as being highly
inappropriate *and* appropriate to desirable femininity. Juliet and Mridula's refusal
does not actually prevent Matt from lighting his splint. While feminine consent is
sought, the refusal can be ignored or taken as having been given – For Matt, their
"NO!" means 'yes' and, if the girls did not intend their "NO!" to be obeyed, then in
this context Matt may be right. The simultaneity of the girls' "NO!" and blowing out
of Matt's splint, their laughter and Matt's smiling and shaking his head (the paternal,
adult man allowing the girls to have their fun?) suggest that this is a well practised,
perhaps even ritualised, bodily and linguistic sequence – these students may well go
through this every science lesson. Rather than contest the desirable heterosexual
femininity that is constituted, in part, through attending to male needs, then, the
girls' laughing refusal to serve in fact inscribes this service as a constitutive element
of desirable heterosexual femininity. And all of these constitutions of desirable
hetero- femininity and masculinity are effected through these students engaging in
the required classroom activity of preparing a Science experiment. Flirting over
schoolwork means that they are certainly not ideal learners, but they are acceptable
students and learners

The minutiae of the apparently mundane practices through which Juliet's femininity is constituted as being not just desirable, but *ultra-desirable*, and the way that Mridula's practices augment this constitution, are evidenced in Juliet's lending of Jolene's rubber. On the surface Juliet's bodily practices infer that Nat's request is an unwanted and inconvenient interruption to her schoolwork. Yet schoolwork seems to be a low priority for Juliet; she has avoided working throughout the lesson and is copying the results of the lesson's experiment out of Mridula's book when Nat makes his request. As such, the way that Juliet responds to Nat seems to have little to do with a desire to work uninterrupted, but does contribute to her constitution as a good(ish) student. The first time that Juliet lends Jolene's rubber she picks it up throws it without looking up from her book. By doing this Juliet's bodily practices suggest that Nat and his needs are of no importance to her, that attending to them is beneath her, but that she is able meet these needs effortlessly. The accuracy of the throw, however, suggests a degree of effort.

Nat, his needs, and her ability to meet them *are* important to Juliet – citing and constituting her effortless fulfilment of Nat's needs and, therefore, her ultra-desirable femininity, the throw would be worthless or even damaging if it missed. The second time that Juliet lends Jolene's rubber she does so without any apparent cue that Nat needs it. The attunement to Nat's needs inferred by this is further citation and inscription of Juliet's ultra-desirable heterosexual femininity – it suggests that she has an intuitive knowledge of Nat's needs and is able effortlessly to fulfil them without being asked. As well as constituting her own ultra-desirable femininity, Juliet's provision of services to Nat is constitutive of his successful heterosexual masculinity. While Juliet ostensibly refused the request for services from Matt, she responds positively to, and even fore sees, the needs of Nat.

Throwing the rubber, at the right time and in the right way is not the natural, effortless and insignificant act which Juliet's body suggests it to be. These practices appear as natural and effortless indicators of Juliet's ultra-desirable femininity. But rather than simply narrating this femininity, these practices cite and inscribe it. Constituted as natural and effortless, this femininity must elide the effort entailed in its constitution – it must appear natural, effortless and integral in order to be ultra-desirable, to be 'truly' feminine.

Mridula and I are enthralled by this encounter – Juliet's bodily exchange is with Nat, but me, Mridula, and the boys at Nat's table are also audience here and our appreciation contributes to the performative force of her practices. The boys' appreciation is constitutive of their masculinity. Similarly, Mridula's and my own appreciation is constitutive of our femininity as well as the impossibility of our being ultra-desirable in this context. Juliet does not acknowledge Mridula's appreciative laugh. She cannot – the appearance that nothing noteworthy has taken place is intrinsic to the ultra-desirable femininity that is cited and constituted through her practices. And it is far more effective than hovering at the boys' table.

When Matt lights his splint from Juliet and Mridula's bunsen burner rather than the teacher's, then, he simultaneously constitutes successful heterosexual masculinity and a studenthood at the boarder of the acceptable learner. Successful heterosexual masculinity is constituted through those practices that inscribe Matt's desire and capacity to engage with and get what he wants from the girls. Studenthood at the border of acceptability is constituted through those practices that inscribe both Matt's relative disregard for the teacher's instruction, and by extension his indifferent orientation to the school, and his compliance and participation in the lesson. Nat's lack of a rubber, that is, his failure to be properly equipped for school, and his borrowing from Juliet can be similarly understood as constitutive of successful heterosexual masculinity (Nat receives the ministrations of Juliet) and borderline acceptability as a student (Nat engages in the set work but is not a diligent and well prepared student). Juliet's location with friends who undertake the set work and are equipped for class and her minimal participation in the set task and copying of results suggest a negative orientation to school but a marginally positive orientation to education. Like the boys, these practices are constitutive of a learner identity at the border of acceptability. Juliet's refusal of Matt's request and apparently disdainful fulfilment of Nat's are constitutive of successful heterosexual femininity, a femininity that deploys marginally acceptable *studenthood* in order to first be asked for services by the boys and, second, to be in a position to provide (or withhold) these.

It is evident that the desirable hetero- masculinities and femininities at stake here are the students' prime concern, whether this concern is implicit or explicit. However, their practices also deploy and constitute particular sorts of students and learners: in constituting themselves and each other within the terms of desirable hetero- masculinity and femininity, Matt, Nat, and Juliet also constitute themselves at the fringes of acceptable *studenthood*. These student-learners are far from the ideal, but they remain acceptable and are not excluded from the educational process.

If these students can be simultaneously desirable hetero-subjects and acceptable learners, might other students subjectivated in ways that exclude them from educational processes also come to be constituted as good students and acceptable learners? Might Steve be adult-hyper-masculine *and* good-student and acceptable learner? How about Phil and Trent? Julie? Luke? Naomi and Marcella?

PART 5: INTERRUPTING EXCLUSIONS

This book has shown how subjects are constituted in the routine and everyday practices of schooling and how these discursive processes of subjectivation are implicated in including some students in the educational endeavour and excluding other students from this. At the same time, the book has recognised and illustrated how students' own concerns and priorities, as these are played out through practices of self, can be divergent to, or at odds with, those of the school. Such divergences mean that as students are constituted inside certain social and sub-cultural identities they are simultaneously constituted outside student and/or learner identities. This is not to suggest, however, a straightforward inverse relationship between school and sub-cultural values. Rather, the book has shown how discursively constituted subjects deploy discourses that render them at once inside both school and sub-cultural discourses and, therefore, subjectivities. Furthermore, the book has shown how constitutions of bad student and unacceptable learner identities are neither constant nor simply taken up. Students have been shown to resist such constitutions and to deploy discourse to constitute themselves *again differently*. That is, students have been shown to act with discursive agency and deploy performative politics.

In the final chapter of the book, then, I will revisit key arguments made over the course of the book in order to explore the significance of these analyses for thinking about the pragmatics of how a performative politics might be put to work in pursuit of a reconfigured inclusive education.

CHAPTER 15

PRACTICING PERFORMATIVE POLITICS FOR INCLUSIVE EDUCATION

INTRODUCTION

I opened this book by setting out my underpinning concern for social justice in education and the constancy with which educational inequalities and exclusions appear to be marked by an array, or more precisely *constellations*, of categorical identities. With this concern, I set out to offer further insight into the processes through which educational inequalities and exclusions come to be entangled with particular constellations of identities and how the day-to-day practices of schooling are implicated in this.

In attempting to address these concerns, I have worked with a selection of theoretical tools for understanding how subjects come to be, and brought these together with methodological tools in order to develop appropriate ways of researching, representing and analyzing these issues. By using these theoretical and methodological tools to guide ethnography in two distinct but related contexts – London, UK and Sydney, Australia – I have been able to demonstrate the cross-national utility of these tools at the same time as making connections between the processes of exclusion and inclusion in each of these research settings. Most importantly, by using ethnography to access the discourses that circulate in schools and undertaking close readings of extended data episodes to interrogate the effects of these discourses, I have been able to offer nuanced insights into the processes through which particular subjectivities are constituted through and tied to educational inequalities and exclusions.

In the first part of this final chapter I will revisit the ideas that are central to the book and the key analytical claims that I make. In the second part of the chapter, I will turn to the pragmatics of translating these insights into a politics that might be engaged by educators.

UNDERSTANDING SUBJECTS AND EXCLUSIONS THROUGH POST-STRUCTURAL THEORIES

Through the analyses offered in the book I have explored the utility of particular theorisations of the subject for making sense of ethnographic data concerned with subjectivities and their entanglement with educational exclusions. I have drawn on the work of Foucault, Derrida and Butler, and Butler's reworking of Althusser and Bourdieu, to understand the subject as an effect of discourse and so subjectivated – made a subject through relations of power that are themselves effected in and through discourse.

By employing these ideas to engage with and analyze ethnographic data, I have demonstrated their utility in making sense of processes of subjectivation and exclusion in schools as well as their usefulness for exposing the limits of these processes and the possibility for these to be interrupted. And in applying these tools to the analysis of ethnographic data generated in the UK and Australia, I have shown the utility of these theories for understanding both the specificities of particular locales and the continuities of subjectivating processes across national contexts. In turn this has demonstrated the continued necessity for school ethnography that can access the everyday micro-processes of schools and test and develop theoretical tools for understanding these.

Within my analysis I have at once adopted and demonstrated the utility of a particular Foucauldian (1990a, 1991) understanding of discourse. This suggests that a discourse is not cited and inscribed in isolation from a broader discursive field. Rather discourses intersect and interact. Furthermore, multiple discourses are cited and inscribed through discursive practices. These practices might be linguistic, textual, bodily, and/or otherwise – verbal exchanges, looks, and deeds all coalesce within constitutive moments, underscoring the importance of attending to the range of practices in researching the processes that constitute schooled subjects. Citations and inscriptions of discourses might be intentional, tacit, and/or unintentional. What is meaningful and, indeed, meaningless within particular discursive frames is variously limited and constrained by their sedimented historicity.

Multiple discursive markets suffuse the school context and the locations, settings and moments within it. The school is not simply dominated by a prevailing or hegemonic discourse. Rather, it is a site of prevailing discourses as well as discourses that might be characterised as subjugated, disavowed, alternative, marginal, counter or oppositional. These discourses combine, coalesce, intersect and interact in various ways. In so doing, possibilities for subjectivities are opened up, limits are demarcated and possibilities for subjectivities are closed down. Nevertheless, particular discourses do seem to endure within the school context and traverse its locations, settings and moments. While these may be nuanced and appear to include adaptation and surprises, a degree of predictability remains.

By using the notion of performative interpellation (Butler 1997a, 1997b, 2004) I have shown how names constitute particular types of subjects – including students and learners – through the citation and inscription of enduring discourses. A name is not guaranteed performative force and, where these performative interpellations are successful, this success remains provisional: their endurance is never guaranteed. The efficacy of performative names is mediated. Crucial to the provisional success of the performative name is its intelligibility; the historicity of the discourses cited through and inscribed by the name; and the specificity of the context in which the name is uttered. My analysis has also shown how these performative practices cannot be understood as being simply linguistic or textual – the embroilment of the body in naming is evident.

Working with the notion of a performative *habitus* (Butler 1997a, 1997b) I have shown how enduring discourses that are constitutive of particular types of subjects are cited and inscribed through bodily practices. I have demonstrated how the subject and the body cannot be understood as distinct, dichotomous or oppositional (as in mind/body, reason/nature), but must both be understood as being constituted in and constitutive of discourse. That is, my analysis has shown how the body is discursively constituted (as a prior, neutral fact) and cannot be said to precede or predict the subject. This analysis insists that discourse cannot be understood as synonymous with language (with the bodily, the social or the cultural residing someplace 'outside' or 'beyond' discourse). Rather, this analysis insists that discourse be understood as being constituted by and constitutive of linguistic, textual, representation *and* bodily practices. By utilising these analytical tools I have been able to demonstrate the nuances and minutiae of a multitude of mundane discursive practices through which particular sorts of subjects are constituted inside schools. I have drawn Ball's (2003) notion of class practices into my thinking about these constitutive processes. Drawing this notion into this post-structural frame suggests that a plethora of discursive practices have class implications, that is, they are class*ed*. And by extension, these (and/or other) practices also prove to be rac*ed* sex*ed*, gender*ed*, special*ed* and so on.

Borrowing from Derrida (1978), Cixous (1986) and others, my analyses have suggested that the performative practices of teachers and students cite and inscribe enduring discourses that are themselves underpinned by and constitutive of enduring hierarchical binary oppositions. I have also shown that each term of these binaries is not singular and demonstrated the complexities and further hierarchies within individual terms. I have detailed the citation and inscription of discourses of discreet, natural races based in phenotypes or physiognomies; dichotomous, biological sex; discreet, oppositional yet complementary genders; sex as causative of gender and normative heterosexual masculinities and femininities; unevenly distributed ability or intelligence; and normalcy and special educational needs. My analyses have suggested that, in citing such enduring discourses, these performative practices tend to constitute student identities within the terms of enduring and predictable categorisations.

The enduring privilege of scientific (biological) discourse has pressed on these analyses. This is underlined by the almost inescapable sense within these data that the categories of sex(-gender); race; and ability/intelligence and disability are absolute in ways that (possibly) sexuality and (certainly) social class are not. I have shown how prevailing discourses constitute race, sex, intelligence and disability as *in /on* the body; sexuality as *of* the body; and social class as *social*, impacting on, but (perhaps) not intrinsic to the body. My analysis has also shown that these are not sealed or unproblematic constitutions – they are fraught by contradiction and contestation. However, the commonsense of this characterisation is illustrative of the endurance of those discourses through which biological categorisations are constituted as *prior* facts from which the very idea of escape becomes unthinkable.

Despite the ongoing tacit citation of these scientific discourses within the data, my explorations of discursive practices have been underpinned by a commitment to the *potentiality* of performatives and the *provisionality* of their constitutions. Within the school there are a range of shifting official and sub-cultural contexts and milieu. These contexts and milieu are constituted by and constitutive of a multitude of discourses. These discourses do not have intrinsic relative values or performative forces. While the historicity of some discourses gives the appearance of particular and abiding meanings and performative force, the different ways in which discourses intersect and interact across contexts insists that meaning and performative force is mobile and subject to change.

In framing the book I proceeded with the uncomfortable necessity of keeping notions of subjectivity and identity simultaneously in play, maintaining the term identity critically and with a sense of its necessity for thinking/speaking about those categories that common sense, identity politics, and population science take as making up the person. I suggested that it is unhelpful, if not impossible, to conceive of such categories of identity in isolation and posited instead a notion of identity constellations. My subsequent analysis of data episodes has shown the utility of this notion. These have shown how multiple identity categories can be constituted through single performatives. The identity category (or categories) to which a performative refers explicitly, frequently is not the only category (or categories) constituted through it. Rather, further categories are often cited and inscribed implicitly, even though these citations may be unintentional and/or unacknow-ledged. Furthermore, identity categories interconnect and interact in particular ways to inform the success or otherwise of performatives.

Throughout the book I have explored the relative status of particular identity categories and the processes through which these are imbued with (or denied) such status. In doing this I have discussed the significance of identity constellations and the discursive fields or markets within which these constellations are constituted and deployed. I have shown how identity categories that are privileged in particular discursive fields can be deployed to mask identity categories that are undesirable with the same discursive field. This can be seen even when the category that is masked appears crucial to the constitution of the category that is deployed. I have also shown how a particular identity category can act to allow and/or disallow coexistence with certain other identity categories. Despite a multitude of moments of (variously successful) resistance, biographical identities that are constituted through intersecting discourses of race, gender, sexuality and social class persist. These axes are open (in varying contexts) to multiple (but not illimitable) provisional constitutions and are pivotal to an array of overlapping and variously constituted sub-cultural, student and learner identities. Through this analysis the centrality of biographical identity categories is underscored. Sub-cultural, student, and learner identities often seem to be constituted through discursive practices which simultaneously and implicitly cite and inscribe discourses which are constitutive of race, sex, gender, sexuality, social class, (dis)ability, special needs.

At the centre of this book has been my demonstration of how student and learner identities are constituted through the performative practices of students and teachers. I have shown how the discursive practices through which privileged sub-cultural and/or biographical identities are constituted can be recuperated and deployed within organisational discourse to constitute bad students and unacceptable learners. Indeed, I have shown how some identity constellations come to be incommensurable with institutional discourses of the student and/or learner and so constitute the subject as an impossible student or learner. This is not, however, a unidirectional process – certain student and learner identities similarly appear to render the constitution of social and sub-cultural subjectivities impossible. In this way I have shown how biographical and sub-cultural identities interact with student and learner identities in particular ways, creating possibilities and setting constraints for various intelligible subjectivities.

The discursive practices of the school organisation seem to suggest a hierarchy of learner identities that is marked by and interacts with students' biographical and sub-cultural identities. Organisational discourses are, in a variety of ways, underpinned by notions, for instance but not exclusively, of ability (intelligence); rationality and self-reflection; good conduct; hard work and commitment; and childhood and adolescent development. As this multiplicity of discourses interact, students and learners are constituted along axes of ability, effort, conduct, compliance – axes which themselves interact with biographical identities through discourses of race, gender, social class, sexuality, disability, special needs. Across multiple discursive fields, some identities are rendered intelligible, legitimate and desirable while others are rendered undesirable, illegitimate and even unintelligible.

Within these constitutions there seems, at times, to be an inverse relationship between status in the mainstream student sub-culture and the organisational discourse of good students and ideal, acceptable and unacceptable learners. Indeed, practices that constitute high status in one of these discursive fields can appear to be the very practices that constitute low status in the other. Yet this is not a direct relationship of inversion. Some discourses do appear to operate as/on planes whose terms are so incommensurable they sheer off against one another to constitute deeply incompatible identities. Yet my analysis has shown that the complex discursive matrices that frame school contexts mean that webs of discourse can be deployed to constitute unexpected inclusions and commensurabilities.

Located (constituted) in these constrained but not determined discursive frames, the subjectivated subject has been shown to retain a significant degree of agency. This subject has intent, but this is an intent that is constrained by the discursive frames through which he/she is constituted and which his/her discursive practices are potentially constituting. And discourses are also deployed tacitly and unintentionally. Whether performatives are deployed unintentionally, constitute subjects as intended, or misfire or backfire to constitute subjects in unanticipated ways, their constitutions are always provisional. In addition, discourses that are potentially constituting of subjectivities that are particularly desirable in specific contexts or milieu may implicitly interact with and cite other discourses which threatened to recuperate these desired subjectivities, or even constitute them as undesirable. There is no once-and-for-all constituting moment that brings a subject to finality or closure.

My analysis, then, has shown how enduring discourses constrain both the intelligibility and commensurability of identities in ways that render some constellations of identity categories traps as the cost of successful subjecthood. These constitutions inadvertently act to pin down, corner, demand, and foreclose particular further identities. Perhaps this need not be seen as misfire or infelicity as the respective analyses of Derrida and Austin might suggest. Rather, this may be understood as *the unforeseen or even acceptable cost of performative constitutions.*

A POLITICS OF HEGEMONY

Throughout the book I have explored the possibilities offered by a politics of performative reinscription (Butler 1997a). My analyses of students' performative practices have illustrated moments of this politics – I have shown students *re*inscribing and *re*inscribed *again differently*, being made or making themselves and/or others something, or someone, they were not before. In this way, within the contexts of specific discursive markets, disavowed identities can be imbued with prestige (if only fleetingly) and coveted identities can be stripped of their status (albeit momentarily).

I have also shown the limits, risks and provisionality of such reinscription. The endurance of prevailing discourses means that these reinscriptions remain open to recuperation. The citationality and historicity of discourse means that they may misfire. The almost inevitable implicit citation of further discourses can contribute further to such misfire and/or recuperation. And so those identities that have been constituted as privileged within and through hegemonic discourses abide and continue to be constituted as such. There is no great throwing off or overthrowing of identities promised here.

Nevertheless, my analysis does show performative politics in practice in contemporary schools and suggests the potential for such a politics to be engaged and/or deployed at the level of policy-making and school practice. Such a take up of performative politics promises to interrupt educational exclusions and make possible student and learner identities that my analyses show to be frequently disavowed. These possibilities respond to demands for a potential strategy for, and practice of, radical educational politics in the contemporary moment (Ladsen-Billings 2004) – a politics that looks to the potential of the performative to reinscribe meaning and subjects and the capacity of deconstruction, after Derrida (1978), to unpick, reverse and displace hegemonic discourses.

The first task of such a politics is to understand, as I have sought to do here, the processes of subjectivation and exclusion inside schools across contexts. This understanding allows the specificities of particular contexts to be made sense of; the commonalities that span these contexts to be identified and, in turn, the impact on localities of globalizing trends to be interrogated; and the theoretical tools being used to be tested, refined and extended. This is one of the tasks that this book has endeavoured to do, offering simultaneously accounts of subjectivating practices and explications of how these are embroiled in educational inclusions and exclusions. This is, of course, a partial account. Focusing as it does on just two locales in the English speaking, post-industrial world and taking account of as many axes of inclusion/exclusion as data and space would allow but, as is often the case when we attempt to cut across received areas of concern, not accounting for nearly enough of these. This then, is an inevitably incomplete account of these processes of inclusion and exclusion and one that I hope that my own future work, and perhaps the work of others, will continue to add to.

This is not simply a descriptive endeavour. This political project is underpinned by the practice and goal of deconstruction. As such, analyses of the discourses that are at play and are constitutive of particular subjects of schooling seeks to *expose* these constitutive mechanisms and so *unsettle and displace* the enduring discourses that contribute to educational exclusions (Derrida 1978 and 1988). Much post-structural educational research moves from such a point of departure, and this point of departure is often pointed to by modernist criticisms that posit the a-political nature of post-structuralism. This criticism is understandable from a modernist perspective, but it is erroneous in that it proceeds from a modernist/structural conception of what politics or action for change might look like. In doing this it missed the crucial point that the practice of deconstruction is itself a political practice, albeit one with reconfigured methods and goals. Continuing to expose the mechanisms of hegemonic discourse and unsettle and even displace these discourses is a politics in education.

This deconstructive politics of hegemony (Butler 1997a) is not simply concerned to replace one injurious name with another which may, or may not, inscribe, or come to inscribe, the injurious subjectivation it was taken up to avoid or resist. Attempts have been made within feminism to severe the link between the biological and the social aspects of sex (male/female) and gender (man/woman). These neither unmoored constraining social structures and practices from the sexed body nor adequately unsettled the abiding belief in the causality between sex and gender in popular, professional and scientific discourses. Likewise, there have been attempts in race politics to reject notions of (biological) race and replace these with either understandings of race as a social construct or notions of (cultural) ethnicity. While this has broadened the range and diversity of identities recognised, it has had limited effects in shifting either common sense notions of biological race or the privilege of Whiteness. Similar attempts have also been made within disability politics where a distinction has been drawn between impairment and disability in efforts to undercut the deficit embedded in notions of the disabled person and highlight the disabling effects of an ableist society. Yet as in the case of feminist and race politics, this shift displaces the encounter with (rather than fundamentally interrupting) prevailing notions of deficit and continues to cite a normative discourse of normal/impaired.

Such limits may be understood as the realities of ongoing provisional and partial identity politics, and are reflective of the revised goals of post-structural politics. Yet more than this, they demonstrate the endurance of normative discourses that reproduce and proliferate hierarchical binaries that act to privilege and exclude. Instead of a male/female binary, 'woman' takes up the subordinate place on the non-normative side of a man/woman binary. Ethnicity takes the place of race in enduring postcolonial discourse that privileges the normative 'White'; and 'impaired' replaces disabled in the subordinate position in a normal/abnormal binary. Accepting Derrida's assertion that such hierarchical binaries are central to Western knowledge and the production of power relations suggests that such slippages are unavoidable.

All of these terms have been deployed, with notable successes, to expose and challenge embedded binaries and force encounters with non-normative and disavowed discourses, but they are also always open to being recouped into the binaries that they challenge and, therefore, into enduring discourse. The practice of seeking a third term that is not reducible to either side of the binary is another promising strategy, and while Wittig's 'lesbian' and Cixous' 'bisexual' appear limited in their capacity to interrupt hetero/homo-man/woman dichotomies, the capacity of 'queer' to do so appears more promising. Yet the risk of a straight/queer hierarchy remains here, a persistence that demonstrates that it is crucial to include terms that have been deployed as part of a resistant or counter-hegemonic politics in the subsequent deconstructive efforts of that politics. I am not suggesting that scholars and activists who have advocated the severing of sex/gender, race/ethnicity, disability/impairment have done so erroneously, far from it. What I am suggesting, however, is that we continue to interrogate the (potentially shifting) effects of these politics and their (perhaps unwanted or unanticipated) performative effects.

I have argued, then, that the shift from a focus on the sexed, raced or impaired might act as a deferral of the encounter with, or even an erasure of, the body rather than an undoing of the effects of deterministic accounts of the limits and meanings of these bodies (see Butler 1993; Fuss 1990). Yet the criticism of the fragmenting of identity categories within identity politics that I have offered here itself runs the risk of enacting a double refusal to engage the body by appearing to advocate neither sex nor gender, race nor ethnicity, impairment nor disability. And this is what I am doing in as much as I am asserting sex-gender, race-ethnicity, and impairment-disability as identity markers that are neither wholly separable from nor reducible to each other. This is to argue that the bodily cannot be extracted from the social, our experiences of the social are embodied experiences. And the social cannot be extracted from the body – the body's meanings are social and any (every) body that precedes (when, exactly?) the social is unobtainable because it only has meaning in discourse.

When I argue, then, that we need to deconstruct the discourses through which students are constituted, and when I argue that it is these discourses that constrain the possibilities for who students can be, this is not to deny a body, or a mind, that can do some things and not others, or be recognised as some things and not others. Rather, I am arguing that what it *means* for a body-mind to be able to do or be some things and not others is due wholly to what that doing or not doing, being or not being, *means* in the prevailing (or other) discourses that frame the context in which that body-mind is inaugurated into the citational chains of discourse and so rendered accessible and meaningful.

CHANGING SCHOOLS

Educators

These understandings of how the subject comes to be marked by social, biographical, sub-cultural and *school* identities might be taken up by educators willing to interrogate how their own practices in the classroom and the corridor, the meeting room and the staffroom, are implicated in the ongoing constitution of subjects inside schools. The notion of the reflexive practitioner (ref) has come to be widely accepted as a model of practice that enhances pedagogy and learning. The analytical-political tools described and demonstrated in this book could be taken up by such reflexive practitioners. Such educators might engage deconstructive thinking to expose how their own practices act to entangle and/or conflate social, biographical, sub-cultural and school identity categories; constitute good and bad students and acceptable and unacceptable learners; and create educational inclusions and exclusions.

With the insights that these exposures offer, these educators might tease apart these entanglements, undo these conflations, problematise these constitutions and interrupt these exclusion. That is, such educators might seek out opportunities for discursive insurrections in the day-to-day practices of schooling, practices that Laws and Davies (2000) have helpfully demonstrated in action. While these possibilities might be available to individual educators who have access to these analytical and political tools, they might also be made widely available through continuing professional development and initial teacher education. Indeed, such deconstructive practices and performative politics might be recast as a central skill and task of the inclusive educator. For instance, returning to the first example of these constitutive practices that I offered in chapter 4 – Steve resists the categories on ethnic monitoring form and Miss Baxter invokes the exotic – I imagine Miss Baxter a reflexive practitioner equipped with these tools of deconstruction. On reflection, she might recognise her intervention as constitutive of fixed, biological races and good and bad students, and she might respond differently next time she is involved in such a classroom exchange.

Pedagogy

Educators engaged in performative politics and discursive insurrections will, in these moments of practice, be demonstrating these to their students. Such demonstrations might be made explicit and become the subject of discussion and analysis in classrooms as educators draw their students into these practices and make explicit processes of subjectivation and performative politics. That is, these educators will be doing deconstruction in the classroom. As a deconstructive pedagogy, rather than cite the Orientalist discourse of the exotic Other, Miss Baxter might invite students to consider the categories as constructs, question what these categories allow and do not allow, and engage the students in the sort of analysis I offered in chapter 4. Indeed, in my own initial and continuing teacher education classroom, I do exactly this with this episode of data. This does not shift the normative use of ethnic monitoring forms or the categories they cite and inscribe, but it does unsettle the self-evident nature of these categories and suggest that they might mean or be otherwise.

Curriculum

Performative politics and deconstruction might also reshape and become part of a curriculum that is serious about interrupting exclusions. By including disavowed and subjugated knowledges in the curriculum and deconstructing their subjugated status, the taken-for-grantedness of prevailing discourses might be called into question and discourses that have been excluded from schools and schooling might become recognisable and even shift the hegemony of prevailing discourse. Likewise, processes of subjectivation and performative constitution might become subjects of explicit study. Clearly, this would need to be neither a tokenistic inclusion of subjugated knowledges that acts only to reinscribe their subjugation, nor a decontextualised expropriation of these. This might seem a long way from the state-mandated curricula that are currently the norm across Western and Westernising education systems. And while the apparent conservatism and instrumentalism of contemporary school curriculum might make these moves seem all but impossible, they may not be so unrealisable – deconstruction is already on the New South Wales high school English curriculum (ref). Furthermore, within the constraints of current prescribed curricular and high-stakes testing, educators concerned to pursue inclusion might still find spaces within the curriculum to explore these ideas and processes with their students. For instance, I am currently working with a team of scientists and educators funded by the Wellcome Trust in the UK who are exploring how learning about the Human Genome Project – which might properly belong across current curricular areas – might not only extend contemporary science to school age students, but also interrupt common-sense understandings of race (and other identities) and raise questions about the status of currently recognisable categories of difference. And education systems such as that of Porto Alegre, Brazil, where the curriculum is developed through thick democratic processes and is wholly concerned with interrogating and destabilizing the normative privileged/subjugated locations of knowledges (Gandin and Apple 2003) offer models for more wholesale moves to a deconstructive education.

Institutional practice

Like educators, institutions might engage in practice of deconstruction in order to identify, understand and interrupt the constitutive effects of institutional practices. Through performative politics that refigure discursive meanings and legitimate new discourses, and through deconstructive efforts that intercept and displace meaning, institutions might pursue a discursive frame that refuses the easy conflation of particular identity constellations with various axes of educational exclusion and instead opens up possibilities for new inclusions to be intelligible. For instance, assumptions about the nature of ability; the organizational and pedagogic practices of differentiation that often follow from these assumptions; and the imagined ideal client (implicitly classed, raced gendered, able-bodied and so on) around whom these practices orbit might be recognised by and unsettled in the alternative practices of educational institutions.

Policy

Just as educators, administrators and institutions might interrogate the constitutive effects of the discourses that they deploy, so policy makers might seek to understand how the discourses that frame contemporary education policy are implicated in, rather than ameliorative of, educational inequalities and exclusions. Policy makers might then recognise how the priorities, goals and practices that they mandate and/or promote for educational sectors and settings are implicated in these inequalities and inclusion. For instance, policy makers might acknowledge that the proliferation of accountability mechanisms and high stakes tests that are at the heart of these are centrally implicated in the re-emergence of notions of fixed, generalised and unevenly distributed ability and the institutional imperative to identify and sort the good and bad student, the acceptable and unacceptable learner. And having recognised these processes, policy makers might endeavour to interrupt these, for instance, they might remove high stakes tests from the educational landscape, they might reconsider the direction and nature of the lines of accountability that they promote. A deconstruction of discourses of market neutrality; accountability; choice; individualism; end user needs and so on would, of course, confront policy makers with the need for currently subjugated and disavowed discourses of equity of outcomes; public goods; compensatory/affirmative action; and progressive and transformatory education to be *re*engaged and *re*legitimated. It would mean taking on analyses of 'institutional' racism, sexism, ableism and so on as *effects*, not as intents, in which their own policies are implicated. And so it would demand the engagement of a performative politics in education.

This is not a romantic plea for return to imagined halcyon days of past educational models, such as the comprehensive school. Rather, it is a call to a performative politics of hegemony that exposes, reverses, displaces, interrupts and *reinscribes again differently* who is and can be a student and a learner inside schools. This is a politics of inclusion that recognises the global and national policy context and looks inside the school to see how the exclusions at the heart of a competitive global market are produced through the daily practices of schools.

CAUTIONARY NOTES

Marketisation and individualisation are integral to the disappearance of biographical identities categories within education policy discourse. Where these have re-emerged in the context of a social inclusion discourse, this has been to recognise the population group(s) excluded (not facing inequalities); remain silent in relation to the structures or practice implicated in creating these exclusions (inequalities); and foreground the individuals responsibility for her/his own inclusion as an active citizen. In such a discursive frame educational inequalities and exclusions, which in earlier times were understood in terms of race, gender and/or social class disadvantage, become individualised. In an increasingly individualised policy context that refuses analyses concerned with groups based on biographical identities, this book underlines the importance of continuing to examine inequality and inclusion in terms of constellations of identity categories and the processes through which these come about.

These analyses, then, have massive implications for policy, both as critique of current policy directions and as a diagnosis of the problematics that policy should engage and attempt to address. Of course, I do not imagine that policy makers will either read or take on these analyses, the discursive capture of the market, and the investment in its terms, is almost certain to be too deep.

Alongside policy makers, school administrators and teachers and students themselves may well be invested, explicitly or implicitly, in the subjectivities this book has explored and, by extension, the educational exclusions it has identified. Interrogating our own practices, as individual educators or as institutions or as government departments, is a deeply discomforting endeavour. And, given the day-to-day, mundane nature of the constitutive practices concerned, it is also potentially a constant task. Furthermore, the absence of a promise of resolution (or revolution), but instead the entreaty to further deconstruction, renders this an unending political practice. This discomfort, coupled with the commitment to a daily politics that does not promise a utopian conclusion, will undoubtedly be taken up by the pessimistic and/or invested as a reason not to embark on such a project and put off even the most motivated of educational activist. And the subjects who might be constituted differently, who might be included instead of excluded through these practices, might resist this changed constitution. Subjectivation of any sort brings with it the capacity to act with intent.

Imagine Steve from Taylor Comp, too masculine to be a good student. If his practices of masculinity were not redeployed by his teachers and peers to cite the bad student, then Steve might be man *and* acceptable learner. This may seem simple. Imagine instead, then, Luke, from Plains High whose specialness is so engrained in school discourse that nothing (no one) else is possible. Would Luke embrace the constitution of acceptable learner if his practices were reinscribed instead of being deployed to constitute his specialness? It seems that in Cath Laws' Sydney school, a 'special school' that in its very existence cannot help but cite the not-normalness of its students, the students practices are taken as legitimate rather than inscriptions of abnormal, and the students do 'do normal' (Laws and Davies 2001).

Given the conditions of the school's emergence and the continued struggle over its proper purposes and governance, it cannot be a site of simple emancipation (Hunter 1996). But it is a site of politics. The analyses offered in this book demonstrate how the school remains implicated in subjectivating particular sorts of subjects and reproducing hegemony. Schooling, from policy maker to classroom teacher, has an obligation to interrogate, and the capacity to interrupt, these exclusionary processes.

REFERENCES

Allen, J. (2002). Actively Seeking Inclusion: Pupils with special needs in mainstream schools. London, Falmer Press.

Althusser, L. (1971). Ideology and Ideological State Apparatuses. Lenin and Philosophy. London, Monthly Review Press: 170-186.

Anyon, J. (1983). Gender and Class: Accommodation and resistance by working class and affluent females to contradictory sex-role ideologies. Gender, Class and Education. S. Walker and L. Barton. Lewes, Sussex, Falmer Press: 19-37.

Apple, M. (1990). Ideology and curriculum. London, Routledge.

Apple, M (2001). Educating the "right" way: markets, standards, God, and inequality. London, RoutledgeFalmer.

Apple, M., Ed. (2003). The State and the Politics of Knowledge. London, RoutledgeFalmer.

Apple, M. W. and J. A. Beane (1999). Democratic schools: lessons from the chalk face. Buckingham, Open University Press.

Aquilina, J. (1997). The New South Wales Government's reforms for the Higher School Certificate: 1-39.

Arnot, M. (1996). Educational reforms and gender equality in schools. Manchester, Equal Opportunities Commission.

Arnot, M. (1998). Recent research on gender and educational performance. London, Stationery Office.

Arnot, M. and K. Weiler (1993). Feminism and Social Justice in Education: International Perspectives. London, Falmer Press.

Armstrong, F. (2003). Spaced Out: Policy, difference and the challenge of inclusive education. London, Kluwer Academic Publishers.

Askew, S. and C. Ross (1988). Boys Don't Cry: Boys and sexism in education. Milton Keynes, Open University Press.

Atkinson, P. (1990). The Ethnographic Imagination: Textual constructions of reality. London, Routledge.

Austin, J. L. (1962). How to Do Things with Words. Cambridge, Mass, Harvard University Press.

Ball, S. J. (1981). Beachside Comprehensive: A case study of secondary schooling. Cambridge, The University Press.

Ball, S. J. (1990). Politics and Policy Making in Education: Explorations in policy sociology. London, Routledge.

Ball, S. J. (1993). Self-doubt and Soft data: Social and technical trajectories in ethnographic fieldwork. Educational Research: Current issues. M. Hammersley. London, Paul Chapman and the Open University Press: 32-48.

Ball, S. J. (1994). Education reform: a critical and post-structural approach. Philadelphia, Open University Press.

Ball, S. J. (2003). Class strategies and the education market: the middle classes and social advantage. London, RoutledgeFalmer.

Ball, S. J., M. Maguire and S. Macrae. (2000). Choice, pathways, and transitions post-16: new youth, new economies in the global city. London, RouthledgeFalmer.

Ball, S. J. and C. Vincent (2001). New Class Relations in Education: the strategies if the 'fearful' middle classes. Sociology of Education Today. J. Demaine. Basingstoke, Palgrave: 180-195.

Barnes, C., M. Oliver and L. Barton. (2001). Disabilities Studies Today. Cambridge, Polity.

Barthes, R. (1983). The fashion system. New York, Hill and Wang.

Barton, L., Ed. (2001). Disability, Politics and the Struggle for Change. London, David Fulton.

Baszanger, I. and N. Dodier (1997). Ethnography: Relating the part to the whole. Qualitative Research: Theory, method and practice. D. Silverman. London, Sage: 8-23.

Becker, H. S. (1970). Sociological Work: Methods and Substance. New Brunswick, NJ, Transaction Books.

Benjamin, S., A (2002). The Micropolitics of Inclusive Education: an ethnography. Buckingham, Open University Press.

Beratan, G. (forthcoming). "'You are who they think you are': Teachers and the transposition of disabled identities." American Educational Research Journal.

Blair, T. (2002). Prime Minister Tony Blair MP's Speech. Technology Colleges Trust Tenth Annual Conference, Specialist Schools Trust.

Blaxter, M. (1976). The Meaning of Disability: a sociological study of impairment. London, Heinemann Educational.

Booher-Jennings, J. (2005). "Below the Bubble: 'Educational Triage' and the Texas Accountability System." American Educational Research Journal 42(2): 231-268.

Booth, T. and M. Ainscow (2004). Index for Inclusion: developing learning, participation and early years and childcare. Bristol, CSIE.

Bordo, S. (1992). "Feminist Studies." Review Essay: Postmodern subjects, postmodern bodies 18(1): 159-175.

Bourdieu, P. (1987) Distinction: a social critique of the judgment of taste. Cambridge, Mass, Harvard University Press.

Bourdieu, P. (1990). The Logic of Practice. Stanford, Stanford University Press.

Bourdieu, P. (1991). Language and Symbolic Power. Cambridge, Mass, Harvard University Press.

Bowe, R. and S. J. Ball with A. Gold (1992). Reforming education and changing schools: case studies in policy sociology. London.

Bowles, S. and H. Gintis (1976). Schooling in Capitalist America: Education reform and the contradictions of economic life. London, Routledge and Keegan Paul.

Brah, A. (1996). Cartographies of Diaspora: contesting identities. London, Routledge.

Brine, J. (1999). Under-Educating Women: Globalizing inequality. Buckingham, Open University Press.

Britzman, D., Kelly, J. (2003). Lost Subjects, Contested objects: Towards a psychoanalytic inquiry of learning. Albany, State University of New York Press.

Britzman, D. P. (1995). "Is There a Queer Pedagogy? Or, Stop Reading Straight." Educational Theory 45(2): 151-65.

Butler, James. (1996). The poof paradox: homonegativity and silencing in three Hobart high schools. L. Laskey and C. Beavis. Eds. Schooling and sexualities: teaching for a positive sexuality, Geelong Vic, Deakin Centre for Education and Change 131-149.

Butler, Judith (1990). Gender Trouble: Feminism and the subversion of identity. London, Routledge.

Butler, Judith (1991). Imitation and Gender Insubordination. Inside/Out: Lesbian Theories, Gay Theories. D. Fuss. London, Routledge.

Butler, Judith (1993). Bodies that matter: on the discursive limits of "sex". New York, Routledge.

Butler, Judith (1997a). Excitable Speech: A politics of the performative. London, Routledge.

Butler, Judith (1997b). The Psychic Life of Power: Theories in subjection. Stanford, Stanford University Press.

Butler, Judith (1999). "Revisiting Bodies and Pleasures." Theory, Culture and Society 16(2): 11-20.

Butler, Judith (2004). Undoing Gender. London, Routledge.

Cixous, H. and C. Clement (1986). The Newly Born Women. Minneapolis, University of Minnesota Press.

Cixous, H. (1986). Sorties: Out and Out: Attacks/Ways Out/Forays. The Newly Born Woman. H. Cixous and C. Clement. Minneapolis, University of Minnesota Press: 63-134.

Clegg, S. (1985). "Quality and Quantity." Feminist Methodology - Fact or Fiction? 19(1): 83-97.

Collins, C., J. Kenway and J. Mcleod. (2000). Factors Influencing the Educational Performace of Males and Females in School and their Initial Destinations after Leaving School. South Australia, Deakin University: 166.

Connell, R. (1995). Masculinities. Cambridge, Polity.

Connell, R. W. Identity, Unpublished paper.

Corbett, J. (1996). Bad Mouthing: The language of special needs. London, Falmer.

Davies, L. (1984). Pupil Power: Deviance and gender in school. Lewes, Sussex, Falmer Press.

Delamont, S. (1989). Knowledge Women: Structuralism and the reproduction of elites. London, Routledge.

Delamont, S. (1990). Sex Roles and the School. London, Routledge.

Delamont, S. and P. Atkinson (1995). Fighting Familiarity: Essays on education and ethnography. New Jersey, Hampton Press.

Derrida, J. (1978). On Writing and Difference. London, Routledge.

Derrida, J. (1988). Signature Event Context. Limited Inc. J. Derrida. Elvanston, Northwestern University Press: 1-23.

Devine, D. (1996). Maximum Security: The culture of violence in inner city schools. Chicago, University of Chicago Press.

DfEE (1997). Excellence in Schools, Cm 3681. London, HMSO.

Epstein, D., J. Elwood, V. Hey and J. Maw. Eds. (1998). Failing boys?: issues in gender and achievement. Philadelphia, Open University Press.

Epstein, D. and R. Johnson (1998). Schooling Sexualities. Buckingham, Open University Press.

Finkelstein, V. (1980). Attitudes and Disabled People. New York, World Rehabilitation Fund.

Foucault, M. (1980). Power/Knowledge: Selected interviews and other writings 1972-1977. New York, Harvester Wheatsheaf.

Foucault, M. (1990a). The History of Sexuality: An introduction. London, Penguin.

Foucault, M. (1990b). The Care of the Self: The History of Sexuality volume three. London, Penguin.

Foucault, M. (1990c). Politics Philosophy Culture: Interviews and other writing 1977-1984. L. D. Kritzman. London, Routledge.

Foucault, M. (1990d). Critical Theory/Intellectual History. Michel Foucault: Politics, Philosophy and Culture: Interviews and other writings 1977-1984. D. Kritzman. London, Routledge: 17-46.

Foucault, M. (1991). Discipline and Punish: The birth of the prison. London, Penguin.

Foucault, M. (1992). The Uses of Pleasure: The History of Sexuality volume two. London, Penguin.

Friere, P. (1970). Pedagogy of the Oppressed. New York, Herder & Herder.

Fuller, M. (1984). Black girls in a comprehensive school. Life in School: The sociology of pupil culture. M. Hammersley and P. Woods. Milton Keynes, Open University Press: 78-88.

Fuss, D. (1990). Essentially Speaking: Feminism, nature and difference. London, Routledge.

Fuss, D., Ed. (1991). Inside/out: Lesbian theories, Gay theories. London, Routledge.

Gandin, L. and M. Apple (2003). Educating the State, Demoncratizing Knowledge: The Citizens School Project in Porto Alegre, Brazil. The State and the Politics of Knowledge. M. Apple. London, RoutledgeFalmer: 193-220.

Gardner, H. (1983). Frames of Mind: The theory of multiple intelligences. New York, Basic.

Gewirtz, S., S. J. Ball and R. Bowe. (1995). Markets, choice and equity in education. Buckingham, Open University Press.

Giddens, A. (1993). Domination and Power. The Giddens Reader. P. Cassell. London, Macmillan: 212-283.

Gillborn, D. (1990). 'Race' Ethnicity and Education: Teaching and learning in multi-ethnic schools. London, Unwin Hyman.

Gillborn, D. (1995). Racism and Antiracism in Real Schools: theory, policy, practice. Buckingham, Open University Press.

Gillborn, D. (2002). Education and Institutional Racism. London, Institute of Education.

Gillborn, D. (2005). "Education Policy as an act of White Supremacy: whiteness, critical race theory and education reform." Journal of Education Policy 20(4): 485-505.

Gillborn, D. and C. Gipps (1996). Recent Research on the Achievements of Ethnic Minority Pupils. London, HMSO.

Gillborn, D. and H. S. Mirza (2000). Educational Inequality: mapping race, class and gender. London, Middlesex University.

Gillborn, D. and D. Youdell (2000). Rationing Education: Policy, practice, reform and equity. Buckingham, Open University Press.

Gillborn, D. and D. Youdell (2004). Teacher, Tests and Triage: standards, high-stakes testing and the rationing of education in the English classroom. American Educational Research Association, San Diego.

Giroux, H. (2001). Theory and resistance in education: towards a pedagogy for the opposition. London, Bergin & Garvey.

Gorard, S. (2000). "One of Us Cannot Be Wrong: the paradox of achievement gaps." British Journal of Sociology of Education 21(3): 391-400.

Gore, J. (1995). Foucault's Post-Structuralism and Observational Educational Research. After Post Modernism: Education, politics and identity: a study of power relations. R. Smith and P. Wexler. London, Falmer: 98-111.

Gramsci, A. (2003). Selections from the Prison Notebooks. London, Lawrence & Wishart.

Griffin, C. (1985). Typical Girls?: Young women from school to the job market. London, Routledge and Kegan Paul.

Grosz, E. (1995). Space, Time, and Perversion. London, Routledge.

Gulson, K. (2005). "Renovating educational identities: policy, space and urban renewal" Journal of Education Policy 20(2): 141-158.

Halsey, A., H. Lauder, et al. (1997). Education: Culture, Economy, Society. Oxford, Oxford University Press.

Hammersley, M. (1989). The Dilemma of the Qualitative Method: Herbert Blumer and the Chicago tradition. London, Routledge.

Hammersley, M. (1990). Classroom Ethnography: Empirical and methodological essays. Milton Keynes, Open University Press.

Hammersley, M. and P. Atkinson (1983). Ethnography: Principles in practice. London, Tavistock Publications.

Hammersley, M. and P. Atkinson (1995). Ethnography: Principles in practice, Second Edition. London, Tavistock Publications.

Hammersley, M. and G. Turner (1984). Conformist pupils. Life in School: The sociology of pupil culture. M. Hammersley and P. Woods. Milton Keynes, Open University Press: 161-175.

Hargreaves, D. H. (1967). Social Relations in a Secondary School. London, Routledge and Kegan Paul.

Hart, L. (1993). Between the Body and the Flesh: Performing sadomasochism. New York, Columbia University Press.

Heath, N. (2005). Comprehensive schooling and choice, unpublished thesis chapter. London, Institute of Education.

Herrnstein, R. and C. Murray (1994). The Bell Curve: Intelligence and class structure in American life. New York, Free Press.

Hey, V. (1997). The Company She Keeps: An ethnography of girls' friendship. Buckingham, Open University Press.

Holland, J., C. Ramazanoglu, S. Sharpe and R. Thomas (1998). The Male in the Head: Young People, heterosexuality and Power. London, Tufnell Press.

Holly, L. (1989). Girls and Sexuality: Teaching and Learning. Milton Keynes, Open University Press.

Holstein, J. A. and J. F. Gubrium (1997). Active Interviewing. Qualitative Research: Theory, method and practice. D. Silverman. London, Sage: 113-129.

Hunter, I. (1996). Assembling the School. Foucault and Political Reason: Liberalism, neo-liberalism and rationalities of government. A. Barry, T. Osborne and N. Rose. London, UCL Press: 143-166.

Jacobson, M. F. (1998). Whiteness of a different color: European imigrants and the alchemy of race. Cambridge, Mass, Harvard University Press.

Jasper, L. and T. Sewell (2003). Look Beyond the Street. Guardian at www.guardian.co.uk/comment/story/0,,1001151,00.html accessed 04/04/2005.

Jones, A. (1993). "Becoming a 'Girl' : Post-structuralist suggestions for education research." Gender and Education 5(2): 157-166.

Kehily, M. J. (2002). Sexuality, Gender and Schooling: shifting agendas in social learning. London, Routledge.

Kieth, M. and K. Pile (1993). Place and the Politics of Identity. London, Routledge.

Lacey, C. (1970). Hightown Grammer: The school as a social system. Manchester, Manchester University Press.

Ladsen-Billing, G. (2004). Just What is Critical Race Theory and What's it doing in an Nice Field like Education? The RoutledgeFlamer Reader in Multicultural Education. G. Ladsen-Billing and D. Gillborn. London, RoutledgeFalmer 49-68.

Lambert, A. M. (1976). The Sisterhood. The Process of Schooling. M. Hammersley and P. Woods. London, Routledge and Kegan Paul: 152-159.

Lamont, M. (1999). The Cultural Territories of Race: Black and white boundaries. Chicago, University of Chicago Press.

Lang, B. (1997). Metaphysical Racism (Or: biological warfare by other means). Race/Sex: Their sameness, difference and interplay. N. Zack. London, Routledge.

Lather, P. (1991). Getting Smart: Feminist research and pedagogy with/in the postmodern. New York, Routledge.

Laws, C. and B. Davies (2000). "Poststructuralist theory in practice: working with "behaviourally disturbed" children." Qualitative Studies in Education 13(3): 205-221.

Lees, S. (1986). Losing Out: Sexuality and adolecent girls. London, Hutchinson.

Leonardo, Z. (2004). The Souls of White Folk: Critical pedagogy, whiteness studies and globalisation discourse. The RoutledgeFalmer Reader in Multicultural Education. G. Ladsen-Billing and D. Gillborn. London, RoutledgeFalmer.

Levitas, R. (1998). The Inclusive Society? Social Exclusion and New Labour. Basingstoke, Palgrave Macmillan.

Lipman, P. (2004). High Stakes Education: Inequality, globalisation and urban school reform. London, RoutledgeFalmer.

Luke, C. and J. Gore (1992). Feminism and Critical Pedagogy. London, Routledge.

Lyotard, J. (1984). The Postmodern Condition: A report in knowledge. Minnesota, University of Minnisota Press.

Mac an Ghaill, M. (1988). Young, Gifted and Black. Milton Keynes, Open University Press.

Mac an Ghaill, M. (1994). The Making of Men: Masculinities, sexualities and schooling. Buckingham, Open University Press.

Mac an Ghaill, M. (1996). Understanding Masculinities: Social relations and cultural arenas. Buckingham, Open University Press.

Mac an Ghaill, M. (1999). Contemporary racisms and ethnicities: social and cultural transformations. Buckingham, Open University Press.

Maclure, M. (2003). Discourse in Educational and Social Research. Buckingham, Open University Press.

Mahony, P. (1985). Schools for the Boys? Co-education reassessed. London, Hutchinson.

Mares, P. (2002). Borderline: Australia's response to refugees and asyluim-seekers in the wake of the Tampa. Sydney, UNSW Press.

Marginson, S. (1997). Markets in education. St Leonards, Allen & Unwin.

Martino, W. (1999). "'Cool Boys', 'Party Animals', 'Squid', and 'Poofters' : interogating the dynamics and politics of adolescent masculinities in school." British Journal of Sociology of Education 20(2):239-263.

Massey, D. (1994). Space, Place and Gender. Cambridge, Polity Press.

Massey, D. (2004). For Space. London, Sage.

McInnes, D. and M. Couch (2001). Quiet Please! There's a lady on stage. Inner Sanctums and bifurcating selves: Navigating cultural worlds and educational contexts, Adelaide.

McLaren, P. (1998). Life in Schools: An Introduction to Critical Pedagogy in the Foundations of Education. New York, Longman.

Middleton, S. (1993). "Feminism and Social Justice in Education: International perspectives'." A postmodern Pedagogy for the Sociology of Women's Education: 124-145.

Miller, G. (1997). Building Bridges: the possibility of analytic dialogue between ethnography, conversation analysis and Foucault. Qualitative Research: Theory, method and practice. D. Silverman. London, Sage: 24-44.

Mills, M. (1999). "Homophobia and anti-lesbianism in schools: challenges and possibilities for social justice." Melbourne Studies in Education 40(2): 105-126.

Miron, L. F. and J. X. Inda (2000). "Race as a Kind of Speech Act." Cultural Studies: A Research Annual 5: 85-107.

Mirza, H. S. (1992). Young, Female and Black. London, Routledge.

Moore, R. (2004) "Cultural Capital: objective probability and the cultural arbitrary" British Journal of Sociology of Education 25(4): 445-456.

Nayak, A. (2003). Race, Place and Globalisation: Youth cultures in a changing world. London, Berg Publishers.

Nayak, A. and M. J. Kehily (1996). "Journal of Gender Studies." Playing it Straight: Masculinities, homophobias and schooling 5(2): 211-230.

Nayak, A. and M. J. Kehily (1996). "Playing it straight: masculinities, homophobias and schooling." Journal of Gender Studies 5(2): 211-230.

Nieto, S. (2004). Critical Multicultural Education and Students' Perspectives. RoutledgeFalmer Reader in Multicultural Education. G. Ladsen-Billing and D. Gillborn. London, RoutledgeFalmer 179-200.

Oakley, A. (1974). Sociology of Housework. London, Robertson.

Oakley, A. (1980). Women Confined: Towards a sociology of childbirth. Oxford, Martin.

Ogbu, D. and A. David (2003). Black American Students in an Affluent Suburb: A study of academic disengagement. New York, Lawrence Erlbaum.

Oliver, M. (1983). Social Work with Disabled People. London, Macmillan.

Oliver, M. (1990). The Politics of Disablement. Basingstoke, Macmillan.

Parsons, T. (1960). The distribution of power in American society. Structure and Process in Modern Societies. T. Parsons. Glencoe, Free Press: 199-225.

Parsons, T. (1963). On the Concept of Political Power. Proceedings of the American Philosophical Society.

Pollard, A. and A. Filer (1999). The social world of pupil career: strategic biographies through primary school. London, Cassell.

Pollard, A. and A. Filer (2004). Identity and secondary schooling: full report of research activities and results at www.regard.ac.uk accessed 03/03/2004.

Power, S. (2001). Missing: a sociology of educating the middle class. Sociology of Education Today. J. Demaine. Basingstoke, Palgrave: 196-205.

Price, J. and M. Shildrick (1999). Feminist Theory and the Body: A Reader. Edinburgh, Edinburgh University Press.

Prior, L. (1997). Following in Foucault's Footsteps: Text and content in qualitative research. Qualitative Research: Theory, method and practice. D. Silverman. London, Sage: 63-79.

Rasmussen, M. L. and V. Crowley, Eds. (2004). Discourse: Sexualities Special Issue 25(4).

Rasmussen, M. L., E. Rofes, et al., Eds. (2004). Youth and Sexualities: pleasure, subversion, and insubordination in and out of school. Basingstoke, Palgrave Macmillan.

Reay, D. (1998). Class work: mothers' involvement in their children's primary schooling. London, UCL Press.

Reay, D. and H. Lucey (2000). "Children, School Choice and Social Differences." Educational Studies 26(1): 83-100.

Renold, E. (2005). Girls, Boys and Junior Sexualities: Exploring Childrens' Gender and Sexual Relations in the Primary School. London, RoutledgeFalmer.

Rich, A. (1980). "Compulsory Heterosexuality and Lesbian Existence." Signs 5(4): 631-660.

Rizvi, F. (1997). "Educational Leadership and the Politics of Difference." Melbourne Studies in Education 38(1): 90-102.

Robertson, S. and R. Dale, C. (2004). Learning Europe: Schooling the Future. American Educational Research Association, San Diego.

Said, E. (2003). Orientalism. London, Penguin.

Saltmarsh, S. and D. Youdell (2004). "'Special Sport' for misfits and losers: educational triage and the constitution of schooled subjectivities." International Journal of Inclusive Education 8(4): 353-371.

Scott, R. (1969). The Making of Blind Men. London, Sage.

Seshadri-Crooks, K. (2000). Desiring Whiteness: a Lacanian analysis of race. London, Routledge.

Silverman, D. (1997a). Qualitative Research: Theory, method and practice. London, Sage.

Silverman, D. (1997b). Towards an Aesthetics of Research. Qualitative Research: Theory, method and practice. D. Silverman. London, Sage: 239-253.

Skeggs, B. (1994). Situating the Production of Feminist Ethnography. Researching Women's Lives from a Feminist Perspective. M. Maynard and J. Purvis. London, Taylor and Francis.

Slee, R. (1995). Changing theories and practices of discipline. London, Falmer.

Sleeter, C. (2004). A curriculum for Imperialism. American Educational Research Association, San Diego.

Snewin, D. (1999). Second National Conference of the Australian Vocational Education.

St. Pierre, E. A. and W. S. Pillow, Eds. (2000). Working the Ruins: Feminist poststructural theory and methods in education. London, Routledge.

Stanley, J. (1989). Marks on the Memory: Experiencing school. Milton Keynes, Open University Press.

Stanley, L. and S. Wise (1990). Method, Methodology and Epistemology in Feminist Research Processes. Feminist Praxis: Research, theory and Epistemology in Feminist Sociology. L. Stanley. London, Routledge: 20-60.

Sternberg, R. and L.-I. Zhang (2001). Perspectives on Thinking, Learning and Cognitive Styles. London, Lawrence Erlbaum.

Stiglitz, J. (2004). Globalisation and its Discontents. Basingstoke, Penguin.

Stonewall (2003). Section 28: An end to a hateful piece of legislation. 2005.

Stronach, I. and M. Maclure (1997). Educational Research Undone: the postmodern embrace. Buckingham, Open University Press.

Sutherland, A. (1981). Disabled We Stand. London, Souvenir.

Symes, C. and N. Preston (1997). Schools and Classrooms: A cultural studies analysis of education. Melbourne, Longman.

Talburt, S. (2000). Identity Politics, Institutional Response, and Cultural Negotiation: Meanings of a Gay and Lesbian Office on Campus. Thinking Queer: Sexuality, Culture, and Education. S. Talburt and S. Steinberg. New York, Peter Lang: 61-81.

Taylor, C. (2002). Geography of the "new" education market: secondary school choice in England and Wales. Burlington, Ashgate.

Taylor, S., F. Rizvi and B. Lingard (1997). Educational policy and the politics of change. London, Routledge.

Thomas, C. (2001). Disability Theory: Key ideas, issues and thinkers. Disability Studies Today. C. Barnes, M. Oliver and L. Barton. Cambridge, Polity: 38-57.

Tomlinson, M. (2004). Reform of the 14-19 curriculum and qualifications. London, DfES.

US, D. o. E. (2001). No Child Left Behind at www.ed.gov/nclb accessed 02/02/2005.

Walkerdine, V. (1987). Sex, power and pedagogy. Gender and The Politics of Schooling. M. Arnot and G. Weiner. Hutchinson, Open University Press: 166-174.

Walkerdine, V. (1990). Schoolgirl Fictions. London, Verso.

Walkerdine, V. (1997). Daddy's Girl: Young Girls and Popular Culture. London, Macmillan.

Weeks, J. (1991). Against Nature: essays on history, sexuality and identity. London, River Oram Press.

Weiner, G. (1985). Just a Bunch of Girls: Feminist approaches to schooling. Milton Keynes, Open Uinversity Press.

Welch, A. (1996). Australian Education: Reform or crisis? St Leonards, NSW, Allen & Unwin.

Whitty, G. (1985). Sociology and School Knowledge: Curriculum theory, research and politics. London, Methuen.

Whitty, G. (2002). Making sense of education policy: studies in the sociology and politics of education. London, Paul Chapman.

Whitty, G. and I. Menter (1989). "Journal of Law and Society." Lessons of Thatcherism: Education policy in England and Wales 1979-88 16(1): 42-64.

Whitty, G., S. Power and D Halpin (1998). Devolution and choice in education: the school, state, and the market. Buckingham, Open University Press.

Willis, P. (1977). Learning to Labour: how working class kids get working class jobs. Farnborough, Hants, Saxon House.

Wittig, M. (1981). "One is Not Born a Woman." Feminist Issues 1(2): 47-54.

Wolpe, A. (1988). Within School Walls: The role of discipline, sexuality and the curriculum. London, Routledge.

Youdell, D. (2003). "Identity Traps or How Black Students Fail: the interactions between biographical, sub-cultural, and learner identities." British Journal of Sociology of Education 24(1): 3-20.

Youdell, D. (2004a). "Engineering school markets, constituting schools and subjectivating students: the bureaucratic, institutional and classroom dimensions of educational triage." Journal of Education Policy 19(4): 408-431.

Youdell, D. (2004b). "Wounds and reinscriptions: schools, sexualities and performative subjects." Discourse 25(4): 477-494.

Youdell, D. (2004c). Bent as a Ballet Dancer: the possibilities and limits for a legitimate homosexuality in school. Youth and sexualities: pleasure, subversion and insubordination in and out of schools. M. L. Rasmussen, E. Rofes and S. Talburt. Basingstoke, Palgrave Macmillan, 201-222.

Youdell, D. (2005). "Sex-gender-sexuality: how sex, gender and sexuality constellations are constituted in secondary schools." Gender and Education 17(3): 149-170.

Zack, N. (1997). Race/Sex: Their sameness, difference and interplay. London, Routledge.

ENDNOTES

[i] The notion of these standardised tests as 'high stakes' has been developed in helpful ways by Michael Apple who has used this term to encompass the variety of standardised tests that are used across contexts and educational/age points while maintaining the commonality of the tests across these contexts – that is, their standardiasation allowing constant comparison and the incredible importance placed upon them and the scale of their impact – they are high stakes (Apple 2001).

[ii] Historicity has usefully been described as: 'what might be understood as the history which has become internal to a name, has come to constitute the contemporary meaning of a name: the sedimentation of its usages as they have become part of the very name, a sedimentation, a repetition that congeals, that gives the name its force' (Butler 1997a:36).

[iii] In *The Archaeology of Knowledge* Foucault describes this method as trying 'to define not the thoughts, representations, images, themes, preoccupations that are revealed in discourses, but those discourses themselves, those discourses as practices obeying certain rules' (Foucault 1972).

[iv] This approach is taken up in *Discipline and Punish* and the *History of Sexuality Volume 1*. It is understood as: 'a form of history which can account for the constitution of knowledges, discourses, domains of objects etc. without having to make reference to a subject which is either transcendental in relation to the field of events or runs in its empty sameness throughout the course of history. (Foucault 1980:117).

[v] *Ecriture feminine* is a movement in feminism, in particular but not restricted to French feminism, that has foregrounded the break with masculinist modes of textual representation. In contrast to the apparently objective, rational and scientific textual codes of conventional, authoritative and masculine texts, *ecriture feminine* offered texts that challenged the boundaries of fiction and non-fiction, academic and creative, evidenced and intuitive in order to create spaces for writing that inscribed the subjugated properties of the feminine and rendered these at once visible and legitimate. See, for instance Cixous and Clement 1986.

[vi] This is primarily, but not exclusively, understood in terms of sovereign and additive models of power.

[vii] Common sense itself is taken here as hegemonic (as opposed to neutral) (Gramsci 2003) and discursively constituted and constituting.

[viii] This ethnography was undertaken for my doctoral research. Taylor comprehensive, and this group of students, participated during 1996-7 in the ethnography I undertook with David Gillborn and published as *Rationing Education* (Gillborn and Youdell 2000).

[ix] This study was supported through funding from a Macquarie University New Staff research grant. Sue Saltmarsh was research assistant to the project and undertook a proportion of the data generation.

[x] Following those theoretical moves outlined in chapter 2, I would suggest that the 'meanings' of speech are impossible to contain (see Butler 1997 and Derrida 1988). Yet while it is impossible to pin down, or fix these meanings, this does not negate the possibility of examining their potential or likely meanings. While I assert that the data has particular meanings and functions, I do not suggest that these are in anyway, exhaustive, final or fixed.

[xi] It must be stressed that the teacher may or may not have spoken to Steve as reported. The 'truth' of the teacher's words and intent, however, are less significant here than the way in which they are received. It is the meaning ascribed to the teacher's words, Steve's response to them, and their location in a chain of signification that I am concerned with here.

xii Steve told me that he and his girlfriend were sitting on a park bench kissing when the teacher saw them.

xiii The interview context may also be influential here. The boys have consented to have the discussion tape-recorded. While they trust me enough to practice the hand-mime, they may not trust me (or each other) enough to call Steve wanker in a way that can be captured by the tape-recorder.

xiv I had only limited contact with Natasha (Mixed-race) during the research. For this reason it is not possible to comment specifically on her disciplinary record, relationship with the school or learner identity.

xv Jasmine is not Black, she is Mixed-race. In mainstream and pupil discourses these race identities are not the same. Rather, while located together in terms of a White/Black binary, the Hierarchy within the Other and the popular discourses of race which it draws upon differentiate between racial sub-categories within the subordinated Black Other. It is arguable that at the level of practice, teachers and students quite literally do not *see* Jasmine as they *see* Marcella, Naomi and Marcia. Phenotypically and physiognomically, Jasmine is not *as* Black as her friends. This is not to suggest that phenotypes and physiognomies convey some inherent racial truth. Rather, it illustrates the sedimentation of the race discourses that are tacitly relied upon and deployed within ongoing constituting practices. The constituting discourses of the student milieu imbue Jasmine with less status and prestige than her Black friends. Simultaneously, this inaccessibility of a Black sub-cultural identity constitutes her as a more desirable learner within the school's institutional discourse – her race identity is not inherently *as* commensurate with a challenge to authority as that of her Black friends. As such, it seems that there may be an inverse relationship between students' status in terms of the Hierarchy within the Other and their status in terms of institutional learner identities.

xvi I would suggest that the rapid rise of marketisation in education and the associated emphasis on benchmark grades means that only students with their heads firmly in the sand are able to dispute the significance of higher grade passes. The adherence to the overriding goal of benchmark grades is not isolated to this group of students but can be seen across diverse studies and groups of students (see, for instance, Gillborn & Youdell 2000 and Gillborn *et al* 1997). As such, a pro-education and anti-school stance is arguably extremely common. Indeed, I would suggest that very few students inside contemporary schools could be understood as anti-education.

xvii It is important to acknowledge that the teacher may intervene more swiftly/harshly because I am in the classroom for the first time, although I do not believe this to be the case given her confidence, seniority, relaxed classroom persona and behaviour during subsequent observations,

xviii It is not within the scope of this discussion to explore constitutions of Ian in this classroom. See Youdell 2004b for a full examination of Ian's resistances to the denigrated homosexual and reinscription of legitimate gay masculinity.

xix Popularised by the media, in the UK in 2005 'Chav' or 'Chavs' resonates with 'Shaza and Baza'. As the discussion took place I recalled with discomfort (and with embarrassment now repeat) the names used by myself and my friends to identify (and constitute) Other students and ourselves in our East Midlands secondary school during the early 1980s. Our Shazas and Bazas were "Sharons and Traceys" whose male equivalents were "Casuals" or "Garys". (It is interesting that Sharon is still around). We believed that we were referred to (constituted ourselves) as "Grebs" and "Trampy Punks". Greb was mostly considered inaccurate (injurious?), Trampy Punk was embraced.

xx This is not to suggest that the feminine and Asian are mutually exclusive constituting discourse, as illustrated by the eroticisation of the exotic Other in Oritamist discourse. Further, the feminisation of Asian boys and, by extension, their lack of masculine and the impossibility of man within such a discursive frame has been documented (see Mac an Ghaill 1988, Gillborn 1990).

xxi My repetition of this demonstrates the success of this unspoken performative and illustrates the potential performative force of silences.

xxii I concur with Butler's (1991) argument in which she outlines the problems involved in retaining the notion of sex as distinct from gender. However, in this section I am concerned to explore the discursive relationship between sex and gender within authorised discourse. For this reason I will use the hyphenated term sex-gender to refer specifically to this discursive relationship.

xxiii It is noteworthy that it is a group of unknown boys who censure Molly's (un)femininity while many known boys appear to have a respectful friendship with her. It is possible that while Molly's masculinity exceeds the traditional masculinity of these unknown boys, it does not threaten the masculinity of the known boys.

xxiv At one level Molly's refusal seems reasonable – her footballing skills are exceptional but her physique is unremarkable in comparison to the other girls in the year group.

xxv As in the case of Molly's body, her school clothes are unremarkable in comparison to those worn by other girls. Indeed, her usual attire of school sweatshirt; black boot-leg trousers; Reebok classics; several gold rings, including one ornamented with the word 'sister'; several gold chains; and gold hoop earrings fits the definition of Shaza offered by the Dir'y 'ippies in chapter 9. The key difference in Molly's appearance seems to be that she invariably wears trousers, does not wear make-up and wears her shoulder length hair in a ponytail without sculpting hair products or ornamenting accessories.

xxvii This masquerade that exposes femininity as a discursive effect reflects that of drag discussed by Butler (1991).

SUBJECT INDEX

NAME INDEX

Printed in the United Kingdom
by Lightning Source UK Ltd.
130654UK00001B/127/A